Conservatives are from
Earth...
Liberals are from
Uranus

by John L. Armstrong

DORRANCE
PUBLISHING CO
EST. 1920
PITTSBURGH, PENNSYLVANIA 15238

Dorrance Publishing Co
585 Alpha Drive
Pittsburgh, PA 15238
Visit our website at *www.dorrancebookstore.com*

ISBN: 978-1-4809-9138-5
eISBN: 978-1-4809-9396-9

DEDICATION

This book is dedicated to my father George William Armstrong, who was the greatest American of my lifetime. Dad was born to parents William Hosea Armstrong and Mae Smith Armstrong in Lawrenceville, Illinois, on August 23, 1923.

He grew up in Arkansas and received a Bachelor of Science degree in Chemical Engineering from the University of Arkansas in 1944. While in college he was an intercollegiate chess champion.

Dad was a common sense Goldwater/Reagan conservative and passed along his values to me through his example. Before his death on June 26, 1969, (age 45) in Houston, TX, he gave to me a gift I know I can never repay: he showed me the way..

ABOUT THE AUTHOR

John Lawrence Armstrong was born in Virginia in 1948. He migrated with his family to the Mississippi Gulf Coast in 1954 where he completed grades 2-12.

He attended the University of Arkansas for two terms--Johnson's and Nixon's--receiving a Bachelor of Science degree in Chemical Engineering.

Armstrong's professional career spanned approximately 3 decades working for two different major oil companies in locations from Freeport, Bahamas, to San Francisco, CA. He retired to his home on the Mississippi Gulf Coast in 1999.

John self-identifies as a Christian, an Eagle Scout, a TEA Party constitutional conservative, and a 4th generation Arkansas Razorback.

INTRODUCTION

Since my collegiate days in the early 1960s and perhaps even before, I have been a lifelong observer of liberals. At first, I found liberals confounding, with no apparent redeeming value. As the years passed, the confounding side of the liberal enigma unraveled itself but the redeemable value remains unapparent.

Liberals are nothing if not predictable. They have the same identical character traits today that they had a half -century ago, only substantially exaggerated. The standard liberal package of character traits includes generosity to a fault with *other* people's money, rights, and freedom. Their generosity leads directly to the secondary trait of moral superiority, egotistical self-delusion and then pathological narcissism. Then in order to maintain the façade of self-delusion comes pathological lying, often times about their motives.

These character traits (flaws) are prevalent in most liberals. But there is a universal cause of all of these liberal symptoms, which is discussed in Chapters 1, 2, and beyond…and sadly why there is no cure for liberalism. In these early chapters we analyze such phenomena as the liberal's compulsion to bully and why liberals are oblivious to allegations of hypocrisy.

What was most baffling to me was not liberal hypocrisy but why conservatives are baffled at liberal hypocrisy. The answer is quite obvious: the conservative mistake is attempting to apply logic to a psychological situation. Liberals simply do *not* function based on logic.

In Chapters 4 and 5 we discuss the attraction of liberals to the fatally flawed concept of *socialism*, which is in reality an attraction to other people's money. Socialism is in fact a centuries-old something-for-nothing Ponzi-like scheme designed to enslave the gullible by the ruling class, as immortalized by the pigs George Orwell's *Animal Farm*. **The diseased socialist brain is far more dangerous than any gun.**

In Chapter 6, we discuss in detail what makes the United States of America by *far* the greatest nation on earth despite liberal propaganda to the contrary.

In Chapter 7, we examine what has become of our federal government "inside the Beltway." It has long- since ceased serving the American people and now serves only itself.

In Chapter 8, we discuss the primary liberal tool for division, disunity, and discontent: victimhood. There are many buyers of this excuse for failure in America, and liberals peddle it in bulk.

In Chapters 9, 10, and 11, we spotlight the individuals responsible for contemporary liberalism's greatest "success" (or more accurately lack thereof) stories. ***Liberals enthusiastically treat failure as triumph out of necessity because that's all they have.***

Then in Chapter 12, we take a look at liberalism's "designated driver" for the now-deceased communism, which collapsed worldwide a quarter of a century ago.

I attempt to infuse humor through hyperbole, metaphoric humor and sardonic sarcasm throughout this composition. I demonstrate the absurd with counter absurdity. That is just my style. But comedy that is not grounded in truth fails. America gets an overdose of that on *every* network late-night comedy show. If Johnny Carson was the father of late-night television comedy, Jimmy Kimmel and Stephen Colbert are its assassins.

The opinions expressed throughout are my own and are clearly identified as such. In virtually all instances, they are supported by *prima facie* evidence. The reader is free to disagree, that is what America is about.

If a unique and brutally honest discussion of these subjects interests you, then you have found the right place. Please read on...

TABLE OF CONTENTS

1. LIBERALISM: THE ENEMY WITHIN

"America will never be destroyed from the outside. If we falter and lose our freedoms, it will be because we destroyed ourselves." – Abraham Lincoln

There is no lethal *external* threat to the United States. Russia, North Korea, Iran and radical Islam are all threats to the United States, but they are not lethal. None of these ill-intended global malefactors can destroy our borders, spend us into bankruptcy, corrupt our media, government and education system, attack our rights to freedom to speech, worship and defend ourselves, or incite civil unrest for the purpose of anarchy.

The greatest threat to the United States is from within…it is liberalism. ***The enemy within is far more dangerous than any external enemy.*** *"The left has destroyed more cities than Godzilla"* – Greg Gutfeld*(12.03.13).

*Greg Gutfeld is the Fox News Channel's resident Martin Riggs (1987 movie "Lethal Weapon") mini impersonator.

Of course, these chunks of urban America are but a warmup for the main event: America itself.

Liberals live here in the United States by the millions. They are outraged by America, at least the way they see it. Ostensibly they seek to destroy America because America is not perfect. Think of the ego it takes to manufacture that thought. Only individuals convinced of their own perfection could look at the greatest nation on earth and then say to themselves, "This does not meet my lofty standards. It is not perfect. It must be destroyed. Then the utopia *I* create will take its place."

Liberals are free to leave for the utopia they long for, but they never do. Instead they seek to "fundamentally transform" America into an egalitarian utopia where all residents have equal outcomes, which they fantasize would preempt all cause for their non-stop personal outrage…a land of rainbows, unicorns, genderless purple penguins, where every kid gets a participation trophy, no one excels causing jealousy and "Kumbaya" is the national anthem.

I have observed this fundamental difference between liberals and conservative thought process: the liberal mindset summed up in a single question is, *"Why can't every day be Christmas?"* The corollary conservative response/question is *"Who's going to pay for it?"*

I have observed other substantial flaws in the liberal thought product: liberals want open borders and an influx of unskilled, uneducated labor while simultaneously demanding an increase in the minimum wage. Liberals demand laws to increase the minimum wage while simultaneously condemning Trump's full employment economy which increases wages naturally through labor supply and demand. Liberals are universally pro-abortion, statistically eliminating their voter base. They oppose tax cuts while claiming to advocate for the middle class. They decry the police shooting of a black teenaged male in the "Hands up, don't shoot!" Ferguson, MO, incident because "Black lives matter!" while ignoring the massive homicide body count in Chicago.

Liberals advocate for women's and gay rights while praising Sharia Law. Liberals demand separation of church and state while full supporting Islam wherein the church *is* the state. They condemn Donald Trump for "Russian collusion" based on no evidence whatsoever and simultaneously have no problem with the phony Michael Steele Russian originated Hillary Clinton financed "dirty dossier." They condemn candidate Trump for refusing to accept a future election result, then reject the same election results *instantly* after *they* have lost. Liberals are for granting "Dreamers" amnesty and an expedited pathway to citizenship while ignoring heinous MS-13 atrocities and the murder of Kate Steinle in San Francisco. Liberals advocate laws which would fine or imprison restaurant employees who give patrons plastic straws while handing out free government financed plastic syringes to drug addicts down the street. Liberals unanimously selected Burger "B" over Wendy's Burger "A" in the 1980s taste test commercial.

These confused, convoluted, and conflicted contradictions are the direct result of substituting emotion for logic, a process that reduces liberals to sloganeering, clichés, memorized talking points, segueing into *ad hominem* attacks, and eventually violence.

We have just finished (2016) an eight-year voyage toward the liberal mythical utopian fantasy land with their chosen Messiah at the wheel. *"We are the ones we've been waiting for. We are the change that we seek,"* Barack Obama informed us on 02.19.08. In the beginning of Obama's *"fundamental transformation of America,"* lofty promises to the American people were as common as pig tracks.

E.g., *"If you like your healthcare plan, you'll be able to keep your health care plan;"* and *"Healthcare premiums will go down by $2,500 annually for a family of four;"* and my personal favorite: *"This was the moment when the rise of the oceans began to slow and our planet began to heal."* – Barack Obama *(06.04.08)*. Allow me to blanket translate these colossal droppings of male bovine fecal matter: "I am a pathological liar. I know I can get away with it because of my skin color. Anyone who challenges me will be pilloried as a 'Racist!' by the MSM, which I control."

Another personal favorite was the Obama job outlook summary during a June 2, 2016 PBS broadcast town hall meeting in Elkhart, IN. Obama informed a local resident whose manufacturing job had just been moved to Mexico: *"...some of those jobs of the past are just not going to come back"*. This also needs translation: "Your job will not be coming back as long as I live in the White House. It is reparation for America's greedy colonial past." He was speaking to a black man.

Promises *kept* were as scarce as Powerball Jackpot winning tickets. *"Shovel-ready was not as shovel-ready as we expected <snicker giggle>."* – Barack Obama (06.13.11)

Now eight years later, there is no aspect of Americans' lives that has not deteriorated significantly… and liberals are more outraged than ever. *"President Obama is the greatest hoax ever perpetrated on the American people"* – Clint Eastwood (09.07.12).

How well we recall the promise of many liberal Hollywood celebrities to move to Canada if Donald Trump won the 2016 presidential election. Apparently America is not big enough for both Rosie O'Donnell *and* Donald Trump. It is *not* because of Trump's weight problem.

We can learn much about liberals from these broken promises: (1) none of the celebrities actually moved to Canada and never intended to, proving they are without exception pathological liars, it was just another acting job; (2) the liberal Hollywood ego to think anyone cares is off the charts. A GoFundMe travel account for this cluster of moral degenerates could have generated millions; (3) *none* of the peripatetic liberal Hollywood carpetbaggers announced Mexico as a destination. Canada is full of white people, cold weather, and a viable economy. Our neighbor to the south, Mexico, is a nation of brown people, warm weather, and a comatose economy. The liberal Hollywood evacuation rhetoric is lousy with the unambiguous stench of racism. However on the bright side, at the rate California is ceding itself to Latin America, it will *not* be necessary for any Hollywood liberals to move at all.

Tragically with the 2016 election result, liberals are yet again denied their long-awaited American death march to Marxist paradise. There must be a new focal point for liberal outrage. Enter stage left from the Cartoon Network Boris and Natasha who obviously colluded with the Trump campaign to "meddle" (as yet undefined) with the election. This is the unanimous conclusion of 17 different federal intelligence agencies (16 too many?) based on evidence no one has ever seen, according to "anonymous sources" who cannot be found.

I personally conclude something entirely different from the liberal post-election obsession with "Russian interference": liberals are about as compatible with reality as vampires are with the noon- day sun. They are, in fact, capable of pretending *anything* that supports the current narrative. They are impervious to accusations of selective outrage, double standard, and hypocrisy such as this because they are single-mindedly focused on *control.*

To the standard issue liberal, the accusation of hypocrisy means nothing derogatory, it is in fact a compliment. It translates to acknowledgement of the *control* they seek. It is public acknowledgement that the rules that govern socially acceptable behavior do *not* apply to them because they are the cool kids in school who have graduated from juvenile delinquency to antisocial public nuisance. Liberals giggle with the pride of accomplishment at being called hypocrites. Allow me to ask a question at this point: does this hypothesis fit *your* observational experience? I thought so.

Liberalism is not an ideology or a philosophy. It is a symptom of acute Obsessive Compulsive Disorder (OCD). While it is typically accompanied by other mental disorders (narcissism, paranoia, schizophrenia, etc.), OCD is the common denominator among virtually *all* liberals.

Liberals cannot compete in the area of ideas because their ideas (e.g., socialism) are vastly inferior. Their preferred strategy is not to *compete* with their opponents, but to *eliminate* them. This strategy led to the murder of over 100 million dissenters by communist regimes in Russia and China alone. In passing, we note there was no 2nd Amendment in either Russia or China. Some would argue that this is a little more than OCD, and they would be correct. But OCD is the universal liberal "starter kit" for liberals, just like socialism is the gateway drug for totalitarian communism.

To reinforce my hypothesis liberalism is *not* an ideology but rather a specific mental disorder, I cite the history of the global communism movement. Although originally documented by Marx and Engels in Germany in the mid-19th century, communism did not gain global traction until the early 20th century in Russia. Then in the late 20th century, even within my lifetime, the global communist delusion died at the Berlin Wall. The *ideology* of communism was put out of its misery, but the *sickness* of liberalism continued to thrive even though its primary vehicle went down in flames. It thrives at this very minute.

OCD dominates every thought, every action, and every syllable uttered by liberals. I have heard the observation that liberals imagine they can detect 80+ different human genders, but they cannot tell right from wrong. It is not that liberals do not understand the difference between right and wrong. It just makes no difference to them because it never enters their thought process, which is overwhelmed by OCD. This is why so little of what they believe, advocate, and say makes any sense whatsoever. ***Any cause that is supported by liberals is either backwards (e.g. "affirmative action") or irrelevant (banning plastic straws).*** The closest hard core liberals ever get to the concept of right and wrong is *"Can I get away with it?"* which is their litmus test.

The primary motivator of the OCD liberal (OCDL) is *control*: *control* of the environment, the future, and most critically other people's speech and even thought. *Control* is the opiate that provides temporary relief for their OCD. In "junkie speak", it is their "fix."

There is no better illustration of the liberal fixation on *control* than their reaction to newly-elected President Donald Trump. Trump cannot be bought, intimidated, bullied, or otherwise *controlled*. He cannot be sabotaged by the mainstream media (MSM) because he can instantly destroy their daily propaganda assault and humiliate them with a truth counterattack via Twitter. Trump has Titter followers numbering well into 8 figures. With re-tweets and the coverage he gets from the reporting on his tweets, his message reaches a secondary 9-digit following instantly. Trump's Twitter following easily dwarfs the *entire* MSM coverage reach.

Let us be clear. As a social medium, Twitter is a sewer of ideas dominated by antisocial toads, "bots" and phony liberal biased censorship algorithms. However, Trump is high profiled enough that his participation and message cannot be adulterated by the liberal Twitter operators.

Through Twitter, he is able to communicate his unfiltered and unadulterated message directly to America, bypassing the uber-left Main Stream Media. Liberals within the MSM who formerly had control of the White House message are now finding themselves *following* the story, no longer in *control*. Loss of message *control* has reduced the MSM into an increasingly desperate and incoherent tower of psychobabble, incapable of distinguishing reality from their latest wet dream. The rest of the left has followed the MSM lead, flopping about on the pier like a fresh landed mullet (the Gulf fish, not the hairstyle).

This complete loss of *control* has turned misdemeanor OCD into the felonious TDS (Trump Derangement Syndrome), which is an acute, chronic, virulent and potentially lethal form of OCD. Witness the 66-year old Bernie Sanders disciple from Illinois who attacked a Republican baseball practice in Alexandria, VA on June 14, 2017 with a rifle. House majority whip Steve Scalise (LA) suffered life threatening gunshot wounds, and the attacker was killed by Capitol Police.

Loss of *control* can literally make liberals scream at the sun, as America witnessed on Nov. 8, 2017, a bright (double *entendre*) liberal idea originated in Boston. There, thousands of liberals gathered at the Boston Common to shriek out loud in solidarity. Liberals nationwide apparently saw value in this futile exercise and joined in the thankfully non-violent display.

Of course, the TDS impaired think *you* are the one with the problem, not them. Screaming at the mid-day sun and shooting up a baseball ball practice are normal. People who object to it are not. We add to this mindset the usual medley of liberal psychological maladies, anger management issues, publicity terrorized law enforcement and a Teenage Mutant Turtle eye bandana and you have the recipe for an Antifa (contraction for "Anti-fascist") riot.

Then on May 16, 2018, President Trump referred to MS-13 gang members as *"animals"* during an event at the White House. This declaration led to a Democrat stampede to the nearest "lights, action, camera" CNN podium. Nancy Pelosi led the herd of usual suspects, countering Trump with *"we are all God's children*"* and *"there is a spark of divinity among every person on earth*, and we all have to recognize that as we respect the dignity and worth of every person*." None* of the victims of MS-13 machete attacks were available for comment.

* Unborn fetuses are excluded from this Democrat proclamation.

This is TDS skywriting. It does give insight into a potentially successful 2020 re-election strategy for President Trump.

As the 2020 election draws near, Trump could resurrect heinous strawmen from the past (Hitler, Nazis, ISIS, David Duke, Satan, Charles Manson, Ted Bundy, etc.) and pronounce them "animals". Out of TDS reflex, Democrats will repeat their MS-13 exhibition and attack Trump like Joey Chestnut on a Coney Island hotdog stand.

This should guarantee yet another election loss.

TDS is the cause of the relentless "fake news" exhibition that America is assaulted with daily. The liberal authors of the daily "fake news" farce would have you believe their problem is *external*, i.e., Trump. Trump is merely the focal point of their advanced OCD, which is an *internal* malady.

The liberal remedy is to *bully* Trump into shutting down his tweeting by ridiculing every single tweet. They envision that if successful, they would return to *control* and manipulation of the White House message.

Their problem is twofold: (1) Trump understands the communication power of social media; and (2) he cannot be *bullied*. There is no satisfactory resolution to this conundrum for the Obsessive Control Disorder (OCD) left. The Trump Twitter phenomena is a primary cause for the ever-worsening outbreak of liberal insanity America is currently witnessing.

What disturbs liberals the most within the current scenario is that Trump has not only the unmitigated audacity to fight back, but the larger-than-life persona to *win*. It is a double header loss for leftists that they (1) lost the election; and (2) are now losing the post-election food fight that they initiate anew daily. They cannot accept that Trump is *not* a punching bag like his Republican Bush predecessors. "It's not presidential!" they shriek in astonishment. Indeed, it is *Trumpian*.

Some liberals seeking relief from the loss of *control*, which is literally consuming them, have called for Trump to be excommunicated from Twitter. That will not happen because this is no longer the Obama Department of (In) Justice Puppet Show. The outlook for the foreseeable future? Trump on Twitter is *not* going away. I look for the liberal hysteria to worsen significantly as they marinate in their own hatred.

The election of Trump meant that liberals had to relinquish *control* of the executive branch of our government and the prestige, power, and symbolism that goes with it. The OCDL reaction that followed was psychotic hysteria: riots euphemistically described as protests, direct televised appeals by "B minus" list Hollywood celebrities (whose *profession* is to convince you that they are something they are not) to hijack the Electoral College and subvert the election result, and a mob of Ashley Judd-led pink-hatted alleged women marching on Washington D.C. They could not articulate why they were marching. I assumed that they were mad the sexist pig Trump won the election. The same gaggle of clucks universally voted for serial sex offender Bill Clinton in the 1990s.

We juxtapose this chaos by the same post-election scenario eight years ago when Obama won the presidency.

Why wasn't the 2008 election of Barack Obama followed by similar conservative antics? Because conservatives are not afflicted with OCD. There is no "Obama Derangement Syndrome."

Eight years ago when Obama won the presidency, there were many Americans just as perplexed that America could be fooled into electing an admitted Marxist and Alinskyite, a self-described "community organizer" who vowed to *"fundamentally transform America"* into our worst nightmare (more on this later). Yet there was *no* rioting in the streets, *no* public appeals to ignore the constitutional election process, *no* massive hysterical temper tantrum of any sort. There was only the Washington mall littered with tons of debris from those who celebrated the emaculation (Rush Limbaugh terminology) of the new "Messiah." Why?

To the conservatives, loss of control of the executive branch of government meant they had to work hard to regain it in a future election. In the meantime, they would just have to muddle through as best they could under significantly less-than-optimal presidential performance. In this case, it turned out to be by far the worst presidential performance in our nation's history. But the 2008 election was not the end of the world; we had suffered through the micro-managing socialist liberal nincompoop Jimmy Carter and the philandering liberal pathological liar Bill Clinton before.

To the Obsessive Control Disorder Liberal, (OCDL) the loss of *control* of the executive branch in the 2016 election resulted in the complete loss of sanity. This cannot be! It is unacceptable NOW!! America must be made aware of its egregious error and it must be corrected NOW!!!

Let us not mistake what this is *really* about. The MSM called the 2016 election for Hillary Clinton immediately after she lost the 2008 Democrat nomination to Barack Obama. The American people did not understand the 2016 election result was not up to Joe Schmo in Kokomo, IN. It was up to the Main Stream Media. Now post-election, the MSM must undo the Joe S. mistake by *removing* Donald Trump from office. The MSM never really cared for the Constitution, anyway. It is just minor obstacle in their pathway to *control*, no big deal.

But for once, the Constitution may actually come in handy, say, if we can somehow get the Electoral College to mutiny their voters and "elect" Hillary Clinton. Having failed at that, there is the 25th Amendment which allows for the removal of a president who is unable to discharge the powers and duties of the office. Defeating ISIS, leading the biggest one-year economic turnaround in American history, securing our southern border by actually enforcing existing immigration laws are all symptoms of diminished mental capacity and advancing Alzheimer's. America *cannot* have such a person in charge of our nuclear arsenal. Besides, according the results of an annual physical exam released on Jan. 17, 2018, President Trump's cholesterol is slightly above average, which means he is dying of heart disease.

The case study of newly-elected President Donald J. Trump yields multiple examples of liberal bullying. An electoral majority, including 30 of 50 states (down from the 57 during the halcyon days of the Obama presidency) elected Trump. Overturning the election would then be the supreme act of bullying and *control* of the majority by the liberal minority. Instantly a liberal national "Dump Trump" obsession is born! The well-being of America and the sanctity of future elections be d@mned. Liberals are perfectly willing to sink the ship (the United States of America) they are sailing to execute a successful mutiny and regain *control* of the bridge.

We need clues of impeachable high crimes and misdemeanors by Trump. During a news conference on July 27, 2016 in Miami, Trump quips, *"Russia, if you're listening, I hope you're able to find the 30,000 (Hillary Clinton) emails that are missing…"* That was the Russian nexus! Trump was overtly soliciting help from his Russian election saboteur comrades!! Trump's joke was actually a "dog whistle" to his Russian comrades in the KGB led by none other than Vladimir Putin!!!

So let me get this straight. Hillary Clinton deleting 33K emails that were under subpoena by Congress as evidence, and coincidently destroying communication devices with a ball peen hammer, scrubbing hard drives with the electronic disinfectant "bleach bit" was *not* criminal…but Donald Trump making a public joke about it *was* a crime? My first reaction to this classic sampling of liberal logic is nobody's that stupid. I then quickly realize my mistake. *You* can't make this stuff up…only a liberal can. *Within the liberal universe of self-delusion, if you <u>want</u> something to be true, then it <u>is</u> true. No evidence or corroboration required.*

Trump's transgression was not taken seriously at the time because (a) it was not serious; it was a rather funny Trump joke; and (b) it was common knowledge Clinton was going to win, making the Trump transgression in Miami moot.

From the Trump joke, we gain insight as to how liberals regard humor: any attempts at humor aimed *at* liberals will offend them to the point of lynch-mob level outrage. Kathy Griffin holding up the decapitated head of President Trump would obviously does not qualify for outrage because the *right* person was targeted, which made it hilarious.

Liberals see no reason for outrage in the case of Kathy Griffin: this is merely the artistic expression of a free-spirited liberal *alleged* comedienne exercising her 1st Amendment right.

But generally, if it is even remotely possible for liberals to be offended, it *will* happen. It gives them the opportunity to *act* outraged, which is their catnip. And *every* liberal acting performance is worthy of an Oscar.

But back to the election result…Clinton lost! Now every pebble, every blade of grass must be investigated to find the "stained blue dress" (formerly known as the "smoking gun") which proves what we all know to be true: the Trump presidency is a Russian conspiracy and an illegitimate fraud. (No, the stain was not pigeon dropping.)

What greater exhibition of *control* than overturning a legitimate presidential election result just because it is therapeutic for your OCD? It would truly be the *"cherry on the doggie do"* (Pelosi-speak) liberals want to serve America.

Tragically for liberals, they have no options. The Robert Mueller investigation will not be the Trump eliminator liberals once envisioned. In oil-drilling vernacular, the Mueller investigation is a "duster." The best outcome Mueller can achieve is that his 2016 election investigation staggers on through the 2018 mid-term election Democrat loss, and his apparatus will already be in place to begin investigation of freshly imagined 2018 "Russian collusion". A permanent "special counsel" branch of government could be established, which in reality is the welfare state for unemployed ex-Obama/Clinton administration deadbeat lawyers (*e.g.*, smarmy Clintonista sycophant schmuck Lanny Davis) waiting on the next Democrat socialist regime to ascend to power. So far Mueller and his merry band of shyster saboteurs have clipped the American taxpayer for $20M in their attempt to manufacture a constitutional crisis out of thin air. There is plenty more cash where that came from.

Mueller has the added incentive to continue the "investigation" of nothing to avoid being investigated for his own misdeeds as FBI Director. His role in the UraniumOne sale to Russia is one high profile example. Any attempt at investigating Mueller before his current lampoon concludes will be propagandized by the left as "obstruction of justice."

And let us make no mistake. The Mueller special counsel is about one thing and one thing only: indicting Donald J. Trump for the *crime* of winning the 2016 election, and punishing the American voter for their feckless choice. Stormy Daniels, Paul Manafort, Michael Cohen, Gen. Flynn, *etc.* are just tools for the job of getting rid of Trump.

Robert Mueller cares *nothing* about justice, he is a paid assassin, a 21st century "terminator". He is not investigating any crime. He is performing government financed opposition research with subpoena and prosecution power for the Democrat Party. Mueller is a contemporary enactment of the Lavrentiy Pavlovich Beria (head of Joseph Stalin's secret police) quote: *"Show me the man and I'll find the crime."* The Mueller investigation and the coup detat it represents is a cancer on America's constitution.

The game is currently on the Democrats home turf: crooked prosecutors, corrupt investigators and activist judges. It is a game of "keep away" from the helpless American voter. This is where the Democrats have the best chance of overturning the 2016 election. Having a competent Attorney General is crucial in this environment of Washington DC lawyer thugocracy. Deputy AG Rod Rosenstein stepping up for the self-recused Jeff Sessions hardly qualifies as that.

As Mueller becomes increasingly desperate, his clumsy flailing becomes more absurd. If he cannot manufacture a legal case against Trump, he will harass Trump until he is fired. Then the battle cry of the ludicrous left will revert back to a favorite "Obstruction of Justice!"

As liberals descend further daily into the depths of Trump-inflicted depression with exponentially increasing velocity like roll of toilet paper reaching its end, their outlook becomes bleaker. The Trump list of accomplishments grows along with his popularity, and the challenge to the OCDL to overturn the 2016 election result increases. This is an opportunity for the bullying obsessed liberal at "minority rule", to defeat the lawful constitution based election process, which is their *gran prix*.

The lynch mob hysteria that instantly follows every allegation of "police brutality" (e.g., *"Hands up, don't shoot!"*) underscores the allegation of liberal non-reasoned over-reaction. Or the ongoing MSM propaganda-driven Russian collusion delusion national farce. Or the "climate change" hoax. Liberals utilize the mob mentality because they know they cannot compete in a logical exchange of ideas. Their only hope is to manufacture a premature populist stampede.

The highest profile apparent target of Obsessive Control Democratic Liberal *control* is speech. America is assaulted daily by the left's outrage at freedom of speech. And since our speech is merely an expression of our ideas, the real transparent target of the *control* and outrage is the ideas themselves...*thought control*. They have been somewhat successful in hijacking the American education system and inflicting thought *control* on generations of Americans too young to defend themselves. By the time they have transversed America's "education" system, America's youth are completely incapable of objective thought. A brainwashed snowflake zombie land is the goal of the liberal education system.

Without question, the millennial-snowflake attitude of self-centered, self-indulgent egocentrism is the direct result of the self-esteem driven education system curricula. Grade schoolers are taught that *their* feelings are paramount and it is their sacrosanct right *not* to be offended by *anything* within their line of sight or earshot. This *right* justifies preemptive strikes if necessary.

The loss of freedom of speech is not a deal-breaker for our liberal comrades. Critical thought and personal responsibility are more of a burden than they are willing to assume. Liberals would gladly accept a government which would relieve them of these overbearing millstones.

Few, if any, issues generate more hysterical reaction from liberals than abortion. It is again about *control*. Through legalized abortion, liberals acquire the godlike power to decide who lives and who dies. It is the ultimate form of *control*.

To a conservative, human life is a miracle from God.

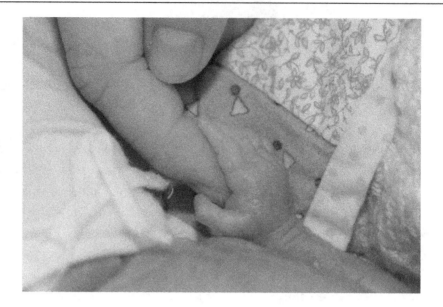

To a liberal, human life is "Parts for Sale." The Center for Medical Progress released an exposé video in April of 2015 that caught the Planned Parenthood abortion business apparently using illegal accounting tricks to hide *profits* generated from the sale of aborted baby parts.

The life of an unborn baby is of no consequence to liberals, particularly when compared to their psychological need for *control*. Tragically, without exception their mothers were *all* pro-life. Perhaps Ronald Reagan summed it up best: ***"I've noticed that everyone who is for abortion has already been born."***

But above all else, abortion represents the liberal rejection of all *personal responsibility*. This true of not only the parents of the aborted human life, but all of liberalism (politicians, schools, clinic personnel, Planned Parenthood, the legal system, etc.) who turn abortion into the hideous big business reality that it has become.

Liberals attempt to put a smiley face on abortion by calling it "pro-choice". It is not "pro-choice", which I will now demonstrate. Sarah Palin gave birth to a Down's syndrome son, Trig Palin on April 8, 2008, less than 5 months before she was nominated by John McCain as his vice presidential running mate.

Ms. Palin learned her child would be handicapped before birth and *chose* life for her son. Liberals attacked her relentlessly after her nomination for her *choice*, proving that they are not pro-*choice*, but rather ghoulishly pro-abortion. There is no such thing as "pro-choice." The attacks did not begin until after Ms. Palin received the VP nomination, proving that they were purely political. They are not fooling anyone with their semantics or motivation.

Capital punishment is the flip side of the same abortion coin. The issue once again gives the liberal the opportunity to *control* life and death, to play God. Like abortion, it is also about the imposition of minority will upon the majority, an overt demonstration of *control*. But the key attraction for liberals again is the total rejection of *personal responsibility*, in this case of the executed criminal. The capital crime was the fault of the weapon, or society, or government. It is never about the individual, which does not conceptually exist to the left.

All of liberalism rejects the capital punishment penalty, which is the ultimate assignment of *personal responsibility*. And as we shall see later (Chapter 6), the left's Bible, *The Communist Manifesto*, destroys the very concept of the individual. The Ebola virus could not keep liberals away from either the abortion or the capital punishment issues.

In truth, capital punishment is a deterrent to heinous crime. I cite the case history of serial killer Dennis Rader, aka the "BTK" (Bind, Torture and Kill) killer in Wichita, KS. During the period 1974-1991, Rader murdered 10 people in and around Wichita. Not coincidentally, the capital punishment sentence did not exist in Kansas during the period 1972-1994. So Mr. Rader's deplorable crimes were committed *only* when there was no capital punishment in Kansas. After it was reinstated in 1994, the BTK murders stopped. Rader was apprehended in 2005 when investigators traced a series of taunting communiques to police and local news services on a computer floppy disk back to him. He is currently serving 10 consecutive life sentences in Kansas state lockup.

Nor does the issue of immigration does not escape the umbrella of *personal responsibility* negligence. The thousands upon thousands illegal immigrants invading America's southern border were coaxed here by Obama's obsession to "fundamentally transform America" into a minority white nation as reparation for some transgression he believes he suffered. With deft sleight of hand, he misdirected responsibility for the invasion during his occupation of the White House with his chronic and habitual *"America's immigration system is broken"* one liner.

This is red meat for your standard issue "blame America first" liberal, who blames American society for the immigration mess. Yes, you and I are responsible, not the stampede of illegal aliens who bear zero *personal responsibility* for breaking our immigration laws…and likewise no *personal responsibility* for Himself for not enforcing the same laws.

We also remember an Obama-led town-hall style meeting (06.25.09) when the Obamacare debate was in its formative stages. A woman asked about a pacemaker for her 100-year-old mother who still had spirit, quality of life, and a will to live. Obama responded with the warmth and compassion of a coiled cobra: *"No, it's better to just give her a painkiller."* And there you have it…not from a trained physician or a clergyman, but from "The Messiah" Himself.

Synopsis: *There is no problem that America has that liberals cannot make significantly worse.*

That liberals seek *control* is only the natural order of things because OCDLs fantasize themselves as superior human beings, a sort of intellectual "Master Race." It is this intellectual superiority that gives them not only the justification to seek the *control* they obsess over, but also the right, the responsibility and the moral obligation to govern hapless mere common folk of inferior intellectual capacity like you and me. Of course, their imagined self-delusional intellectual superiority is nothing more than a dangerous egotistical fantasy. Thus we may add self-delusional egomania to the lineup of typical liberal psychological maladies.

The battle against liberal insanity is a test of wills that America simply cannot afford to lose.

2. THE LIBERAL INDICTMENT: GUILTY ON ALL COUNTS

"The trouble with our liberal friends is not that they are ignorant, but that they know so much that isn't so." - Ronald Regan (10.27.64)

The primary purpose of this book springs from a desire to elucidate the truth about a subject which has interested me deeply: exposing liberalism and its perpetrators for what they are…about how they can be so consistently and profoundly wrong while simultaneously being so completely oblivious to reality and so condescending about it. How is it that their ideas have a virtually 100% failure rate and yet they never seem to learn or even acknowledge it, with the omnipresent exception of blaming their failure on their political opponents (*e.g.*, "the vast right wing conspiracy," "Russian hackers," Rush Limbaugh, Fox News Channel, the ubiquitous "racism," misogyny, George W. Bush, Donald Trump, etc.)? Without question, liberals have the Midas touch…everything they touch turns to mufflers.

America is undergoing constant metamorphosis that might be better described as liberal schizophrenia. In the 2008 election campaign, we were told by Barack Obama *"Yes we can!"* In the 2012 election campaign, that was revised to *"You didn't build that!"* a line he plagiarized from "Native American" Senator and fellow Bolshevik ideologue Elizabeth F. Warren. The concept he was peddling in 2012 was government dependency, the antithesis of his 2008 *"Yes we can!"* message. Of course, it was nothing more than another teleprompter read to our historic first self-identified Marxist president.

In the 2012 campaign we were told *"The Cold War is over."* Perhaps this is why Barack Obama's foreign policy was patterned after Neville Chamberlain in the 1930s…the strategy of appeasement that accelerated Hitler's Third Reich and gave birth to World War II. Playing golf was rebranded "strategic patience."

But post the 2016 election, Russia threatens the very fabric of our democracy. Now enters the confluence of liberal wet dreams and reality: Trump's public call for assistance from his Russian cohorts, a neurotic wildly-biased MSM referencing imaginary "unnamed sources" who appear out of thin air magically whenever their narrative needs a refresh, and a heavy dose of paranoid schizophrenia which led to the reincarnation of Russian operatives (now "meddlers") Boris and Natasha from the Cartoon Network.

It is also the perfect recipe to get ordinary everyday Americans to turn off the newly-christened "fake news" altogether.

Without question the MSM has great animosity toward Donald Trump. It is highly visible, but is dwarfed by America's contempt and hatred toward the egregiously biased and corrupt MSM. The MSM tactics will continue to backfire on themselves until they understand the ricochet effect they have created. Barring major missteps during the Trump first term, it will be a significant factor in his 2020 re-election.

America has seen this movie before. Our minds drift back to the good ole days of the 2000 presidential election…pre-9/11, pre-Iraq War, pre-Katrina, pre-housing bubble collapse, and pre-historic first affirmative-action president. You remember. The good ole days of "hanging chad," which begat Bush Derangement Syndrome (BDS), the ancestor of Trump Derangement Syndrome (TDS).

What makes TDS so much more devastating to liberals is the ascent of alternatives to the Main Stream Media former monopoly since the Bush years. Social media, talk radio, and the Fox News Channel have all effectively cut into the traditional MSM market share to the point that their propaganda no longer *controls* American public opinion. The 2016 election result is Exhibit "A."

It must be acknowledged that liberals are controlled by emotion because they are incapable of logic. This results universally in a hysterical rush to judgment which is virtually always wrong because it is politically motivated by people who seek to *"fundamentally transform America"* for errant political reasons. It may be basically summarized as the "mob mentality."

America has seen the staged "mob mentality" show many times before. It is the political version of *"Groundhog Day."* Notable recent episodes include *"Hands up, Don't shoot!"* in Ferguson, MO, the Duke "rape" case, the Freddie Gray death in Baltimore, the Trayvon Martin death in Florida, the San Bernardino massacre, the Orlando massacre, the Las Vegas massacre, Obamacare. The objective of each "mob mentality" episode is to produce an emotional irreversible political outcome before logic and reason can influence the result. Twitter has made the flash mob as quick and easy as broadcasting a one line "bat signal" to a standby rabble of warm bodies.

We recall the Ferguson, MO, riots. How much destruction occurred there before it was revealed that the *"Hands up, don't shoot!"* eyewitness was lying? ***"Never underestimate the power of stupid people in large groups."*** — George Carlin.

The events surrounding the August 2014 street shooting fatality of black teenager Michael Brown in Ferguson, MO, near St. Louis is an interesting case study in *perspective*. Not every American will evaluate perceived "facts" the same way.

Allow me to illustrate with six (6) widely-varied perspectives on the same event, same set of facts. An FPD police officer, Darren Wilson, fired multiple shots and killed a young African-American male Michael Brown who was a suspect in an earlier convenience store strong-arm robbery. The police officer *first person/* eyewitness perspective and eyewitness testimony that the shooting was justified self-defense.

Another African-American named Dorian Johnson gave a *second person* bystander eyewitness perspective. He stated that the shooting victim was no threat to the police officer, <u>running away</u>, hands raised, hollering *"Hands up, don't shoot!"* Mr. Johnson later sued the city of Ferguson for $25K. The suit claimed Officer Wilson stopped the men *"without justification and unreasonably detained [them] before discharging his weapon, killing Brown."* Johnson's testimony was later discredited by the coroner's report which confirmed that Brown was *not* shot in the back. We were yet again treated to another perfect example of why America hates lawyers. The Johnson lawsuit was an exercise in the Rahm Emanuel postulated axiom: *"You never let a serious crisis go to waste."*

Riots, burning businesses, looting immediately followed the liberal media's *third person* perspective accounting of these preliminary "facts," and serious trouble continued sporadically for months afterward.

To liberal journalists, the point of the *"Hands up, don't shoot!"* narrative was not whether or not it was true. The point was it *could* have been true. The point was liberals *wanted* it to be true. All they have to do to bridge the gap between fantasy and truth is close their eyes and click their heels three times. ***"Never let the facts get in the way of a good story."* – Nucky Thompson (*Boardwalk Empire*).**

And so *"Hands up, don't shoot!"* became a national liberal rallying call. Victims of America unite!

A *fourth* reasoned legal perspective was delivered when a November 2014 *grand* jury with its typically low threshold of probable guilt did *not* indict the police officer for *any* crime.

A *fifth* political perspective came from the Obama-Holder Department of Justice (DoJ) investigation of the incident: although the DoJ supported the FPD officer's claim and grand jury conclusion of self-defense, they coincidently determined that the FPD had engaged in *misconduct* against the citizenry of Ferguson by among other things discriminating against African-Americans and applying racial stereo-types, in a *"pattern or practice of unlawful conduct."* America is very fortunate that Attorney General Eric Holder sent his team of investigators to Ferguson to find evidence of the conclusion he had reached while he was a freshman at Columbia University occupying the campus ROTC building during a 1969 protest of who-the-hell-knows-what. Not surprisingly, the DoJ reached the same conclusion in Fer-guson, MO, that President Barack Obama reached five years earlier in the Cambridge, MA 9-1-1 call incident. To wit: *"The Cambridge police acted stupidly."* And *"...there's a long history in this country of African Americans and Latinos being stopped by law enforcement disproportionately."*

My personal *(sixth)* perspective was to withhold judgement in lieu of non-biased facts, given the virtual 0% historical accuracy of the Main Stream Media (MSM) in any racial matter (e.g., the Duke lacrosse "rape" case, Trayvon Martin, Tawana Brawley, Freddie Gray in Baltimore, etc.)...actually, *any* matter whatsoever. In any racial matter, I use the garrulous blowhard Al Sharpton as a windsock. If the blovi-ating race hustler arsonist Sharpton interlopes with a narrative, I know to bet the *hacienda* on the 180° opposite eventual outcome. By the time the truth becomes apparent, Sharpton will be long gone pour-ing gasoline on the next racial fire.

The recurring riots in Ferguson, MO, were tragic and heartbreaking for many Americans. On a positive note, a GoFundMe account was set up for *"Natalie's Cakes and More"* on behalf of African-American Ferguson bake shop proprietor Natalie Dubose, who lost her new business in the chaos. She quickly met her $20K goal with $272+K in donations. In the interest of full disclosure, I was touched by her despair and made a modest donation.

All liberals wallow in the popularity of giving other people's money away. If some is good, more is better. British Prime Minister Margret Thatcher explained the liberal mindset so eloquently: *"The problem with socialism is that eventually you run out of other people's money to spend."* PM Thatcher was the first to articulate the socialist's one trick pony act: spending other people's money. Alternatively posed, what compassionate American is going to show up in poll survey against "free ____ for everybody!" Insert your own metaphor.

Money is also a key obsession of the OCDL because money equals power, which can easily be converted into *control*. The most common and abundant source of money to the OCDL is the American Taxpayer, i.e., the public trough. This, then, is a primary attraction of liberals to socialism: not only the power and *control* that results from redistribution of taxpayer revenue (called "graft"), but also redistribution of wealth from *future* taxpayers to liberals' current *persona grata* supporters. The national debt becomes a fresh cash cow for legalized embezzlement from future generations by present day parasites.

Victimless crime? Not a crime at all to a parasite. To liberals, America's unborn future citizens have no legal standing, unlike illegal aliens. This is how they get away with it. OCDL socialists love increasing the national debt because it satisfies their *control* addiction, however temporary the relief may be. Eventually the product of the national debt and the interest rate will mathematically cause the government to go bankrupt. At that point the government must enslave the population through confiscation of private property to save itself and your freedom will be a thing of the past. In the meantime, leave it to the conservative icon Margret Thatcher to buzzkill the party with reality.

Money and power are prerequisite tools to the *control* OCDLs must have in order to maintain any semblance of sanity. Moreover, the *control* they are seeking must be transparent and overt, frequently forcing people to do something against their will.

This brings us to the topic of taxes. Liberals, socialists and Democrats are universally against tax *cuts*. Why is that?

First and foremost, liberals are helpless snowflakes who want the government to take care of them with somebody else's money. To the extent the government is deprived of funding, our liberal comrade is reduced to foraging on her own. In contrast, our fellow conservative is predominantly self-sufficient and wants little government interference in his life because he knows it leads directly to indentured servitude.

Conservatives view money as earnings resulting from the individual's work product. Liberals view money as the property of the government to be rebated back to the individual only as necessary. Money should be used for the benefit of the collective, *not* the individual. Of course that is only after the government pays itself for the service of handling the people's money. This is why Washington D.C. is and always will be recession-proof.

The liberal view is that the government knows better how to spend the taxpayer's money than the taxpayer does. This is how "Shrimp on a Treadmill" projects get funded. The $682+K frivolous government grant to study "Taking the Pulse of Marine Life in Stressed Seas" was granted to College of Charleston biologists in 2011. The individual taxpayer is just too stupid to see public benefit in understanding shrimp cardio-vascular health. I know I am.

It is a major stretch for liberals to acknowledge the individual at all. *The 10 Planks of the Communist Manifesto* will provide more insight on this mindset (Chapter 6). And after all, the government incurred the burden and expense of printing the money, why shouldn't the government reclaim what they merely loaned to the American people? More oxymoronic "liberal logic."

This is part of the advertised liberal aversion toward tax cuts, but it is not the whole story. To liberals, there is no such thing as a tax cut. In the liberal vernacular, there is only a "tax cut *for the wealthy.*" The point being the words "tax cut" and "wealthy" are inseparable to a liberal. It is the inverse of "radical Islam," which does not exist within the liberal lexicon...the words "radical" and "Islam" will *never* be found together in any sentence uttered by a liberal. The word "wealthy" in the liberal dictionary means "anyone with a job."

A virtually universal characteristic of liberals is that they are not proficient in the sciences, because science requires logic. But if we examine the data, we will find that our liberal comrade might have inadvertently swerved into a modicum of truth for the first time ever. Facts are friendly: 50% of Americans pay *no* income tax at all. The top 1% of American income earners pay 50% of all income tax; the top 10% of income earners pay 80% of all income tax— a lot of numbers that add up to the simple fact that it is only the "wealthy" who pay any income tax in the first place.

Then who should rightfully benefit from an income tax cut? The 50% who didn't pay *any* income tax? An emphatic "Yes!" replies our liberal comrade to this rhetorical question.

The people who pay the most income tax now are also America's wealth *creators*. The money they save on an income tax cut is spent on things other people of lesser wealth must produce through their *employment*. If our affluent countryman buys a new Cadillac Escalade, someone was employed in Arlington, TX to assemble the vehicle. Countless others nationwide are employed to manufacture its component parts. That creates jobs. "*…the number one job facing the middle class, and it happens to be, as Barack says, a three-letter word: jobs. J-O-B-S, jobs.*" – Joe Biden (10.15.08). They also spend their money on business investment which is the capital for yet more job growth. *The wealthy employ people. The poor do not.*

This entire line of thought led to the economic boom of the 1980s under the leadership of President Ronald Reagan…the decade that liberals today pretend never happened. The 1980s were so economically successful that the economic prosperity carried forward into the 1990s, making Bill Clinton look good outside of his personal sex scandals.

Democrats know this. To prove this assertion, I point out a television ad I have seen frequently for the Democrat-controlled state of New York. Perhaps you have seen it too. The state of New York advertises a 10-year state tax holiday for businesses that will relocate or start up in one of their designated "tax free zones." Don't ask what happens after the 10-year period has expired. If you have to ask, you can't afford it. Their intent is to replace the tax-based businesses they are hemorrhaging to zero-income states like Florida and Texas. Good luck finding suckers for that "bait and switch" deal!

The point here is that liberal schemers in New York know full well that the way to be competitive in attracting new businesses is to offer them reduced taxes. Meanwhile, New York senators and representatives argue the Trump proposed income tax plan, which includes massive income tax cuts for individuals and businesses alike, is a scam that will undercut the middle class. Of course that is what doubling the standard deduction for couples from $12K to $24K will do…anyone who can count beyond their fingers and toes will very quickly see through this sinister Trump ruse!

Aside from the absurd demagoguery, the hypocrisy, and the ignorance of historical tax-cut success, why do liberals oppose *every* tax cut? First and foremost, they oppose tax cuts because *they know it will work*, a fact clearly demonstrated by the afore- mentioned "New New York" campaign tax break ad. A successful Trump tax plan means a two-term Trump presidency just like the two-term Reagan presidency in the 1980s. This is a liberal's worst nightmare: having to pretend yet *another* eight years of American prosperity resulting from conservative tax cuts did not happen even before the Reagan era has been forgotten. Americans have short memories...but Baby Boomers remember. A second Reagan era in a single liberal lifetime may be more than their fragile Marxist psyches can handle.

But there is an even more fundamental ideological driver for their opposition to *all* tax cuts: it is because money equals power, which equals the *control* they obsess over. Even if Democrats are not currently in power, they expect to return to power sooner rather than later. They delude themselves constantly with the fantasy that America will get over the Obamacare debacle and that their time will come with the next election, as if they have done ever done *anything* to earn the vote of the American people.

Democrats are quick to point out their eternal lead in the generic poll taken at the corner of Broadway and 116th St. in Harlem, New York City (polling only Democrats) as conclusive evidence that they are about to sweep the next election cycle. The polling question might as well been *"Are you for Santa Claus or against? Check D for and R against."* The polls are *prima facie* evidence that Santa Claus remains popular, nothing more. In this post-Obama era, Democrats must take refuge from the Obama trail of destruction where they can find it.

The Democrats showed the same generic ballot polling advantage throughout the eight-year Obama era and lost first the House, then the Senate. Aside from Obama, who was elected exclusively because of his skin color, the Democrats have suffered catastrophic elected-office damage during the Obama presidential years.

When (and if) they return to power, they want an overbearing tax structure already in place. They want an impoverished citizenry dependent on government entitlement spending already in place. To return to the majority and then immediately raise taxes to increase their *control* over the American people would be political suicide in the epic-fail range of Obamacare.

They want the money to be able to *control* the American people with redistribution of America's confiscated wealth. They would clearly rather sacrifice America's prosperity for the *control* and power higher taxes gives them. This is completely the result of OCD, and their number one obsession, *control*.

"A government big enough to give you everything you want, is a government big enough to take away everything that you have." – **Thomas Jefferson**.

It should be pointed out that here again, the liberal prefers rhetoric over results...form over substance.

The liberal *control* motive is also the genesis of leftist hatred of corporations, which have brought unprecedented prosperity (jobs) to America. Corporations threaten big government's (the word is "*Bolshevik*") insatiable appetite for *control*. *Prosperity is the mortal enemy of big government.*

The purpose of corporations is to make a profit. Profits help feed and provide a living for employees, shareholders, and investors. More profits mean less government dependency. Liberals disdain, detest, and universally denounce the word "profit" and all the independence from government it represents like the Pope denounces Satan.

Nor do liberals have any use whatsoever for entrepreneurs, who are the creators of successful businesses. These businesses lead to profits and many eventually metastasize into evil corporations providing products and services that people want at a price they can afford. All *bad*! All of this should be the function of a dysfunctional liberal-run government.

In summary, leftists are against anything that will lead to capitalist success because it is a vector of opposition to government *control*. If this diatribe sounds a little harsh, I challenge any liberal to give me an example of where it is errant.

So now we get the most transparently absurd rationale for opposing major tax cuts for the American people proposed by Trump ever: in one of the greatest 180° political whiplash turnabouts in American history, liberals oppose tax cuts because "it will increase the budget deficit." Forget the positive dynamic impact that the tax cuts of the Reagan years and the Bush years had on the deficit and national debt. Those never happened; they were conservative hallucinations.

Yes, the same people who virtually doubled the national debt from $10.6T to $19.1T during Obama's two terms have suddenly grown a conscience and decided stealing from their own grandchildren is a bad idea? Hardly. The issue here is *who controls* spending the money. Democrats are no longer in *control* of this sacred government function, so now it is a very BAD thing. It has gone full circle from George W. Bush (deficit spending BAD!) to Barack Obama (deficit spending GOOD!) to Donald Trump (deficit spending BAD again!).

On the other hand, perhaps Democrats are just lying and will do anything, including sabotaging the financial well-being of the American people, to make sure Trump does *not* succeed so that they can recapture the presidency? ***Liberals lie about their motives 100.000% of the time.***

As reinforcement for this broad brush indictment, ask yourself this question: "How many times have I seen Democrats maneuver to postpone a key vote or policy enactment until *after* the next election?" Or the corollary question "How often have I seen Republicans press for a key vote *before* the next election?" The reason for these tactics is all too obvious: full disclosure of motives to the voter.

The truth is that the Trump tax cut will pay for itself and further pay down the national debt through economic growth, which liberals will never understand. During the Reagan administration, annual federal income tax receipts grew from $618 billion to $991 billion (an increase of 60%) due to growth of the American economy. The concept of economic growth is about as compatible with the fundamentally myopic and static liberal principle of the "zero sum game" as a tire iron in my garbage disposal.

Control is the same liberal motivation that spawned Obamacare. There is no better tool for *controlling* the population than through government healthcare, which incidentally carried with it the additional *control* benefit of a substantial incremental tax burden. Government healthcare was never about healthcare...it was always about government.

Control is also the origin of their never-ending obsession with "tail wags the dog" minority-rules causes: transgender bathrooms, depriving fertile California farmland of water for an insignificant fish no one has ever seen or heard of, blocking American energy independence and jobs by obstructing the Keystone pipeline due to imaginary worst-case scenario environmental damage, banning 16 oz. soft drinks, forcing Christian bakeries to bake cakes for gay weddings against their religious beliefs, banning the film classic *Gone with the Wind* from theaters, removing elephants from the circus, forcing Americans to support abortion against their religion with their own tax dollars, removing Civil War hero statues from display, banning the name Washington "Redskins," etc.

To most Americans, many of these causes seem childish and petty. However, to the OCDL they sustain the purpose of their very existence. It is the insatiable need for this elusive confirmation that their life has relevance and therefore meaning. For with no valid spiritual base, the OCDL is completely dependent on an *external* source of relevance validation. They are attracted to high-profile meaningless emotional causes like a swarm of termites to a 2 x 4, allowing them to showcase their moral hubris, which is now known as *"virtue signaling."* From this we may also accurately conclude that liberalism is a desperate scream for attention: "LOOK AT ME! I AM RELEVANT!!!"

To OCDLs, failure is not an option because their psychological well-being is at stake. There is no cause too petty or too absurd, and all combat is either to momentary victory or to self-delusional denial.

It is this hopeless quest for relevance that drives all liberals to relive the "Golden Age of Liberalism," the Civil Rights era of the 1960s.

This retro movement can be accomplished three different ways:

1. By self-delusion, at which liberals are exceptional. Pretend we never left the 1960s: the fascist threat to the liberals' exalted "social justice" is ubiquitous. For example, let's imagine the Omni-

present menace of the KKKlan (Robert C. Byrd?) still lurks among us. Or let's imagine a neo-Nazi (George Soros?) in every bush. Or let's imagine card-carrying NRA members (Sarah Palin, Dana Loesch and Ted Nugent?) have their crosshair sights set on *innocent* liberal "protestors" (Antifa on the Berkeley campus?). Then too, America is populated with various and assorted "bitter clingers" and TEA Party Neanderthals. All of these "deplorables" have been emboldened by the election of white- supremacist Donald Trump, and it is now open season on minorities. "Racism!" in America has made a full comeback.

We can imagine that innocent liberal "protestors" are being threatened by the growing menace of the imaginary neo-Nazi movement. The remedy is clear enough: ban freedom of speech and the Confederate flag. Remove all statues and monuments of Confederate war heroes followed by removal of monuments to America's slave-owning founding fathers, followed by removal of statues of explorers, followed by removal of statues of anyone white. This is not "mission creep." It is OCD run amok. The cheerleading liberals get from the biased far left MSM not only condones but *encourages* them to find even more absurd causes.

This "clear and present danger" to American freedom by white supremacists must be crushed: a (masked) strike force which can oxymoronically attack preemptively in "self-defense" at events such as the hate speech of neo-Nazi Ben Shapiro (who diabolically disguises himself as a Jew) on the University of California Berkeley campus. Think of the damage this Nazi blowtorch could do to the precious snowflakes there with a few heinous syllables! There must be an intervention by the Antifa Thought Police!!!

"We cannot continue to rely only on our military in order to achieve the national security objectives that we've set," Obama read from his teleprompter during a 07.02.08 campaign speech in Colorado Springs, CO. *"We've got to have a civilian national security force that's just as powerful, just as strong, just as well-funded."*

Antifa was made to order for this task. "Antifa" is a contraction for "anti-fascist." It is about as anti-fascist as the "Affordable Care Act" is affordable. It is the most egregious oxymoron this side of "liberal logic." The masked Antifa-ites (who were obviously childhood Zorro fans) identify potential hate speakers and pre-emptively attack them in "self-defense". They are the sole arbitrators of first the hate speech itself, and then who is likely to be the next hate speech offender, and finally the appropriate pre-emptive violent attack. Antifa is a unique blend of the McCarthyism spirit of the American 1950s, the thuggery of Hitler's Brown Shirts during 1930s Nazi Germany, and the stealth active wear of modern day ISIS. We now understand what Obama had in mind in his 2008 speech about a *"civilian national security force."*

The truth is that America already has such a civilian national security force. They are called "bikers". Many are Vietnam veterans. And if it devolves into a showdown, your rent-a-thug mob will be wearing a "Rolling Thunder" tire facial.

2. The return to the 60s could be facilitated by importing a whole new minority class which needs liberal civil rights advocacy. These could be Mexican migrant workers, Mexican drug gangs, Middle Eastern ISIS infiltrators, Central American MS-13 *animals*, etc. The imports must be *non*-white, non-English speaking, have *no* education or job skills, and have *no* intention of ever assimilating into American society to qualify for this role.

    This resume will guarantee the new immigrant need of government for *everything*. It is the perfect recipe for liberal co-dependency: the American liberal politician in need of new voters and the new minority in need of American taxpayer largesse.

    "When the people find that they can vote themselves money, that will herald the end of the republic." — Ben Franklin.

    The liberal politician has no concern for the long-term survival of the republic. He (she or it) is only concerned with satisfying the immediate obsession for *control*. It's all good because the liberal doesn't have to pay for any of it herself; there is an infinite public trough to cover her re-election funding needs. That is what deficits are for.

3. America can return to the 60s by recreating the racial tension of the 1960s through "community organizing" America into a race war on law enforcement. It starts with rhetorical sniper fire like *"The Cambridge police acted stupidly,"* and *"If I had a son, he'd look like Trayvon,"* on open law enforcement matters.

    Then a corrupt Department of Justice (DoJ) investigates local law enforcement in matters that have racial implications. The DoJ investigation result is cookie cutter: although there was no criminal wrong-doing in the original incident under investigation, there is "systemic racism" in the police department (based on evidence that is not released to the public). The investigation-targeted police department must submit to new DoJ requirements under penalty of forfeiting federal government funding. This is obviously not extortion if the government is the perp...who is going to prosecute the DoJ for extortion or coercion?

There is no one as judgmental as liberals. Their judgments are typically instantaneous, erroneous, and irreversible. This leaves them constantly covering up the last mess. Their consistently poor judgment results from their inability to reason, which is undermined by their OCD. It puts them on the wrong side of every major issue such as abortion, gun control, immigration, national defense, fiscal responsibility, etc.

The American Culture and Faith Institute recently released a patriotism poll documenting what **liberals** think are the most patriotic American institutions and people: the Democrat Party, Colin Kaepernick, the U.S. Supreme Court, Planned Parenthood, Michael Moore, the New York Times, and the NFL. Surprisingly, Anthony D. Weiner (aka "Carlos Danger"), the New Black Panthers, Kathy Griffin, Antifa, Rosie O'Donnell, the Council on American-Islamic Relations (CAIR), Jeffrey Dahmer, and Charles Manson narrowly missed the cut.

Liberals are perpetually seeking excuses for their failures because they are perpetually failing. They are accomplished at excuses out of necessity. Barack Obama spent eight years blaming his socialist economic failure on George W. Bush. Hillary Clinton will spend the rest of her life dreaming up new excuses for her failure in the 2016 presidential election. My personal favorite is "Macedonian content farmers." Anyone who can locate Macedonia on a global map wins a chicken dinner.

Her first book on the subject is titled *What Happened?* America prays that it is her last.

Liberals project <u>themselves</u> onto their political opponents. That is to say liberals project their own bigotry of racial low expectations onto conservatives. They project their own "Russian collusion" onto conservatives. They project their own "obstruction of justice" onto conservatives. They project their own fascism onto conservatives. Etc. They are licensed to do that in the court of public opinion because they are prolific at giving other people's money away, which is the root of their popularity...plus a major assist from their corrupt accomplices in the MSM, who also think that giving away money that other people earned is "BIG fun." *"Laissez les bons temps rouler"* – Cajun French expression meaning *"Let the good times roll."*

The post-2016 presidential election aftermath is a classic example of liberal delusional denial in lieu of failure. The OCDL had over-invested all psychological capital in the defeat of Donald J. Trump. For them, election defeat was beyond comprehension. And yet it happened.

Post-election OCDLs were divided among three basic delusional mindsets: (1) those who thought the election had not yet happened and remained in campaign mode, like Hillary herself; (2) those who thought they won the election like Chuckles-the-Clown Schumer; and (3) those who sought to "correct" the bogus election result by manufacturing another imaginary Trump scandal, *vis a vis* "Russian hackers" like the rogue FBI leadership cabal. Curious behavior indeed from the same sanctimonious herd who bleated in synchronized indignation when Trump who refused to answer "Yes" to the question "Will you accept the election results?" during a pre-election debate. By his treasonous response, Trump had "disqualified" himself from the office of the presidency from that moment forward...a menace to "our democracy" itself! Now that it is Democrats refusing the election result, it is "patriotic." No hypocrisy to see here America...just move on.

All three of these mindsets can be clinically diagnosed as "denial." Let us be clear: the first two are merely delusional, and some may succumb to reality in due course. It is the third mindset which actually poses a clear and present danger to our democracy.

Because the Democrat party is leaderless, the far left-controlled Main Stream Media (MSM) has expanded itself to fill the vacuum. Congressional Democrats are now their puppets. This is the lay of the landscape in the wreckage and political wasteland left behind by the scorched-earth Obama regime.

America is gob-smacked daily with the MSM slanderous/libelous dump bomb designed to confuse, anger, distract, demoralize and otherwise punish Americans for the felony of electing Donald J. Trump president. This campaign of misinformation is nothing new for the MSM based on over a century of leftist propagandist history. Actually, the process has become quite streamlined now that it is entirely contained within the MSM, i.e. no need to coordinate with extraneous irrelevant groups such as the Democrat National Committee (DNC). I mean, who would you even talk to at the DNC, the monosyllabic refugee from a 1940s creature feature movie "F-bomb Tom" Perez?

The MSM dump bomb *de jour* begins with alleged anonymous-sourced information which always precisely fits the target narrative. This should raise suspicion in the mind of anyone capable of critical thought, which automatically excludes the left. The narrative is quickly picked up by other MSM comrades, twitter being the usual conduit of choice. From there it metastasizes like stage-8 brain cancer. In reality, it is a desperate daily exercise of throwing as much Trump slanderous mud (choose your own metaphor here) against the wall as possible to see if *anything* will stick. Guilty until proven innocent, no evidence necessary, is the standard for the daily "Trial by MSM."

There is no better example of this journalistic malpractice than the accusation that Trump had ordered the statue of Dr. Martin Luther King removed from the White House immediately after the inauguration. The purpose of this particular dump bomb was to sabotage relations between the new administration and the African-American community. It was also a completely clumsy MSM attempt at mitigation for the childish Obama blunder of returning the bust of Sir Winston Churchill to England immediately upon entry into the White House in January 2009.

The MIA-MLK bust story was front page above the fold for two days before anyone in the media acknowledged that the statue was right where it had always been. The reporter who tweeted the initial accusation later explained he could not see the statue because someone was standing in front of it… who knew?!?!? No apology was ever given for the misinformation or its spread. ***"A lie can travel around the world and back again while the truth is lacing up its boots."*—Mark Twain.**

So the MSM gets another failing grade for that malicious stunt. On the "J-school fool" grade scale, it is *magna cum laude*. Their performance has deteriorated noticeably since then as their desperation anxiety has increased.

It took a massive quantum leap on November 8, 2016, when the MSM was unable to prevent Trump from winning the White House. What we are now seeing in the antics of the left led by the MSM media is ever-increasing desperation resulting from their failure to stop Trump first from getting the

Republican nomination, and then from winning the general election. More fundamentally, it is the reality that they have lost *control* of the artificial narrative they fed daily to the American public for over a century. Narrative *control* is absolutely crucial to the OCDL.

We digress briefly for a recent case study in narrative *control* abuse by the left. America has been awash in positive news during the second year of the Trump administration: economic performance and consumer confidence are at high water marks for the 21st century; peace and denuclearization on the Korean peninsula appear to be within reach, ISIS virtually defeated in the Middle East, FBI and Department of Justice (DoJ) corruption is finally exposed to the cold light of day via the flawed Inspector's General report on the Hillary Clinton email scandal, etc.

The American people *must* be distracted from anything positive associated with Trump. This is a key job responsibility of both the MSM and congressional Democrat hecklers. Stormy Daniels (who gives a whole new perspective on "Silicone Valley") is old news, criticism Melania's shoes backfired rather spectacularly. Criticism of Melania's accent when speaking English (her *fifth* language) by the MSM (whose *second* language is Pig Latin) is an insightful exhibition of oxymoronic "liberal tolerance". And now the Mueller probe is fading faster than the Wicked Witch of the West in a drive through car wash.

We need an *issue*. How about the cruel and unusual separation of invading Central American "families" at the US southern border? (Incidentally, all credible accounts are that 80+% of the "families" are *not* families at all.) Yes, that's it! Liberals *never* pass up an opportunity to use children as human shields, this is no exception. Children are always the perfect prop for any propaganda campaign, as we witnessed in the post Parkland, FL high school shooting gun control revival. Invading hordes of Central Americans masquerading as families are separated into adults and children for required legal processing before adjudication for entry into the United States. This is what current law requires. For anyone who is genuinely concerned about these invading "families", the relevant question is "What kind of parents would give their child up to strangers to make the perilous 2,500 mile journey from Central America to the coveted asylum in the United States?" The journey to the United States is not about asylum, because our Central American pilgrims bypass 2,500 miles of Mexican asylum to get here. It is about access to the American treasury. It is the same reason homeless drug addicts are attracted to San Francisco and Seattle. ***"If you want more of behavior x, subsidize it."***

Democrats will gladly give away the American treasury, or for that matter America itself, in exchange for votes. Such is their obsession with power.

Now I would like utilize imagery to juxtapose genuine American family separation (below upper) with the left's fake family separation temporary child detention center near the Mexican border (lower).

The left does not understand why President Trump cannot just waive the law the way Obama did when it did not suit his political whim. They also do not understand why Trump cannot unilaterally make new immigration law by executive order the way Obama did with his Deferred Action for Childhood Arrivals (DACA) proclamation. The chorus of criticism from the left is deafening, successfully hijacking the news cycle away from all the positive events that should be headlining the news cycle. Any positive news has been exiled back to somewhere after the obituaries and the delinquent tax notices.

The overview of this propaganda farce is actually quite stunning. Democrat lawmakers are relentlessly criticizing the president for enforcing laws *they* passed. They are criticizing him for *not* ignoring the laws *they* passed. They refuse to work with him to pass laws that would be better for everyone, including their under aged human shields. Their co-conspirators in the media hysterically cheerlead the propaganda effort.

The purpose of the liberal farce is threefold: (1) distract America from Trump's many spectacular successes; (2) manufacture an issue they can utilize in the 2018 mid-term elections, regardless of where it dangles off the palate of American voter priority; and (3) overrun America with what they envision as their future voting base. *This* is the imaginary "blue wave" of liberal lore.

And make no mistake about it, liberals have precisely zero concern for the non-American children for whom they "lament". It is all yet another acting job, at which they regard themselves as supremely gifted. "Based on what evidence?" you may ask. Liberal overwhelming support of Planned Parenthood and partial birth abortion would be my response.

Now Democrats attempt to manufacture a populist themed mirage for the 2018 midterms, "Abolish ICE!" (Immigration and Customs Enforcement) emerges based on a single primary election result.

Yes, attacking law enforcement has long been the "go to" stratagem of the Democrat playbook. It plays well in NY 14th District (east Bronx/north Queens), which is one the most egregiously liberal districts in America… at least among 12% of the voters who turned out in the last primary election there. The NY-14 upset of incumbent Joe Crowley by Alexandra Ocasio-Cortez is instantly extrapolated beyond infinity, and liberal losers so starved for anything that might work at the polls head for their nearest ICE office with pitchforks and flaming torches in hand. Liberals need a strawman to burn. Tag, ICE… you're it!

Like sharks on bloody chum, our irrationally OCD infested Democrat strategist/wind sock envisions the same non-reasoned emotional anarchist "Abolish ICE!" message will work nationwide. Yes, in Joplin, MO it will surely carry Claire McCaskill to a re-election landslide victory as incumbent red state Missouri senator. In reality, it is coastal demented elitist "fool's gold". And Ocasio-Cortez, who has and economics degree from Boston University but doesn't know a profit from a prophet, is *not* the next liberal Messiah despite her abundant identity qualifications (female, minority). It is more likely that her degree is in *Grubering* (see Chapter 11). She is *not* ready for prime time, and "Make America Venezuela Again!" is not gonna sell anywhere outside coastal urban cesspools.

Or perhaps Democrats will pick up the lead of New York Governor Andrew Cuomo who declared *"America was never that great,"* in an August 15, 2018 speech before a women's rights group in Manhattan. His declaration was a refreshing contrast to the stodgy Donald Trump 2016 campaign slogan *"Make America Great Again"*. It surely will sweep Cuomo into the White House in an election coming to you soon.

After realizing that his initial attempt at manufacturing a campaign "drop the mic" moment failed miserably, Cuomo stated the very next day *"I want to be very clear: Of course America is great and of course America has always been great,"* in a follow up attempt to mitigate the self-inflicted gunshot wound to his very own *gluteus maximus*.

Of course you are as full of cr@p as a 5¢ burrito, Cuomo. *This* is what being hoisted the petard of your own Trump Derangement Syndrome (TDS) looks like.

And once again we scratch our heads wondering what Democrats are actually *for*. There are an abundance of issues where they have made it known what they are *against*: tax cuts, border enforcement, freedom of speech, constitutionalist SCOTUS nominations, the 2nd Amendment, Israel, etc. The things they are actually *for* cannot be disclosed in public.

But at this point Democrats need a strawman to burn down for their 2018 midterm pep rally. Clearly America is not going allow the Mueller Russian collusion delusion to serve that purpose, it is wearing on everybody's nerves. So the battle cry *de jour* "ICE gotta go!" becomes the latest liberal manufactured political rabbit hole. Desperate people do desperate things.

There is another component to the NY-14 election aside from the gross rejection of American sovereignty and law enforcement. Joe Crowley is a 56 year old liberal white male Democrat in exalted standing with his party: pro-abortion, anti-Trump, socialist, higher taxes, increased government spending, anti-military, anti-law enforcement, anti-2nd Amendment, etc. In short, Crowley was fully vested in doubling down on what has gotten America into its current liberal induced mess.

Crowley was first elected to congress in 1999 and held various chairmanships within the Democrat Party. It was widely understood that he would pose a viable challenge to Nancy Pelosi's Democratic House leadership position in the foreseeable future.

Alexandra Ocasio-Cortez is a 28 year old Puerto Rican descended radical socialist with virtually no experience in politics. Aside from the difference in age, experience and radical militancy, there is likely little philosophical difference between these two contenders.

The key election outcome determinant between these two contenders was skin color and gender discrimination among voters as surely as your property taxes are going up again. Joe Crowley is the first of many white male Democrat politicians who will become extinct sooner rather than later.

Democrats have spent well over a generation sabotaging America's heritage, including our (white male) founding fathers and our Constitution. You can bet Crowley condoned if not encouraged this disrespectful revisionist propaganda. Crowley's election loss is an unintended consequence of this lifetime crusade. Congratulations, Joe. You have officially been hoisted on your own liberal petard.

White female Democrats like Nancy Pelosi and Elizabeth F. Warren, who think they are safe in this game of identity politics Russian roulette because of their gender, will eventually become extinct as well. Hillary Clinton learned this lesson all too well in the 2008 Democrat primary (Chapter 8: Victimology).

For decades, the MSM has envisioned itself the godfather of American politics. They have been able to manipulate the American electorate with strategic miss-information and thus nudge marginal elections to the left. This power and *control* has undergone a steady erosion for the last quarter century due to the emergence and ever increasing popularity of talk radio, the Fox News Channel (FNC), and particularly the Internet.

"Rathergate" is a vivid illustration of the powerful role the Internet now has over the news cycle. Late in the 2004 Bush v. Kerry presidential campaign, the MSM kingpin CBS News-produced "60 Minutes" indicted incumbent president George W. Bush with fraudulent memos impugning his Alabama National Guard service. The documents were quickly spotted as illegitimate by an internet blogger based on the bogus typing font of the earlier era. This revelation spread throughout the Internet like HIV in a 1980s San Francisco bathhouse. "60 Minutes" was instantly on the defensive. The feature narrator, Dan Rather, quickly exhausted all credibility capital attempting to defend the indefensible. Despite eventually apologizing profusely for being caught, his reputation was destroyed and the reputation of "60 Minutes" was mortally wounded. It was at this point that the MSM was served notice that it no longer had *carte blanche* to inseminate the American people with artificial information. Mr. Rather became the first casualty of the internet phenomena we now know as "fact checking." In Mr. Rather's case, it was swift and lethal. It has since evolved into instant and lethal. Internet 1, MSM 0.

From the perspective of the MSM, the loss of power and *control* has gotten substantially worse since then. For them, the situation has reached critical mass. They envision returning to the era 30+ years ago when they had complete *control* of the flux of information to the American public. Those days are gone forever.

So what we are witnessing now from the MSM is the meltdown that results from OCDL loss of *control*. It is no different from the reaction of any other OCDL individual; it is just more visible.

The vehement protests over Trump on Twitter by the MSM, Democrats, and other leftists is identically rooted. When Trump tweets, they cannot edit, coalesce, and distort his message to conform to their agenda. They have lost *control*. This literally drives them insane. They must force him to stop tweeting his unadulterated message directly to his millions of followers or face psychological as well as political destruction. Trump realizes the power of Twitter, and there are no indications that he will succumb to the self-censorship demanded by OCDLs. Sadly for them, it is not possible to extort a multi-billionaire.

There is a further complication. What if Trump's success in defeating the MSM emboldens other conservatives to defy the MSM? What if Republicans see Trump winning the crucial narrative battle and grow a spine? To lose the narrative battle will surely bring on other challenges to the media's power and *control* of their propaganda monopoly. Trump's leadership could trigger an anti-media tsunami and turn the MSM into a ridiculous clown car.

This just in: The Trump media rebellion has already happened!

It must be noted here that Trump has a near-perfect profile of the prototypical contemptible OCDL strawman villain: white, septuagenarian, multi-billionaire, Christian, loud, opinionated, braggadocio, successful alpha male…a demographic which OCDLs and Oprah alike would agree should be expunged from the face of the earth. Two hundred and fifty years ago he could have been a founding father, perhaps even a slave owner.

The point of this protracted example is to elucidate the liberal obsession with *control*, and the type of behavior that results when they do not have *control*. Trump will be a tough nut to crack for OCDLs both in and out of the MSM. He has clearly demonstrated that he cannot be intimidated. Unlike the Clintons, he cannot be bought. He took the job and the accompanying pay cut (he is now working for zero compensation) because he seeks to improve the lives of everyday Americans and for the country he loves. These are uncharted waters for the left and the MSM. They have never faced an opponent with these motives, resources, and determination before.

Most likely scenario? Trump was elected by the American people against the headwinds of the profoundly-biased MSM and rigged election polls. That hasn't changed. The attacks we see daily by the MSM are not just attacks on President Trump; they are attacks on the voters who elected him…the millions of unwashed and uneducated American voters (like myself) who have the audacity to think that the election result was up to them. They clearly did not get the memo. The function of the MSM is not to inform the American people; it is to *control* them.

Another high-profile case history serves to illustrate the liberal obsession with *control*: Barack Obama was clearly the most liberal president in U.S. history.

What were his key priorities? Government healthcare, gun *control*, climate change, and open borders. Each of these priorities is aimed at only one thing: *control* of the American people.

Obama did not think of himself as president for 8 years. He thought of himself as ruler for life. This became evident to me when he abandoned the legislative process completely for executive order rule-by-fiat two years into his presidency. "After all, how could America pass that opportunity up?" the pathological narcissist asked Himself. We can guess what His gushing retort to Himself was. So He envisioned Himself in it for the long haul. In that scenario, disarming the people you want to *control* has to be the top priority, just like it has been for dictators throughout the ages.

The script for the liberal gun control play never changes. It is classic political opportunism from the Rahm Emanuel playbook – *"You never let a serious crisis go to waste."*

Within minutes (seconds?) of a mass shooting, the next gun *control* sales pitch is set into motion. Within hours, before any of the victims or the shooter is even identified, the usual suspects are in front of a camera trying to convince America that "the gun did it" and the 2nd Amendment is evil (just like the rest of our constitution). All liberal politicians are frustrated actors, you understand. Chuck "Hole" Schumer (D-NY) even turns on the tear spigot when his rhetoric fails. The tears stop 1 Nanosecond after the camera is turned off. I award Schumer my personal maximum rating for his comical tearful performance:

"Something *must* be done now!" bleats out the leftist politician protected by *armed* body guards, just to emphasize what she thinks of you. *"More gun laws!!"* (which have worked so well that Chicago is now a third- world combat zone). There is never any mention of the *existing* laws that were already broken in the commission of the tragedy.

During a *single* weekend in August 2018, 70+ people were shot and 12 died. However, all is not lost for besieged Mayor Rahm Emanuel: (1) Chicago remains a sanctuary city (for illegal alien criminals, *not* resident American citizens); (2) Chicago remains a "Trump free zone"; and (3) the 12 latest deceased shooting victims will be voting Democrat for the duration. Chicago has been run by Democrats since dead people acquired the right to vote there in the early 20th century.

"If we can only eliminate guns, the slaughter would instantly stop!!!" we can imagine Adolph Hitler imploring citizens in 1930s Nazi Germany. Gun control in Nazi Germany was soon followed by the greatest mass shooting in human history.

THIS is why we have a 2nd Amendment. *"Political power grows from the barrel of a gun."* - Mao Tse-Tung (1949). It is even more effective when your political opponent has been disarmed.

When the American wilderness was settled, there was no law. The law was provided by your gun. Vast areas of America remain that way today. Coastal and urban liberals do not understand that fact because they don't want to. But this is why we continue to need a 2nd Amendment today. ***The reason we have a 1st Amendment is because we have a 2nd Amendment.***

Freedom is *not* free. An armed citizenry is the worst enemy of a wannabe dictator who would socio-pathically weaponize the government against the people to corrupt the election process. It is a major obstacle to the control and power he lusts for. If America is to remain free, we must remain armed and find workable solutions to mental illness which drives mass shooters.

Immediately after their December 7, 1941, attack on Pearl Harbor, the Japanese considered an invasion of the United States West Coast. The idea was rejected because of the American citizenry armed *via* U.S. Constitution 2nd Amendment. The Japanese understood America was *not* a "gun free zone."

As usual, the real target of liberals is hidden from the view of the American people. Their stealth targets are the 2nd Amendment of the Constitution, which dominoes into the Constitution itself. And the National Rifle Association (NRA), which supports the 2nd Amendment is also a target along with any political candidates who oppose gun *control*. Thus the NRA becomes the essential focal point for liberal OCD hatred. At this point I think it appropriate to ask some questions: How many mass shootings in America have been perpetrated by NRA members? How many mass shootings in America have been truncated by NRA members…or other American hero *with a gun*? How many mass shootings in America have been perpetrated by psychotic liberals? How many mass shootings in America have occurred in "gun free" zones? What would America's murder rate be if the five cities with the highest murder rates (Chicago, Detroit, Washington DC, St. Louis, New Orleans) were deleted from the nationwide statistic? Who runs these cities?

Liberals at all times need a strawman *piñata*. On gun *control*, the NRA is it. Condemning the NRA for every gun-related death beyond the Chicago city limits is the complement to abdicating the personal responsibility of the shooter.

Make no mistake about it, the American left wants to disarm law-abiding conservatives. Even liberals understand that criminals will not disarm because criminals, like liberals, have no respect for the law in the first place. This disrespect is psychologically rooted like every other liberal character malady. When the law conflicts with the liberal's convoluted obsessively compulsive sense of "justice", the law is *wrong* and can therefore justifiably be ignored or broken. This disrespect for the law is a unique liberal blend of sociopathic egomania and the basic requisite obsessive compulsive disorder.

Guns are the tools of the criminals' trade, and their guns are all illegal already.

There are workable solutions to America's school shooting problem that do not involve confiscating the guns from law abiding citizens. One such solution would be school marshals who operate on the same basis as air marshals. The left counters with a heaping helping of "liberal logic": "More guns in schools are <u>not</u> the answer!" To the typical superficial liberal thinker, it sounds superficially reasonable. This is classic liberal conflation to make a perfectly *in*valid point. **"Never argue with idiots…they will drag you down to their level and beat you with experience."—Mark Twain.** Sage advice.

On that same basis, the police should disarm before entering a school in response to a shooter because it would introduce more guns into the school. Also, the Capitol Hill Police officers who gunned down the psychotic Bernie Sanders supporter at a Republican baseball practice on June 14, 2017 in Arlington, VA should never be allowed firearms. The would-be mass shooter opened fire critically wounding Congressman Steve Scalise. The victims had baseball bats and had the shooter outnumbered; that should have been good enough, right? Also, the Secret Service who protect the president should disarm immediately. There you have it. "Liberal logic" hits yet another new low.

Seriously, if you are the victim of a home invasion robbery and a gunfight breaks out, do you want to be the only one there *without* a gun? No, I have chosen a different strategy.

Yes, liberals do *not* want heroic Parkland, FL assistant football coach Aaron Feis, who saved school children's lives by absorbing mass shooter gunfire with his body, to be able to defend himself and his students. The simple truth is that by the time armed police show up at the next "gun free zone" massacre, the damage is *already* done. Response time statistics prove this point: the typical mass shooting is over in less than 5 minutes. The typical law enforcement response time is more than 5 minutes. That makes an onsite defense plan the *only* plausible effective deterrent. *A gun in the hand is worth more than the entire police force on the phone.*

The left rejects this solution because they are <u>not</u> interested in protecting school children; they are only obsessed with "gun *control*," ultimately leading to gun confiscation. This is why liberals reject any and all mass shooting solutions short of nationwide gun *control*. A *workable* solution such as hardening the target dismisses the issue, and the liberal has then squandered the opportunity to leverage mass shootings into their obsession of national gun *control*. This is a chronic and habitual characteristic of the liberal thought process: they prefer issues, *not* solutions.

Mass shooting victims such as school children of Parkland, FL are simply expendable collateral damage *en route* to their *control* obsession. Sadly school children are now being "community organized" into the next radical leftist national protest group called "Every Town," the sequel to the George Soros financed OWS and BLM. It has quickly been identified for what it is, a thinly-disguised Alinsky-ite attempt to utilize school children as human shields to advance the radical left's gun *control* obsession. Of course, the child student's reasoning capacity is not yet fully developed, which is why the legal voting age is 18 and the legal age for alcohol consumption is 21. At high school age, they are more interested in the "Tide Pod Challenge" than constitutional rebellion. Their age makes them easy prey for evil Alinsky-ite "community organizers" in search of "useful idiots." The truth is quite hideous, but typical of the liberal obsessive-compulsive-disordered thought process.

So we rhetorically ask ourselves "How can any sane person think that way?" Applying Occam's razor we conclude that they cannot. However, we should never expect liberals to "rethink" their position on mass shooting remediation, or anything else for that matter. That is because they didn't think it through in the first place. Thinking is a product of the individual mind which does not exist within the parallel liberal universe. Liberal positions are instead distributed to them by a central propaganda source.

Then on March 18, 2018 about a month after the Parkland, FL mass shooting, Washington DC ABC affiliate WJLA aired a video showing approximately 7,000 pairs of shoes on the Capitol lawn.

Presumably the shoes represented the number of children killed in U.S. shootings since the 2012 mass shooting at Sandy Hook Elementary School in Newtown, Connecticut. The memorial was created by OCDL organizers advocating for gun reform (translation: gun *control*).

I have some problems with absurdly irresponsible attempt at propaganda: (1) the 7,000 figure is over-stated by a factor of 50 making the WJLA video <u>*VERY*</u> fake news. There have been in fact 138 school shooting deaths in America since the December 14, 2012 Sandy Hook mass shooting; (2) there was no mention of the countless thousands of Planned Parenthood victims since Sandy Hook who *never* got the chance to wear shoes. I personally reject any "morality" based argument for gun *control* from *anyone* who advocates the wanton slaughter of human life via abortion; (3) there was no mention of the *millions* of shooting victims in the "gun free zone" of Nazi Germany.

Without doubt, liberals are believers in the quote of their comrade Joseph Stalin: *"A single death is a tragedy; a million deaths is a statistic."*

During the aftermath of the Parkland, FL tragedy, the corrupt liberal MSM worked overtime to ignore the role of government that failed at *every* level to protect the Marjory Stoneman Douglas High School students. The local Broward County Sherriff's office received many tips in 2016 and 2017 about the shooter's (Nikolas Cruz) threats to carry out a school shooting. The FBI learned that a YouTube user named "Nikolas Cruz" posted a message *"I'm going to be a professional school shooter"* on September 24, 2017, but the agency "could not identify" the user. Then in January 2018, a direct complaint of a death threat by Cruz was not forwarded to the local FBI office by the FBI tip line. According to the post-massacre FBI statement *"The caller provided information about Cruz's gun ownership, desire to kill people, erratic behavior, disturbing social medial posts and potential of him conducting a school shooting."* Apparently the FBI had bigger fish to fry with Trump surveillance.

An armed Broward County armed officer arrived quickly on the scene and took up a defensive position rather than entering the school to confront the shooter. He was reprimanded by Broward County Sheriff Scott Israel (Democrat), who also later participated in televised anti-gun protests. Yes, despite the dozens of felonies the shooter committed, more gun laws are obviously the answer.

And then there was President Obama's "Promise" program which reduced the reported number of school suspensions, expulsions, and arrests in an effort to alter the "disproportionate" minority crime statistic rate. Without doubt it played a role in keeping Nikolas Cruz under the law enforcement radar in the run up to the 2018 Valentine's Day mass shooting in Broward. What exactly is Obama's "promise" to the 17 dead and 14 wounded at MSD High School?

Throughout the post-shooting coverage, the media barely identified the murderer or the stunning failure of local and national government. Instead, their focus was on the NRA and gun *control*.

Could it be that mass school shootings are in part the result of removing God and prayer from America's schools? This thought will *never* occur to a liberal.

Liberals are not problem *solvers*; they are problem *creators*. Do not look to leftist front kid David Hogg for answers. Liberals make their living at perpetuating problems, by relentlessly flailing away at a goal they never reach because they don't want to. Their first great illusion is convincing enough people that they care, that they are trying and should therefore should be re-elected. Their second great illusion is convincing America that a very small underwhelming liberal minority is actually an overwhelming majority. In reality, they have only fooled themselves as Barack Obama did for eight years.

A classic example of liberal problem solving ineptitude is their "War on Poverty," a Democrat brainchild of the 1960s. Now 50+ years and $20+ trillion in expenditures after the opening salvo of the war under the administration of Lyndon B. Johnson, the poverty rate remains unchanged. An abysmal failure by any measure? NO! The *stated* intention was to reduce poverty. The *real* intention was to create a class of voters dependent on an ever-expanding government which would carry Democrats (synonymous with liberals) to election victory in perpetuity. In that sense, the *"War on Poverty"* has been an unqualified success. As Lyndon Baines Johnson (LBJ) so eloquently put it in this reported early 60s quote: *"I'll have them n*****s voting Democrat for the next 200 years."* These are *not* my words; they are the words of the 36th President of the United States, a Democrat no less. Moreover, anyone who acknowledges the truth about the *"War on Poverty"* is a heartless, soulless, greedy *racist*, and will be pilloried in the court of public opinion by left's enforcer apparatchiks, the Main Stream Media (MSM).

What other lessons do we learn from the liberal "War on Poverty" wasteland? That liberal self-delusion with failure is rooted in the definition of failure itself: for the liberal, success or failure is *not* related to results, but rather *stated* intentions. As it turns out, within liberal lexicon the proverbial "promised land" *never* equals the delivered land...but nobody ever seems to notice, which is why they never go away.

An orangutan flipping a coin is right 50% of the time. A stopped watch is right twice a day. How is it that liberals *never* get *anything* right? Could it be that we should *not* take their stated intentions at face value, that there is actually sinister deceit in play? LBJ's 1960s testimonial to his *"War on Poverty"* just might be a clue.

We also learn that the universal liberal response to every problem is to throw other people's money at it, then it will magically disappear. I think the brilliant Ms. Thatcher would agree.

There is no better leverage for extortion *control* of the people *that you have now disarmed* than deciding who gets healthcare and who is denied. This tops even Obama's politically-weaponized IRS which used its intimidating bureaucracy to sabotage Obama's political opposition in the 2012 presidential campaign. Obamacare was to be only a stepping stone, a way station on the journey to the leftist final destination of a single-payer healthcare system. Once arrived at single payer, the Washington DC bureaucracy would be in complete control of your healthcare decisions. Then your healthcare decisions would be handled with all the impartiality and compassion of the IRS under the control of Barack Obama in the 2012 election campaign. Instead of the IRS, the HHS will become the leftist bureaucrat's weapon of choice. Imagine this setup in the hands of Obama. This is what the left's end game looks like.

Liberals are enthusiastically for mass transit. People are herded onto vehicles of mass transit like animals. They are confined and *controlled*. They are transported according to a schedule provided by a central authority. This is the psychological attraction of mass transit for liberals.

Mass transit works just fine in densely-populated Western Europe, Japan, and specific American urban locations. But costal and urban liberals do not understand why mass transit will not work in West Texas any more than they understand why someone would need a firearm in West Texas. They have no concept of the vastness of America beyond their liberal enclaves. They have no concept of *anything* beyond their own personal urban costal experience, which they seek to impose upon America at large. And of course, they are always constrained by their "one size must fit all" mentality.

"Climate change" (the 21st century iteration of "global warming"), covers the contingency of any deviation whatsoever from 72°F and mostly sunny. It can be utilized to *control* not just the nation's vital energy sector, but also the entire national economy. There is no sector of the American economy that does not depend on energy.

"Climate change" has the added feature of the perfect phantom strawman: an imaginary global temperature rise of .2 °C in the year 2075. Don't like those numbers? Pick your own! No one here now will be there then to call you a liar. In terms of made-to-order strawmen, "climate change" tops even the imaginary "Russian collusion" delusion.

All you need is an alleged computer model, a white lab coat, a plump government study grant and a pair of coke bottle glasses to become a government-paid thinkofant. Yes, the same computer model that cannot predict where a hurricane is going to hit day after tomorrow is now going to predict the global (whatever that means) temperature 50+ years into the future. The only thing you need to know is that as a government-financed thinkofant, your financial security depends on coming up with the answers liberal politicians want to hear.

"Ninety-seven percent of climate scientists agree on the basic science of climate change, and we've been hearing their warnings for years…" Barack Obama (05.03.14). How could anyone question the consensus of *"97% of climate scientists"* our climatologist in chief referenced?

Here is a prime example of a classic liberal debate technique: the hearsay testimonial of an absent anonymous amorphous alleged "expert witness." The unidentified "expert witness" is never present, so he/she/it can never be cross-examined and his/her/its alleged testimony cannot be challenged. I am not a lawyer, but I have to wonder if this is why hearsay is excluded from the courtroom.

Moreover, this assertion has been made by our historic first black president. To challenge his claim would clearly be "Racist!" The MSM is waiting to pounce on anyone who disagrees with Obama with the "Racist!" accusation. Try washing that one off. Obama knows he will get cover from the MSM on "climate change" because they got him elected, and they are fully invested in his *perceived* success. Therefore, *they* manufacture the perception you need.

Never mind *"If you like your healthcare plan, you can keep your healthcare plan, period"*; and *"ISIL is the JV team"*; *"Not a smidgen of corruption in the IRS"*; *"You can't drill your way out of this"*; and *"The 1980s are now calling to ask for their foreign policy back because…the Cold War's been over for 20 years." You* obviously took those soundbites "out of context."

The truth is that Obama is a technical illiterate Marxist propagandist who does not know the First Law of Thermodynamics from his first cr@p. I refuse to hand over my country's energy and economic future to a man who thinks "Integrated Kinetic Energy" is a Red Bull and vodka on the rocks.

Or that *"Quantum Mechanics"* is a transmission and muffler repair shop out past the caution light.

A better question of Mr. Climatefixit might be "How about naming one of your alleged 97% 'expert climate scientists'?" That question will produce 20 minutes of embarrassing stammering by President Teleprompter, but no names.

Obama's priorities on the stage of global terrorism also serve to illustrate the OCDL obsession with *control*. Obama never acknowledged the worldwide menace of radical Islam. Moreover, he could not even speak the words "radical Islam" for whatever reason. Most likely his sympathy and covert affiliation came to him in a "Dream from My (Muslim) Father," and from his obsession with skin color.

From Obama's perspective, the radical Muslim threat was very remote. It was a distraction. He lived in the White House surrounded by a fence (which he raised in his second term) and heavily-armed Secret Service agents...the same arms he sought to deny rightful American citizens. Radical Islam did not pose a threat to his *control* of the American people or to him personally. Quite to the contrary, Obama saw an opportunity to provide America with one of his all-too-classic "teachable moments" by demonstrating how to peacefully coexist and even "partner" with Islam. This he would be able to do based on the keen insight he acquired from his Muslim heritage and the awesome power of his speechwriter's rhetoric read off a teleprompter. For the first time ever, Islam had a dependable ally in the White House, one of its own.

Of course, this misconceived stratagem was a colossal failure and led to disasters in Iraq, Libya, and Syria. The real catastrophe was putting Iran on an expedited path to a nuclear weapon, including financing with a cargo plane of cold, *untraceable* cash delivered secretly in the middle of the night. It is uncertain if there were simultaneous *other* untraceable cash deliveries to the Bahamas or Cayman Islands during this clandestine cold cash operation. The Obamas' net worth has been reported north of $40M today.

But none of these sophomoric clownish misadventures in Middle Eastern foreign policy impacted Obama's obsessive *control* of the American people. After all, the Muslim menace was half a world away. Even the full radical Islam assault on Western Europe was still a full ocean away. The evergreen affirmative action "get out of jail free" card from the MSM is the accelerant that kept Obama's ongoing dumpster fire burning for eight long years. ***"The media is Obama's scandal condom."*** – Greg Gutfeld.

As the radical Islamic menace and ever-worsening Middle East crises grew during his presidency, Obama focused like a laser on America's real enemies: "climate change" and Republicans. As the newly-minted radical Islamic terrorist group ISIS was beheading, drowning in cages, and burning alive Christians in the Middle East, Obama was warning the world of the danger of "climate change." Dead Christians meant nothing to him. On the other hand, "climate change" was his opportunity to *control* the global energy sector which cascaded directly into *control* of the global economy. What Marxist wouldn't sell the soul he never had to Satan for that?

Republicans were an existential threat to Obama's McGuffin: *control* and domination of America's political landscape. For an OCDL, this obstruction is a capital offense. When Republicans attempted to participate in the legislative process on issues such as healthcare early during the Obama administration, they were dismissed with condescending one-liners like *"Elections have consequences,"* and the supercilious *"The election is over, John (McCain)."* The result was the partisan "stimulus" (aka "Porkulus") and Obamacare legislation smash-and-grab jobs on the American treasury. Looking back, the only detectable results from these early Obama-driven legislative fiascos was a significantly higher national debt and a crippled healthcare system.

On the other hand, the big-ticket items NOT a priority for Obama were equally revealing: jobs, America's exploding national debt, military support, support of law enforcement, confronting radical Islam, support of our Middle Eastern outpost for Western democracy, Israel, *et. al.* He showed little interest and zero passion for any of these issues which are the top issues for polled Americans and critical to the well-being of America. They were not a priority for Obama because they have little impact on the *control* of the American people he obsesses over…in some instances, they are countercurrent to his *control* focus.

The only positive development for America was that Democrats were promptly relieved of their majority in the House two years after Obama took office. The Senate is more difficult to turn over because Senate terms are 6 years. The Senate fell from Democrat majority control four years later in 2014. The Democrat legislative disasters begat election losses which resulted in loss of Congressional power and *control*. Obama's second term became an exercise in executive orders (*"I have a cell phone and a pen"*), mostly illegal.

Finally America's "Nightmare on Pennsylvania Avenue" was over when Obama nominated Merrick Garland to the Supreme Court to replace the deceased Antonin Scalia in early 2016. Republican Senate leader Mitch McConnell told Obama to "go pound sand" citing the "Biden Rule" precedent from 1992: *"The Senate Judiciary Committee should seriously consider not scheduling confirmation hearings on the nomination until after the political campaign season is over."* The Shakespearian-quoted expression *"hoisted by his own petard"* comes to mind. Another anonymous quote *"Karma is a bitch"* may also be appropriate.

Like watering holes on the African Serengeti, liberals tend to collect and congregate in enclaves which are sheltered from all reality. These enclaves include academia, journalism, Occupy Wall Street (OWS) séances, broadcast media, sports, the legal system, social media (Twitter in particular), Black Lives Matter (BLM) riots, liberal arts, performing arts, crack houses and Democrat campaign rallies, all of which attract liberals like Bill Clinton to a White House intern. There the world's problems can be solved by clueless clucks on a performing stage (e.g., classroom, movie set, courtroom, etc.) with no real direct personal physical harm done. There is no required attachment to reality. Utopia thrives, Marxism works, and common sense is exiled to Pluto or even better, to Texas.

Let us dissect the motives in academia as an insightful case study. There Zen master tenured professors who have taken the student's grade point average hostage have the freedom to inseminate young formative minds with whatever convoluted cr@pola that suits their fancy. Aside from the sciences, our free spirited keepers of the knowledge range from leftist to radical leftist. As a rule of thumb, the further the subject matter drifts from relevance and reality (e.g., political science, sociology, philosophy, gender studies, African-American studies, urban education, media studies, toxic masculinity, etc.), the further left our self-esteemed academic titan gravitates. Finally you reach the intergalactic "Lost in Space" territory of Marc Lamont Hill. I would attribute this trend a quote of multiple origins: **"Idle hands are the devil's workshop."** Or, when you "teach" nothing of substance, you have plenty of time for idle leftist mischief.

What propels our academic mastermind universally toward liberalism? Trust me, it is not compassion for their fellow man. My personal theory is that:

- They do not actually earn any money, therefore they have zero respect for it. As a result, they have no problem giving away the money that *other* people earned. Redistribution of wealth is the foundation of socialism. Simultaneously they award themselves a moral superiority merit badge for this "social justice" based redistribution.

- They are government employees. They have no problem with their employer, the government, growing larger and more powerful. The term for this is "Bolshevik". They have no problem with ever increasing tuition for an ever decreasing quality of education which leads to an unemployable graduate. Increasing tuition equals increasing professorial pay. They have no problem with the government taking over the student loan franchise to finance student inculcation with the socialism they are peddling. Although they advocate the Marxist principle "to each according his needs from each according to his means", they would *never* consider "teaching" *pro bono*. I am aware of at least one Harvard professor (whom I long ago dubbed "$h!tt!ng Bull") who received a $400K salary for teaching a *single* course by utilizing cultural misappropriation charade. Perhaps most curious of all, these college professors of liberal insanity are also free to relocate to the socialist paradise of their choice worldwide, but they never do.

- They perform their jobs in a bubble which is perfectly insulated from reality. A bubble in which Marxism, Keynesian economics, the Communist Manifesto, global appeasement, solar powered 747s and lofty empty rhetoric works. A parallel universe where diversity, self-esteem and equality of outcome outweigh freedom of speech and the rights documented in the United States Constitution. These theoreticians are in charge of shaping a future that *never* arrives. They are *not* responsible for making anything work *now*. They are in charge of changing the name "Washington Redskins" and transgender bathroom policy, not leading a response to a terrorist attack in Benghazi. Thankfully America has just survived an eight year excursion into this navel gazing faculty lounge.

- They are the masters of the intellectual universe and they have the documentation (sheepskins) to prove it. As such, they are deeply disturbed that they have not been compensated for their incomparable intellectual greatness. Academians could never support *any* socio-economic system that would reward Donald Trump with billions in fortune plus the presidency while ignoring its chosen intellectual standard bearers. American capitalism is at fault for these insufferably egregious transgressions. It therefore deserves the death sentence by any means necessary, including anarchy.

- Academia is its own self-contained world, virtually isolated from the real world. It is the ultimate gated community. As such, it will forever remain remote from the potential damage it wreaks onto America at large. This licenses Academians to pot shot America with total impunity.

A similar analysis is possible on any liberal enclave that is isolated from America. What do all of these enclaves have in common? Two things: (1) they are all stages which require a "performance"; and (2) no human life is ever at stake. There is no way American society is ever going to entrust a life-or-death situation to oxymoronic "liberal logic," or to a mob of Hillary supporters gathered to scream mindlessly at the sky on the first anniversary of her historic defeat.

On the other hand, conservatives are typically doctors, police, firemen, military, engineers, businessmen, etc. They deal in situations where real lives and futures are at stake. Liberals may be likened to "reality TV," conservatives to reality.

Although mental disorders like OCD are not clinically contagious or infectious, liberalism can easily be spread in these liberal enclaves. This may be attributed to liberal susceptibility to propaganda which results from the total absence of critical thought skill, no longer taught or encouraged in America's education system. In contemporary vernacular this is called "group think."

The idea that socialism equals "equality for all" is the result of a corrupt liberal education system. Young students in their intellectually formative years are bombarded with propaganda about "equality," "diversity," "conflict resolution," and "social justice" at the expense of learning the basic building blocks of a good education: reading, writing and math. In the socialist context, "diversity" means skin color, ethnicity, gender and sexual orientation, *not* of thought. Anyone who thinks socialism is the preferred socio-economic system (a) does *not* understand what it is; because (b) they are a product of the corrupt liberal education system.

What third-grader would ever oppose socialist propaganda cloaked within the façade of "equality" or "social justice"? Sadly, this toxic soufflé of propaganda seasoned with mindless zombie like conformity is the prime commodity of the contemporary American education system.

This is seed of the current bumper crop of millennial Bernie Sanders supporters. To the new wave of mis-educated socialist advocates the solution to all of America's problems are as simple and obvious as Bernie's plan for energy independence.

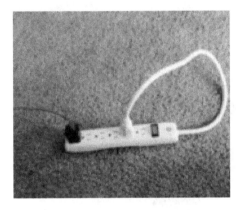

In a single sentence, their plan is "Free _____ for everybody!"

Liberals are very accomplished at faux-branding and marketing (e.g., *"The Affordable Care Act,"* the Dodd-Frank *"Wall Street Reform and Consumer Protection Act,"* the *"Fairness Doctrine," "Net Neutrality," "the Southern Poverty Law Center", "democratic socialism", "affirmative action"*, etc.) because propaganda requires no logic. It doesn't even require a brain.

They understand that 80+% of their supporters will never read beyond the label due to attention-span deficit, a characteristic of most liberals. Far too many young students are never able to recover from the K-12 brainwashing they are inseminated with by propagandist "educators." Far too many then make their way to the "Big Show" (baseball analogy) of college to be further inculcated by malcontent

Marxist college professors. What awaits them after they receive their B.A.B.S. degrees is a five-or-six-figure college debt, and the qualifications for a McJob to pay it off with. So the long and miserable road to liberal education failure ends up sleeping on an air mattress in their parents' basements.

OCDLs are natural aggressors. Their mental disorder drives them to reject the *status quo* under all circumstances. *"Doing nothing is not an option!"* becomes the bumper-sticker quality justification (cleaned up version of "bull $h!t one-liner") for liberal-induced chaos. This is how America winds up with Obamacare, which is light years *worse* than nothing. The same people who had no health insurance before Obamacare still have no health insurance *and* now are paying an ever-increasing fine for that privilege. However, our brilliant Supreme Court has ruled it a "tax" and not a "fine." That makes everything OK for the American living paycheck to paycheck and now paying the Obamacare fine. The eventual goal of Obamacare is a government-controlled single payer system…VA quality healthcare for everyone financially overseen by the Internal Revenue Service (IRS).

Although liberals are in perpetual motion to correct *externally* what they perceive as America's problems, their own *internal* problems are out of reach. To start with, they do not think they have a problem. Their ongoing mental turmoil produces a basic incompatibility with all things current, resulting in aggressive behavior.

It is also this dissatisfaction with the status quo that causes leftists to be perpetually negative. What is actually happening is that through their negativity they are attempting to offload their mental illness onto you. In this sense, liberalism is in fact contagious.

My personal anecdote for the liberal illness is (1) prevention by avoiding liberals; (2) less MSM news; and (3) a daily dose of Rush Limbaugh.

Liberal aggression is almost exclusively directed toward their political opponents, whom liberals see as malevolent trolls obstructing the pathway to Utopia.

Synopsis: For over half a century virtually all evidence has mounted against liberals: highly suspect motivation, faulty ideas and premises, an ancient and corrupt playbook amplified by Barack Obama and the Clintons, and abysmal results. All could be summed up in a single word: "Detroit"…or if a second word is required, "California," which is a contemporary re-enactment of the 1950s socialism-run-amok Ayn Rand novel *Atlas Shrugged*.

3. BANS AND BOYCOTTS:
THE LIBERAL BULLY'S WEAPONS OF CHOICE

"Pick the target, freeze it, personalize it, and polarize it. Cut off the support network and isolate the target from sympathy" – **Saul Alinsky (*Rules for Radicals*).**

The OCDL's necessarily invasive nature all too often takes the form of a ban or a boycott. The perpetual calls for bans are clearly an open declaration of self-moral and intellectual superiority. This is the liberal justification for encroaching upon the freedom of others. They are also often comical attempts at relevance by people who cannot accomplish anything meaningful in a positive way because they are in truth irrelevant.

With each and every negative incident of national prominence that occurs in America, the liberal reflex reaction is "What do we need to ban next?" This reflex is *not* rooted in public well-being. It is rooted in the need for public admiration of the relevance, leadership *(control)*, and selflessness of our self-centered Pecksniffian pinheaded liberal.

Ignoring them is a personal insult which they cannot and will not tolerate. To ignore liberals forces them to redouble their efforts to become your problem. It becomes a revitalized stimulus for their bullying; it is gasoline on their fire.

The top priority of the OCDL is to turn their problem (OCD) into your problem. This is the fundamental objective of the ban tactic, regardless of any other advertised motives. Liberals lie about their motives 100.000% of the time. Their obsession with control hangs in the balance. Bans are nothing more than the OCDL overt demonstration of *control* by bullying.

Liberalism is about encroaching upon the freedom of others to assert *control*. Liberals are de facto compulsive bullies. They utilize "minority rights" and advocacy as a justification for bullying. The truth is they care nothing about minority advocacy; they care about bullying because it has therapeutic value for their OCD.

As evidence of this assertion, I ask two questions, one difficult and one easy. First the easy question: what was the last liberal organized ban you recall? Now the difficult question: what was the last conservative organized ban you recall?

Liberals do not utilize logic, which takes time, effort and deliberation. They are characteristically emotional, reactive, mercurial, and shallow. This is why liberal "causes" are spur-of –the-moment, rush to judgment, superficial, and dysfunctional like the impassioned outcry for gun control instantly after every mass shooting. ***"Strike while the iron is hot." –* Richard Edwards (*Damon and Pythias - 1566*)]**

Liberal bans typically target free speech. Methods used are public ridicule, mocking, slander, liable, fake news, coordinated Twitter thuggery including flash mob harassment, blackmail, extortion, etc. The technical legal term for this genre of offense is *coercion*.

In the area of speech *per se*, liberals attack with an ever-changing Rolodex of clever (not to be confused with "smart") terms to describe free speech that irritates them. It is ever-changing to give old ideas a fresh coat of paint because liberals do not get any new ideas. ***Liberals were out of ideas in the 19th century.***

That is why liberals call themselves *"progressives"* instead of *"liberals"* now. Same old idea, fresh coat of paint. That is why *"global warming"* has been rebranded to *"climate change."* Fresh coat of paint. That is why *"illegal aliens"* have been rebranded *"undocumented workers."* Fresh coat of paint. Perhaps a reasonable compromise would be *"undocumented illegal aliens,"* which is 100% accurate.

Word bans, "free speech zones," "hate speech," "micro-aggressions," "cultural appropriation," "shadow banning" (Twitter), and *"dog whistles"* are all covert body-slams which describe the same thing: "We cannot compete with you in the arena of ideas; therefore *you* must shut up." It is liberal self-appointed supervised *censorship*, which they rebranded "political correctness." President Harry S. Truman had perhaps the most insightful and surgically accurate explanation of "political correctness" in this September 01, 1945 communique to Gen. Douglas McArthur: *"Political Correctness is a doctrine, recently fostered by a delusional, illogical minority and promoted by a sick mainstream media, which holds forth the proposition that it is entirely possible to pick up a piece of $h!t by the clean end!"*

I reject <u>all</u> these forms of liberal censorship. My freedom of speech will *not* be sacrificed for your liberal OCD. ***If you hear dog whistles, you are most likely a dog.***

The concept of "free speech zones" should be particularly obnoxious to Americans. In order to protect millennial snowflake liberal college students from the plague of non-liberal ideas, universities have designated miniscule "free speech zones" where anyone is free to exercise their 1st Amendment right of free speech, *even* conservatives. This is truly one of the most magnanimously conciliatory gestures I have ever heard of, at least since the Japanese surrendered in 1945 to end World War II.

Of course, the fallacy here is to accept the liberal premise, which is *always* a mistake. ***Never accept any liberal premise because it is based on liberal logic, which does not exist.***

In this case, the premise is that the university is separate and apart from the United States of America, is self-governing and self-constituted (e.g. the People's Republic of Missouri at Columbia). Therefore, the United States Constitution does not apply. Try arguing that one before the Supreme Court of the United States (SCOTUS).

In the fantasy land of liberal utopias like Missouri-Columbia, the 1st Amendment does not exist at all. Neither does the United States Constitution, or the United States for that matter.

This just in: there is only one *"free speech zone"* in our country. It is called the United States of America. PERIOD!!! With this declaration of truth, we have rejected the liberal premise.

At this point in the conversation the typical OCDL will recite the classic pseudo-logical rhetorical talking point that *"You can't shout 'Fire!' in a crowded theater."* The OCDL then extrapolates this irrelevant distraction to infinity and concludes that it is common practice to ban words or speech. It therefore follows by extrapolation *beyond* infinity that *anything* the OCDL *wants* banned *is* banned. With one specious sentence the OCDL has successfully invalidated the 1st Amendment of the Constitution. Viola! ***By "Liberal logic," <u>any</u> exception may establish a new rule. Conversely, <u>any</u> rule may be invalidated by a single exception.***

"Liberal logic" is the most egregious oxymoron in the American vernacular.

Now a return from liberalism to reality: the word "fire" is *not* banned *anywhere*. What is banned under this particular circumstance in the theater is committing the crime of "reckless endangerment," or, at the very least, "disturbing the peace." The word "fire" is part a larger context that *might* be criminal. It does *not* mean that "I will start a fire in the barbeque pit" is verboten because of the word *"fire."*

Likewise, you cannot walk into a bank and say to the teller "I have a gun; give me all of your money." *None* of these words are banned *per se*, but under these circumstances collectively they become a felony called "armed robbery."

"Hate speech" is yet another masterpiece of liberal misdirection. What sane American would not oppose "hate speech?" It's "common sense," right???

Then you find out that the definition of "hate speech" is any speech that liberals hate. That could be further clarified to anything that comes out of a conservative's mouth, e.g., "Stop spending money we don't have," or "Build the wall," or "All lives matter." So we quickly arrive back at the "free speech zones" which are designed to accommodate and *contain* these egregious examples of "hate speech." Small world.

"Micro-aggressions" are a liberal invention to criminalize speech that offends anybody (predominantly *them*) for any reason. It protects liberal snowflakes with the imaginary Ameritopian (plagiarized from the Mark Levin book *"Ameritopia"*) constitutional amendment against *any* speech which offends *any* liberal for *any* reason.

The 1st Amendment of the American Constitution (the *real* one) gives *all* Americans the right to freedom *<u>of</u>* speech. In the parallel and 180° bassackward, out of phase and upside down liberal universe there is the Ameritopian constitutional amendment that gives all Ameritopians (aka "snowflakes") the right to freedom <u>*from*</u> speech, entirely at their discretion.

The 1st Amendment of the *real* constitution also gives all Americans the right to freedom <u>*of*</u> religion. It was been ruled by the Warren SCOTUS in 1962 that the 1st Amendment actually meant freedom <u>*from*</u> religion, and moreover that freedom <u>*from*</u> religion trumps freedom <u>*of*</u> religion. This idea provides liberals the precedent they need to displace reality with their fantasy of censorship.

Suddenly snap! Poof!! And just like that, the *real* 1st Amendment is gone. Snowflakes of the world, unite!!! The ban of "micro-aggressions" is now the law of the land!

And furthermore, if we have been misreading the Constitution for lo, these many centuries, what other liberal misinterpretations are waiting for us? Liberals will inform us in due time.

"Cultural appropriation" is the imagined mockery of one (non-white) "culture" by another (white) "culture." It is monitored by liberal self-appointed "political correctness" police ("PC Nazis").

Typical offenses included wearing a *sombrero* on the 5th of May (*"Cinco de Mayo"*); eating watermelon or fried chicken at a family picnic; wearing a barrel marked *"MTY"* and a gaudy brightly-colored sequined cowboy hat to a Halloween costume party;

doing the 'tomahawk chop' at a Florida State football game; joining the Washington Redskins marching band.

"Shadow banning" is a recently-discovered Twitter phenomena. Liberal Twitter monitors are able to censor conservative twitter users based on algorithm alerts without the conservative's knowledge. Our fellow conservative user thinks he or she is broadcasting a tweet into the Twittersphere, but the tweet is only seen by the author. Clever indeed! Liberals have no problem with "shadow banning" because *they* are not the ones targeted.

At this point, I will recount my own personal experience on Twitter, which has now banned the words "illegal alien" as hate speech. I found it somewhat entertaining and posted my thoughts for a few months. I was following ~100 people, and I had ~200 followers which was steadily growing. Then mysteriously my account was suspended for a few days. I was reinstated and tweeted for a while, then I was suspended again. This happened several times. No reason other than generic "Violation of Terms of Service (ToS)" messages were given. Attempts to find out what specific ToS violations I committed were futile because there is no one at Twitter to communicate with…you are effectively the victim of invisible liberal censorship. At this point, I realized my violation was that I am a conservative. So I abandoned Twitter and authored a book with my ideas. Censor this, Twitter!

If a conservative finds something objectionable (e. g., MSNBC, CNN, the New York Times, Stephen Colbert, Kathy Griffin, etc.), he avoids it. If an OCDL finds something objectionable, it must be banned or outlawed (e. g., the American flag on a T-shirt, the NRA, the television series *The Dukes of Hazard*.)

If a conservative finds a law objectionable, he works to change it. If a liberal finds a law objectionable, he (she or it) simply ignores it. This is their way of illegally asserting *control*. Example: Barack Obama refusing to enforce immigration law at our southern border because *"Our immigration system is broken."* Mysteriously, our "broken immigration system" fixed itself on January 20, 2017, the day Donald Trump took office.

Reasons given for bans are typically as absurd as the ban target itself. The point of the bans is *not* the alleged public benefit; it is the gratification of the OCDL's insatiable psychological need to *control*.

Some notable recent examples of OCDL ban targets:

- The professional football team name Washington "Redskins" – like all word bans, an assault on the 1st Amendment.

- Red meat – to save the planet from "global warming" (which has since been renamed "climate change" to cover the contingency that the planet continues to cool noticeably), and to save mankind (now "humankind" thanks to the compassionately inclusive Justin Trudeau) from an imaginary health risk: saving the planet from asphyxiation from cow flatulence. Liberals care even if you don't.

- 16+ oz. soft drinks in NYC – to curb obesity.

- Salt – to curb high blood pressure.

- DDT – an alleged carcinogen— and other alleged detrimental environment effects. This ban is probably the single greatest factor in the world-wide malaria epidemic.

- 100 Watt incandescent light bulb – "climate change." Moreover, Thomas Edison should be banned from history books.

- Elephants in the circus – animal "cruelty". As a symbol of sadistic animal cruelty, are the University of Alabama mascot's days numbered?

- Killer whales at sea world parks – animal "cruelty."

- Coconut oil for popping popcorn – cardiovascular health.

- Children's toys in McDonald's happy meals – childhood obesity.

- Plastic straws and bags in San Francisco – general "save the planet." Simultaneously, the city of San Francisco is giving out free hypodermic syringes to hard drug mainliners. I wonder what they think the syringes are made of?

- Bottled water in San Francisco – more "save the planet" hysteria.

- Toy guns – indirect assault on the 1st *and* 2nd Amendment.

- Horse-drawn carriages in NYC – fewer horse droppings. Meanwhile the homeless can now *legally* "relieve" themselves anywhere in NYC???

- Goldfish in San Francisco – still more animal "cruelty"...how compassionate these people are!

- Barbie dolls in West Virginia – emotional stress to young girls striving for the unreachable 44-22-34 figure.

- Crosshair symbols on maps – This was the "dog whistle"* used by Sarah Palin to attack Arizona congresswoman Gabby Giffords...another direct assault on the 1st Amendment, plus an indirect assault on the 2nd Amendment.

*During the election run-up to the 2010 mid-term, Sarah Palin's PAC put out an ad "targeting" certain Democrat-held congressional seats for take-back by Republicans. Gabby Giffords (D-AZ) was one of them. Ms. Giffords was shot near fatally on Jan. 8, 2011 soon after the election at a constituent meeting in a Tucson supermarket parking lot. Liberals put these two facts together and assigned responsibility for the aggravated assault on Sarah Palin and the gun (*not* the actual shooter).

- Confederate flag – the rallying battle flag for neo-Nazis, white supremacists, NRA Neanderthals, and TEA Partiers...1st Amendment assault again.

- "Welfare" (the word) – You guessed it. The word has a negative connotation for the majority of liberal voters. They have no problem with actual welfare (the handout). To be clear, liberals are on welfare. Conservatives pay the welfare bill. Liberals resent that.

- "Snowflake" (the word) – The word is insensitive and hurtful to the delicate psyche of today's young people, college students in particular. *Liberals think it is unfair that life isn't fair.*

- "Yoga" – The meditative exercise represents white (because only whites are allowed to do it?) "cultural appropriation" from the colonialized Indian culture. This could be useful to Hillary Clinton, who now has an alibi for deleting the 33,000 subpoenaed email messages from her illegal server...she was correcting her own "cultural appropriation."

- "Chain immigration" – The term is offensive to African-Americans who "immigrated" to the United States in chains, according to Sen. Dick Durbin (D-IL). It is rather amazing that there are still some alive.

Clearly singers Aretha Franklin (*"Chain of Fools"* – 1967) and Sam Cooke (*"Chain Gang"* - 1960) did not get the email. For the record, Sen. Durbin is a 73-year-old white liberal *alleged* male who has committed the heinous felony of misappropriating the cause and culture of 19th century black slaves for his own personal political gain.

The city of San Francisco appears to be leading this "Back to the Futuristic" stampede of liberal obedient conformity toward George Orwell's "1984". It is *not* because San Francisco is populated with rugged, self-reliant, patriotic Special Forces types. Liberals are rapidly turning San Francisco into a latrine (literally!) as America looks on in astonishment. Its city government overhead cracks down on plastic straws while Market Street turns into a sewer.

Yes, these are the compelling issues of our time displacing the exploding national debt, border security, jobs, opiate addiction, the economy, Iranian nukes, *et. al.* from the American public view. In rides the OCDL cavalry on its high horse to save America from these ubiquitous injustices. We must stop asking the question *"How absurd can these liberal crusades get?"* Far too many liberals are taking this rhetorical question on as a personal challenge.

The point of these ever increasingly absurd bans is *not* any positive effect they may have on anyone's lives. It is about proving to one and all that they can force ludicrous whim upon you because they *control* you. Therefore, the more asinine the ban rationale, the more clearly their *real* point is made.

The liberal narrative can only be enacted with the co-dependency of the liberal Main Stream Media (MSM). Thus we are treated to a lecture on the "global warming" from our Climatologist-in-Chief while Christians are being beheaded, drowned in cages, and burned alive by ISIS in the Middle East.

The imaginary doomsday strawman "global warming" of 50 years into the future can be confronted and "defeated" with rhetoric from a teleprompter. ISIS, the perpetrator of psychotic radical Islamic mayhem and murder, not so much. This sets the liberal priority of "global warming" at the very top. Liberals would much rather do battle with the imaginary opponent "global warming," which will no doubt lead to imaginary victory, than the all-too-real ISIS.

The recent #MeToo campaign, triggered by the philandering adventures of Hollywood serial sex offender Harvey Weinstein is an example of narrative *control*. #MeToo should not be confused with #U2, which is an Irish rock band.

We should also note that # is a symbol which means "pound". So #MeToo should not be misinterpreted as the declarative sentence "Pound me too." This would counterproductive in the extreme.

The #MeToo campaign accomplishes multiple liberal objectives: (1) it is a demonstration to liberal self that they still *control* the narrative. They can redirect the public narrative and cable news cycle in any direction they choose; (2) it deflects the ongoing sordid debauchery and disgusting morality crisis away from uber-liberal Hollywood; (3) it provides Hollywood with a platform for a "moral superiority" demonstration of "zero tolerance," boldly taking the lead for America and elevating themselves to hero status. A "teachable moment" for America as it were in the grandiose production technique of Obama's "beer summit"; (4) it is an attack on "toxic masculinity," i.e. an attack on (white) males by the effeminate left.

The leftist controlled narrative is stealthy maneuvered from Hollywood criminality to (white) "toxic masculinity" in general and the boorish sexcapades of Donald Trump in particular, which will no longer be tolerated in America. Never mind that virtually all the #MeToo offenders (Weinstein, Matt Lauer, Tom Brokaw, et. al.) were liberals and Hollywood was the epicenter of the morality meltdown. Never mind that any Trump "sexcapades" were consensual, juxtaposed to the rejected sordid trysts of serial sex offender Bill Clinton. Somehow these immaterial factoids didn't make it into the script. *This* is the advantage of having control of the narrative.

The liberal MSM has bigger fish to fry. They are on vigil for the next outbreak of (white) "toxic masculinity" like those heinous stains on America's blue dress of virginity: the Duke Lacrosse team "rape" case, the UVA frat "rape" case, Tawana Brawley, etc. Even beyond that, all of America's "founding fathers" were white males. Many owned slaves. So #MeToo becomes America's moral counterbalance to "toxic masculinity", the same evil malady that corrupted America at its inception and ever since. This crime has gone unpunished for centuries. The liberal of today will correct this overdue egregious social injustice with a nationwide "all-(white)-males-are-rapists" campaign. A key component of the campaign is the guilty-until-proven-innocent standard that worked so well at Duke and UVA. When you control the narrative, you also control the burden of proof standard.

The lesson of all of this is that with malicious narrative manipulation, the clever liberal can distort the Harvey Weinstein portfolio of sexual misdeeds and return an indictment against all (white) males, our sitting president, America's founding fathers and America itself. And the ham sandwich was indicted for murdering a pig.

Liberals can only successfully peddle the #MeToo nonsense if *you* buy it; it will only live on if public opinion allows it to. I personally have zero interest in checkout counter *he said/she said* tabloid #MeToo sleaze.

And let's not kid ourselves about the liberal-coined term *"male toxicity."* It is "dog whistle" dogma for "<u>white</u> male toxicity" exclusivity. You will not find any liberals utilizing their term *"male toxicity"* to describe any non-white males. No one understands better than liberals that would be *"Racist!"* which is the *numero uno* liberal capital offense.

It is more than a coincidence that most of these ban targets involve either taking away our basic rights such as freedom of speech so that the oppressed and abused victim class will be spared further humiliation; or making the "right" choices for us to protect our health because we are too stupid to do that on our own; or saving the environment from the cretin conservative mongrels because that is what liberal "virtue signaling" superheroes do.

Nothing is more sacrosanct to the liberal than her superhero status. It must be reaffirmed at every opportunity, including opportunities manufactured out of a vacuum by our superhero herself. For example, attacking a statue of Andrew Jackson in New Orleans. Imagine the courage it takes to pour a gallon can of red paint on a statue in the dead of night! Our troops who landed on Omaha and Utah Beaches in Normandy were cub scouts compared to the 21st century liberal warrior/snowflake.

Fundamentally, liberal bans are all aimed at eroding American freedom, and installing liberals in control over your life. Of course, this list could go on *ad infinitum*. The point has been made. The ban targets are mostly inconsequential. The rationale cited ranges from superficial to borderline-absurd, in truth no more than an excuse for OCDL interloper bullying.

Moreover, if all these fantasized bans were enacted today, the OCDL would find little comfort because it is not the result that brings psychological relief for OCD; it is the act of bullying itself. It is the public demonstration of *control*. This is why liberals are perpetually roiled. And let us be clear about this hypothesis: what roils the OCDL is not anything *external*; it is an acute mental illness which is *internal*. This is why there is <u>no</u> external remedy. ...banning the Confederate flag is *NOT* a cure for your OCD.

If the professional football team name "Washington Redskins" was banned tomorrow, the team name "New Orleans Saints" would be instantly besieged by OCDLs claiming the name is offensive to Muslims. If not the "Saints," the "Arkansas Razorbacks" could be a target. Muslims are highly offended by pigs, you understand. The Cleveland Indians, the Boston Celtics, the Atlanta Braves, the Notre Dame Fighting Irish, the Cleveland Browns, etc. could all be fungible in this role. The particular targeted team name matters little to the alleged slurred victims and it matters not at all to the OCDL.

What matters is forcing minority rule upon the majority against their will. It is the opiate that relieves the symptoms of OCD, however temporary it may be. The smaller the minority, the greater the psychological boost to the OCDL. For example, "transgenders" are approximately 0.3% of the American population. To the OCDL, it is perfectly logical that the other 99.7% of the American "cisgenders*" should therefore conform to an "anybody-in-any-bathroom-at-any-time" law to accommodate the 0.3% transgenders' whim *de jour*.

The OCDL must win this battle for their opiate daily or face psychological destruction. Make no mistake about it, the OCDL is engaging in bullying the majority solely for the sake of demonstrating *control*. Because their gratification is inversely proportional to the size of the majority they bully, the 99.7% "cisgender" majority they offend is the Heisman Trophy of liberal pinheaddery.

* "Transgender" referring or relating to people whose sense of personal identity and gender does <u>not</u> correspond with their birth sex. "Cisgender" denoting or relating to a person whose sense of personal identity and gender corresponds with their birth sex.

Apparently inclusion is critically important in America *especially* in bathrooms. Thus the liberals' "Big Tent" strategy becomes the "Big Outhouse" strategy.

I am waiting for the first liberal proposed "perfect solution" to the burning issue of our time to hit the MSNBC prime time suggestion box: destroy half the bathrooms in America and *force* everyone to use the lone remaining bathroom. Then the unisex bathroom becomes a giant step forward toward the liberal egalitarian utopian dream! *"All for one and one for all..."* – Alexander Dumas (*The Three Musketeers*).

I am so ancient that I came from an era where choosing which bathroom to use was probably the least controversial thing anyone ever did. It leaves me wondering what transgenders did for bathroom facilities during the terms of the first 43 American presidents...then along came 44...

The transgender bathroom dilemma has the added value of a much-needed break for liberals from demolishing statues and monuments of our forefathers. They could demolish latrines for a change of pace. However, the whole issue mysteriously disappeared into the ozone when Obama left office, similar to the ISIS crisis.

The left has a great deal of political capital invested in the attack on the name "Washington *Redskins.*" They have been at it for a number of years now. Since they have made it such a high profile issue, it is worthwhile to spend a little ink on the background.

The team was founded as the Boston Braves in 1932. Soon thereafter they hired William "Lone Star" Dietz, who was part Sioux Indian, as head coach. To honor their new head coach the team was renamed the *"Redskins."* Apparently Coach Dietz was unaware of his victimhood status and was not a liberal, so he did not object.

Now passes the better part of a century, and liberals find the name *"Redskins"* offensive to the point of panic-attack-induced hysteria. To the race-obsessed liberal, "red" and "skin" cannot be spliced together into a single word without a major cataclysmic event on their psychological Richter scale.

Never mind that virtually no Native Americans came forward to protest the name. There are 300+ million Americans, and among us there are approximately 2.5 million Native Americans. Surely there is one Native American willing to feign displeasure and support the liberal uprising? Did anyone talk to Elizabeth F. Warren about this travesty of social justice? That was *not* the point. In lieu of Native American outrage, Liberals are offended in proxy.

On the other hand, if virtually zero Native Americans are offended by the name "Washington *Redskins,*" is it fair to strip the memory of Native American Coach Dietz of the honor bestowed upon him early last century?

The "Washington *Redskins*" controversy is precisely the type of issue Obama could not resist. Our intrepid community organizer-in-chief cannot avoid social injustice issues like *"If I had a son, he'd look like Trayvon,"* or *"The Cambridge police acted stupidly,"* or *"Growing income inequality is the defining issue of our time."* **When you are incompetent, you "focus" on the irrelevant.**

The point here is that our historic first Muslim descended president cannot solve a *real* problem, and he knows it. He can only create problems. In lieu of *real* problem solutions, he must distract you with meaningless drivel elevated to problem status with the help of a complicit MSM. Enter the words "Washington Redskins", which have zero impact on *anyone's* quality of life, onto the national stage.

So as the national debt approaches $20 Billion, the Middle East is in complete and utter chaos and getting worse by the minute, Obamacare is imploding, American employment and race relations reach a 50 year low, Obama is all over the Redskins "controversy" like a vodka martini on an olive.

Personally, I am a great deal more offended by individuals who misappropriate someone else's culture to land a high pay/low work tenured professorship at Harvard than I am by the exalted Washington football franchise name *"Redskins."* There is *nothing* fraudulent about the *"Redskins"* rich franchise history or the origin of the name.

In 2015, Obama unilaterally instructed the U.S. Trademark and Patent Office to cancel the team's logo patent, which is a multi-million dollar a year marketing asset. Many months of litigation followed.

In the end, the plaintiffs withdrew their litigation when it became obvious that the 2017 SCOTUS (Supreme Court of the United States) was going to rule in favor of the team's 1st Amendment right protecting freedom of speech, as opposed to an imaginary nth amendment right protecting *anyone* from *ever* being offended by the speech of *anyone* else.

This became apparent from the SCOTUS 8-0 ruling in the *"Slants"* case. In this June 19, 2017 decision, the SCOTUS extended trademark protection to words and names that *may* be offensive, ruling that the 1st Amendment right to free speech allows the Asian-American band from Portland, OR to call itself the *"Slants."* This decision sounded the death knell for the *"Redskins"* plaintiffs. And once again, Obama demonstrated that he knows less about constitutional law than my late cat, "Lucy."

But anyone who thinks this Quixotic exercise in overbearing government d!p$h!ttery was about Native Americans has been badly fooled by the left. ***Liberals lie about their motives 100.000% of the time.***

What it is actually about is minority (no matter how small) *control* of the majority; it is about censorship, which is a form of *control*; it is about bringing down an icon of American culture that has stood for almost a century as a means of demonstrating sanctimonious self-importance; and it is about attacking the 1st Amendment of the Constitution and the entire Constitution itself by extension, because it is the Constitution that stands between far leftists like Barack Obama and the *control* of the American people he obsesses over; it is yet again about liberals confiscating *your* rights in sacrifice to *their* obsession.

Native Americans were merely the prop *de jour*, the human shields of choice on this particular day. Tomorrow it could be transgenders, Syrian refugees, or women wearing pink vagina hats in a protest march for reasons *they* cannot even intelligently guess at… apparently no one explained to them that they were the latest failed iteration of the anarchist left's useful idiot-victim parade-response to the 2009 TEA Party movement. "Occupy Wall Street," utilizing the class warfare meme and "Black Lives Matter," utilizing racial victimhood were earlier George Soros-funded failures at counterpunching the TEA Party. The latest iteration in this parade of liberal insanity is the oxymoronic "Antifa" (Anti-Fascist). Antifa is about as anti-fascist as the Affordable Care Act is affordable. *They are* the fascists.

So why does this oversized gaggle of clucking ducks protest? They protest because they *can*. They live in the greatest country on earth that allows them to do so, and they have convinced themselves that they hate every second of it. But they would hate anywhere they live because it is their mental disorder that causes their hatred and rage, *not* the United States of America.

There is no "Riot Act" in the United States as there is in Great Britain. Quite to the contrary, the 1st Amendment of the Constitution of the United States explicitly states *"The people shall not be restrained from peaceably assembling…"* Liberals agree with that wholeheartedly, except for the word *"peaceably."* Liberals hate our constitution and would abolish it in a New York nano-second if they could, because it is a roadblock to the *control* they lust for.

But this is their 15 minutes of fame, their opportunity at faux relevance in a lifetime of abject irrelevance. They do not want to miss this shot at the "Big Time" while the CNN cameras are focused on them. They wake up each day outraged, they spend their day seeking a scapegoat for their outrage and they go to bed outraged. It is nothing short of miraculous that they can sleep at all. Looking in the mirror will *never* occur to them. ***"The superior man blames himself. The inferior man blames others"*** **- Don Shula.**

Allow me illustrate this point with evidence of President Donald Trump's nomination of SCOTUS justice Brett Kavanaugh on July 9, 2018. Hours before the announcement of Trump's choice, an oversized gaggle of motherless clucks gathered in the name of the "Women's March" on the steps of the

Supreme Court building. They were beyond rowdy, they were threatening to the point that FNC shut down a live on site broadcast due to personnel safety concerns. Printed flyers were circulated among the mob and released to the press condemning SCOTUS nominee "xx" as a threat to America. The nominee's name would be filled in after Trump's announcement.

"WOMEN'S MARCH STATEMENT ON TRUMP'S EXTREMIST SCOTUS NOMINATION

Washington, DC – In response to Donald Trump's nomination of XX to the Supreme Court, the Women's March released the following statement:

'Trump's announcement today is a death sentence for thousands of women in America. Etc., etc., etc.'"

This was a thuggish mob in search of a piñata, a strawman to torch. The truth is this mob represents a far greater threat to America than any candidate of Trump's list. It represents anarchy.

This vignette illustrates multiple relevant points: (1) Liberal rage is already there 24/7/365, it just needs a focal point. In this case it was SCOTUS nominee "xx"; (2) *"Liberals are too stupid to be embarrassed"*; (3) Losing has become a liberal way of life since the 2012 presidential election. They are now 0 for the last 6 years; (4) intimidation through mob rule is at the top of the liberal playbook; (5) in lieu of winning an election, the judicial branch of the government is the last hope for liberal victory, at least until enough illegal aliens can be shepherded to the polls to win an election; and (6) desperate people due desperate things.

We should be clear: the name "Washington *Redskins*" is just a warm-up for the American left. In addition to the 1st Amendment, the eventual co-target for their disordered minds is the game of football itself.

Why? Football is enormously popular in America among both sexes. But more importantly, it is uniquely American; it is a cornerstone of our culture. For six months each year, Americans are devoted to the sport. For the other six months each year, they lie in wait of the next playing season. Moreover, American football is substantially increasing in popularity worldwide. The National Football League (NFL) has been expanding venues to locations like London, Mexico City, and Tokyo with unqualified success.

This icon of American culture cannot be allowed to infect the entire planet, where soccer is the almost universally preferred sport. "Other countries should not be playing American football; America should be playing soccer," thinks your basic OCDL. This is *ipso facto* a rejection of American exceptionalism.

In recent years, we have seen the left attack the sport. We remember the 2014 NFL draft when an openly gay University of Missouri defensive end Michael Sam was drafted 249th of 256 players drafted, then kissed his boyfriend on stage after the announcement. The 248 players drafted ahead of Sam, and all the hard work they put in to get there were virtually ignored by the left wing media covering Mr. Sam's triumph over "homophobia" and "bigotry." I still do not understand why Mr. Sam's sexual orientation is relevant at all. From my perspective, there were 248 stories of athletic achievement at this event more deserving to be told. To elevate draft pick number 249 to the sports section front page above the fold because of his sexual orientation was discriminatory, a violation of the 1964 Civil Rights Act.

Two years later we watched while San Francisco Forty Niners quarterback Colin Kaepernick refused to stand for our National anthem, "taking a knee" instead. This protest was mimicked around the league as players saw the favorable MSM press Kaepernick was getting. By midseason the NFL's television ratings had dropped precipitously, and the left-wing media had no clue why.

It was probably due to the presidential election. Yeah, that's it! People were too busy watching Hillary Clinton delivering a speech with all the aesthetic value of a mortally-wounded screeching pterodactyl at one of her many overflow campaign rallies (yeah, I missed that one too) to watch pro football.

In all, live game attendance was down 10+% to its lowest point this century. The drop in ratings for the far-left sports network ESPN Monday Night Football was far more dramatic.

I know why I quit watching, and it was *not* to watch Hillary Clinton campaign rallies. I refuse to watch the anarchist "Black Lives Matter" hijack the NFL to perpetuate a phony "social justice" narrative. I refuse to watch a cluster of overpaid professional athletes disrespect the national anthem, the flag, and the country that made them all multi-millionaires with this contemptable and insulting pre-game gesture. I refuse to watch selfish self-centered thugs disrespect our military who volunteered to keep our nation safe and free, protecting their 1st Amendment right to make these stupid public gestures. ***Irony is ALWAYS lost on the stupid.***

It is no coincidence that 70+ percent of NFL players are black. Could it be that the real issue here is lack of "diversity," which we know is a prime obsession of the OCD liberal?

I think it is safe to say the idea of leaving America for another country where they could earn just as much pay *plus* the "social justice" they seek *never* occurred to *any* of them. Cuba beckons. The Havana Jalapeños ("Racist!" again!!!) are always on the lookout for good ballplayers.

Now the left is eying a new silver bullet to bring down the game of football entirely: brain concussion damage. The drumbeat gets louder; studies reminiscent of the "global warming" hockey stick hoax of a few years back begin to surface; and liberal crosshairs are steady on the target. I personally expect that government will sponsor a be-all, end-all study within a few years about the time the next Democrat is elected to the White House, a morbid thought for sure. The study results will drive the stake in the heart of America's beloved game. At that point, NFL protestors will have no venue to protest from...back to the hood and total obscurity.

But OCDL ban attempts have gone on throughout recorded history. It will continue as long as there are OCDLs and majorities to be bullied with the liberal fallacy that majority *noise* from the minority equals a majority.

In 2017, a new ban target has arisen in the sights of liberal destructive insanity. Like a school of sharks in a bloody feeding frenzy, the liberal psyche needs fresh targets. Historical statues which commemorate Civil War heroes of the Confederacy are now the "focus" of the psychotic left in their daily obsession to find a new source of their rage and destroy it. Of course this is pure symbolism for their need to antagonize and bully anyone who would dare to oppose. The Antifa fascists know they will have the cover of the equally fascist MSM. Any confrontation initiated by the rent-a-mob Antifa fascists will thus be amplified and transformed into the exact opposite of what it really is by their comrades in the press.

Leftist fascist riots are not a new tactic. We saw the same thing during the run-up to the 2016 presidential election. The ex-Nazi sympathizer George Soros-funded rent-a-mob masked fascists showed up at announced Trump campaign rallies in Chicago and San Diego to "protest" (translation...riot). For the majority of them, it was the closest thing they ever had to a job. Anyone who attended the

Trump rallies to show support were attacked by the rent-a-mobsters, then vilified by MSM propaganda machine in a process now known as "fake news." Now the rent-a-mobsters have a name: Antifa.

We could go back further in time to the Antifa fascists' ancestors in 1930's Germany, Hitler's brown shirts. The tactics are identical: mob intimidation and violence to force political change which eventually begat World War II.

So the Antifa fascists would have us believe they are out to save America from a miniscule minority of "white supremacists," who are probably actually outnumbered by transgenders. To elucidate the fallacious nature of the Antifa strategy, we should examine their "focus": statues and monuments of the Confederacy. They are the very definition of the rhetorical "strawman," scorn-worthy *inanimate* objects which cannot defend themselves. I personally am completely underwhelmed by the "bravery" of the Antifa fascist warriors.

We note here the "focus" of the left is on the *past*, statues which commemorate our *history*. This is not an accident. They "focus" on irrelevant ancient artifacts in lieu of contemporary *solutions* to real problems because they have none. The "focus" on the past serves to distract America from the truth that can only deliver anarchy, chaos, and the misery of collectivism to America's future. America has just endured an eight-year sample of liberal visionaries. They deliver the promise of devolving America into Venezuela the way they did to Detroit and are now doing to California.

Rewriting history is always easier than pathfinding the way forward. Liberals are experts at this.

So the left's shiny object of distraction in elections of the foreseeable future will be "White Supremacy," racism, bigotry, and Nazism. I have to wonder how much Democrats paid the consultant who came up with the idea that calling voters who elected Trump in 2016 "White Supremacists" and "Nazis" will convert them to voting Democrat in future elections. I would liken that "strategy" to walking up to Osama Bin Laden, calling him gay and then asking him to fetch you a "sex on the beach" cocktail.

I have no crystal ball, but I think anyone with an IQ:Body Fat Ratio > 1.0 (math speak...liberals will not understand because math* is a pure science requiring logic) would give both of those ideas a very low probability of success. However, after eight years of Obama domestic and foreign policy failure, this is apparently all they have left.

*I considered starting a Remedial Math, Ciphering and Tax Service for Liberals at 1-800-4JETHRO but quickly gave up on the idea due to an intellectually infeasible customer base.

Do not look for the Confederate statue issue to go away anytime soon. It contains too many of the classic OCDL attractions. (1) Because removing the statues is polling at 3 to 1 against, we have the textbook "minority rule" liberal-bullying opportunity, always at the top of the liberal cause shopping list. (2) It provides a highly visible platform for the obligatory sanctimonious "virtue signaling" faux-moral superiority performance. Liberals *never* pass up the opportunity to "perform" before the CNN cameras. All liberals are actresses, you understand. There is *no shortage of prima donnas* or *divas*. Their goal is to convince you with each performance that Hollywood made an egregious mistake when they were overlooked for a leading role. No, nobody made a mistake. They think they can cover up any lie or blunder (e.g., Benghazi, a felonious email scandal, FISAgate, Obamacare, etc.) with sheer acting ability. The acting "superpower" is a major factor in liberals' compulsion to lie, which is now known as *"Grubering"* (Chapter 10). Divorce from reality is *de facto* a way of life for these liar savants. (3) With subversive MSM support, it can be amplified beyond all reason into an emotionally-charged nationwide crisis, like the recent transgender bathroom "crisis" was. The centuries that passed peacefully when everyone seemed to know which bathroom facilities to use before transgender crisis status must be ignored as an inadvertent oversight on somebody's part. (4) Nationwide there is a virtually limitless supply of "strawman" statues for the OCDLs to target. Failure at any given location simply means liberals move the drive-by attack to the next location. It does *not* mean the *program* has failed. (5) It provides a crucial distraction from *real* news that liberals want to bury, *i.e.* the weekend body count in Chicago, where the *Chicago Tribune* obituary section is approaching the size of my hometown phonebook. The Chicago headline is their gallant struggle against evil racist America to maintain "sanctuary city" status, *not* insignificant murder victims. (6) America has an oversupply of "snowflakes" whose right it is to be offended by anything within reach of their five senses or imagination. They have been taught this right by an education system obsessed with participation trophies, delusionary narcissistic self-esteem, conflict resolution, social justice, etc. There are plenty of "useful idiots" willing to perpetrate the liberal statue assault d!p$h!ttery in order to bond themselves to the 1960s Civil Rights movement and forever implant themselves on the "right" side of history (which they are ironically eradicating). This places them in an elite category alongside the Taliban in Afghanistan, who saw fit to destroy *all* Buddhist monuments there. *"Islam is a religion of peace."* — Muhammad Ali.

Then, too, it must be recognized that there is zero historical significance attached to these statues by today's collegiate snowflake. They have been taught that history began the day they were born and that they are the center of the universe by a dysfunctional education system. The desecration of historical statues is the "new beginning" of history for the bed-wetting genderless Inner-city Culture major. It is the metaphorical equivalent of a stray dog marking his territory.

Targeting Confederate statues and monuments is only a starter kit for the left. Confederate monuments will quickly domino into America's founding fathers because many of them were once slave owners. Their monuments gotta go!

America's founding fathers were obviously evil. By extension their work product, America's *Constitution* and other founding documents are also evil. By liberal logical extrapolation, America itself is evil. Evil people do evil deeds. Another domino tumbles!

Eventually, all monuments to anyone who does not qualify for liberal-assigned victimhood status (translation…all white males) must go. All issues real or imagined in the OCDL mind ultimately revert back to racial and social justice, and the relentless liberal struggle to wipe America clean of bigotry personified by the statues of these grotesque white males. This justifies dynamiting Mount

Rushmore, destroying the Ronald McDonald (fictional character) statues in front of the fast food restaurants, renaming John Wayne Airport in Orange County California and removing his statue, removing Monument Park at Yankee Stadium, destroying the Christopher Columbus statues and renaming "Columbus Circle" "Malcolm X Square" in New York City, destroying the Rocky Balboa (fictional movie character) statue in Philadelphia, removing bottles of Mr. Clean (fictional product icon) from retail outlet store shelves, removing the Vince Lombardi bust from the Pro Football Hall of Fame, tearing down the Paul Bunyan (mythical character) statue in Brainerd, MN, eliminating the Oscar award (which is gold, but race-obsessed liberals imagine it to be white), razing the Statue of Liberty (with its imagined Caucasian facial features), sandblasting the Confederate soldiers off of Stone Mountain, GA, *etc.* Nor is there anything that limits this Talibanesque assault insanity to just statues and monuments, or just the Constitution. ***"Every record has been destroyed or falsified, every book has been rewritten, every picture has been repainted, every statue and street and building has been renamed, and every date has been altered. And that process is continuing day by day and minute by minute. History has stopped."*** **– George Orwell (*1984*).**

The OCDL opportunities here are pretty much limitless, but make no mistake about what the primary targets are: white males, the 1st Amendment, and the *Constitution* followed by anarchy. All of this must be sacrificed for the sake of protecting American snowflakes from things that *might* offend someone somewhere somehow. Liberals are just looking out for the rest of us, you understand. No, they are in fact *bullying*, which is their national pastime.

One thing we know for certain based on a lifetime of observational experience: liberals will *always* overplay their hand. If they are able to advance a position, it immediately establishes a new status quo with which they are completely dissatisfied. This is a direct byproduct of OCD.

Liberals will upgrade a cause to a crusade for the purpose of bullying based on three primary factors: (1) the *Majority: Minority ratio* or count; (2) the *common sense* discount factor; and (3) the *disruption* factor. These can best be understood through an example.

For this we will return to the white hot transgender bathroom "crisis". It reached critical mass during Obama's second term when he had *"more flexibility"* which actually translated to zero accountability to the American people.

Statistically it has been estimated that 0.3% of Americans are transgender. This means that 99.7% of Americans are not. (I refuse to use the term "cisgender.") We crunch the numbers which give us a *Majority:Minority ratio* of 332.3 (=99.7/0.3). The OCDL bully's antenna are up, this ratio is exceptional.

From the standpoint of *common sense*, what could *possibly* go wrong with an anybody in any bathroom at any time policy? It is lawyer Nirvana. Think of the lawsuits that could be filed when a seven year girl is raped in a women's restroom by a 50 year old male serial sex offender. The rapist could immediately file a sexual harassment lawsuit against the child for the "hate crime" of gender discrimination. The rapist becomes the victim. The ACLU would be on that heinous violation of civil rights like a hobo on a southbound freight train in winter.

As for *disruption*, all Americans use public restrooms at some point so all will be impacted by the policy. This gives the "crisis" ultimate visibility and therefore awards ultimate relevance to the otherwise irrelevant OCDL inciter. Virtually no one in America is safe from the menace created by the OCDL bully.

I discount males who, aside from a little embarrassment, are in no real danger of physical, emotional or psychological harm. They can take care of themselves. But what male does not know a female who is a potential victim of this liberal insanity?

"This is the price America must pay for imagined generational transgender discrimination," our comrade OCDL bully rationalizes. Our liberal superhero stakes out the moral high ground for him/her/itself with a full throated chorus of "virtue signaling". And yet again liberals have overcome bigotry in America.

Yes, the transgender bathroom "crisis" is the "happy hunting ground" (Elizabeth F. Warren speak) of liberal nuisance crusades, their trifecta based on the criteria I have listed. Could anything be more asinine? No, but the liberal scouts keep searching because it provides relief from their oppressive OCD burden.

Sooner or later, liberals will wither in the face of disgusted public opinion as their insatiable demands grow. This is what naturally follows an overplayed hand. After the disintegration of each asinine failed campaign, the next asinine liberal crusade is triggered. This is as certain as Occupy Wall Street (OWS) was followed by Black Lives Matter (BLM), which was followed by Antifa. You can bet the Antifa sequitur has already cleared the design phase by now. The asinine crusades never go away because the OCD never goes away.

Liberal boycotts are the first cousin of the ban. The primary difference is that ban is usually aimed at everyone while the boycott can only include willing participants. Liberal bans have produced some of the most hilariously spectacular epic failures this side of the Jimmy Carter malaise days.

The 2012 attempt to boycott Chick-fil-A (C-F-A) for their alleged animosity toward LBGTs is a notable case study. Liberal activists decided to boycott the national fast-food chicken restaurant because of statements by C-F-A President Dan Cathy and disputes over C-F-A's charitable contributions to *alleged* anti-LGBT organizations. The boycott was clearly another case of coercion.

Such actions are used as leverage, to force the victim (C-F-A) to act in a way contrary to their own interests. In addition to the boycott, new C-F-A franchise locations were denied in Boston, Chicago, and San Francisco by local politicians grandstanding for moral superiority applause. In Chicago, Mayor Rahm Emanuel pontificated "*Chick-Fil-A values are not Chicago values,*" as the murder rate there continued to soar.

In response, several high profile conservatives (Mike Huckabee, Sarah Palin, Rick Santorum, *et. al.*) led a counter-protest effort including a "Chick-Fil-A Appreciation Day." The counter-protest was far more effective than the protest. C-F-A sales for 2012 hit record levels with a 12% increase over the previous year, while the company's privately-held valuation reached record levels. It was the worst year in the history of chickens since Harland Sanders was promoted to colonel.

Post controversy, public opinion polls showed C-F-A at 61% favorable, 13% unfavorable (almost 5 to 1 for our low-math-skilled liberal comrades). Translation of the polling data: this was a case of classic liberal minority bullying of the majority.

The vast majority of liberals never understood the C-F-A "issue" at all, and still don't. The "issue" was *never* about LGBT rights because LGBT rights were never threatened. The only right ever threatened was Dan Cathy's 1st Amendment right to express his opinion about LGBTs or anything else in his purview, and to donate to the causes he wishes to support. The fact that he could legally and morally do this and simultaneously increase CFA sales volume by 12% increases his value as an employee, and is probably deserving of a bonus. Full disclosure: I am now a CFA customer for life and will go out of my way to find one…still more bad news for chickens!

Sadly, liberals will <u>not</u> understand this even after it is explained to them. Instead, they will invoke the nonexistent "hate speech" clause of the *Constitution* in condemnation of C-F-A with all the legal expertise of Saul Goodman (*Breaking Bad* legal counsel *emeritus*). **If it is possible for a liberal to misunderstand, she will. It provides an essential ongoing source of outrage. It is also an omnipresent demonstration of the difference between ignorance and stupidity.** Or, in Biblical terms, *"Hear now this, O foolish people, and without understanding; which have eyes, and see not; which have ears, and hear not."* – Jeremiah 5:21

Another interesting case study of liberal bullying is that of "Memories Pizza" in Walkerton, IN., near South Bend. "Memories Pizza" is a small family-owned-and-operated business. Indiana governor Mike Pence signed into law a religious freedom bill on March 26, 2015, modeled after the federal *Religious Freedom Restoration Act*, which President Bill Clinton signed into law in 1993. The Indiana law simply states the government cannot interfere with people and businesses exercising their religious beliefs. The Indiana bill was hardly pathfinding, and made Indiana the 20th state in the nation to adopt such legislation.

A few days later Alyssa Marino, a local reporter for ABC 57 News out of South Bend, went trolling for an ambush victim for her storyline about non-existent "LGBT persecution." She walked into "Memories" and confronted Memories employee (and daughter of the owner) Crystal O'Connor with the hypothetical question *"Would Memories cater a gay wedding?"* The 20-year-old Ms. O'Connor politely declined.

WHOA!!! This was capital offense perpetrated by Memories Pizza! The social media shitzkreig that followed was so devastating that business owner Kevin O'Connor was forced to close down his business. Threats, phony take-out and delivery orders, Yelp attacks, telephone harassment were the punishment for truthfully answering the reporter's question and exercising what is unquestionably every American's 1st Amendment right.

Memories Pizza was *coerced* out of business by a coordinated crucifixion aimed at the first business to deviate from the liberal script. The attack by the self-appointed liberal "thought Gestapo" was so egregious that the story quickly went national. A GoFundMe account was set up for Memories. The stated purpose of the account was "to relieve the financial loss endured by the proprietors' stand for faith."

Within days the account reached $842K+ (versus the initial goal of $200K) and was shut down. Once again the American people were polled and responded with contribution dollars. Full disclosure: I made a modest contribution to this account in support of the 1st Amendment right of *all* Americans, even the Nazi Nano-witted Alyssa Marino. ("Nano" is a mathematical prefix meaning "one billionth." To call Ms. Marino a "halfwit" would overstate her intellect by approximately 50 %.)

Although these spectacular backfire failures would discourage, embarrass, and humiliate virtually any normal American, they have little if any impact on the convoluted liberal psyche. *Liberals are too stupid to be embarrassed.* The OCDL mindset is that of a radical Islamic terrorist: they only have to win a single battle to be able to claim victory in America's culture war because anything vaguely resembling "success" will be amplified *ad nauseam* by their cheerleading MSM.

The pattern of the liberal boycott style attack is always the same: the initial attack appears to be momentarily successful due to biased MSM coverage. Then they are quickly punched into oblivion by a counterattack of American common sense and decency. The MSM is never around to cover the defeat.

So it is merrily on the way to their next drive-by crime scene, propelled by their OCD. So powerful is the force of their disorder that liberals are oblivious to *any* sense of fairness, right or wrong, or even legality...and much less any "double standard" or "hypocrisy" criticism regardless of validity.

What they cannot achieve at the ballot box with tactics like illegal voter registration, voter fraud, and rigged super delegates, they seek to achieve through the legal system stacked with activist radical leftist judges who have the same mental disorder. Then after failing at all three branches of government, they predictably move on to the boycott/ban strategy.

In reality, the threat of a boycott is a far more effective weapon for their coercion/extortion schemes, in the same way that the threat of a strike is very often a more effective weapon than the strike itself. They become victims of their own propaganda. The liberal mind proudly and boastfully thinks of itself as "thinking outside of the box." To the extent they are actually capable of thought, they *are* the box.

The final resort in the standard liberal playbook is rioting and fascist Antifa-style street thuggery. Liberal MSM-biased coverage is a crucial component of this tactic.

SYNOPSIS: Throughout it all, there is one lesson of critical importance that OCDL's never learn: not everyone thinks the way they do or has the hatred in their heart that they do. As obvious and fundamental as this point is, the concept completely eludes OCDLs, which is why their boycotts almost never work.

4. SOCIALISM: THE EGALITARIAN LIBERAL UTOPIA

"In practice, socialism didn't work. But socialism could never have worked because it is based on false premises about human psychology and society, and gross ignorance of human economy." – **David Horowitz**

Horowitz' quote nails the content of this chapter precisely.

Socialism is a socio-economic system wherein wealth is confiscated from producers and doled out to non-producers in exchange for votes, i.e., bribery. It is legalized slavery. *Socialism is the number 1 enemy of civilized people.*

Liberals do not have any real problem with slavery. They have no problem with censorship, a centrally-controlled economy or being told what to think, which relieves liberals of their greatest burden after OCD. It simplifies life. How simple was life in "Oceania" in George Orwell's "1984"? Liberals are very much into *simple*: no surprises, no risk, no reward, and no critical or analytical thought. This is also the perfect description of my two Persian chinchillas, "Gypsy" and "Voodoo."

My apologies for any demeaning comparison, ladies.

The prime movers who advocate socialism are very "compassionate" people. They care deeply for the disadvantaged, the downtrodden, the "underdog," and the "victims" of oppression. Their faux "compassion" is 100.000% financed by redistribution of *other* people's wealth.

In truth, socialism is a colossal bunco scheme by self-appointed oligarchs designed to swindle the citizens of a country out of their wealth, which equals power which equals *control*. The bunco scheme is peddled on a façade of fairness, equality and social justice which are the mask over poverty, slavery and hopelessness. We observe that *no one* has ever escaped America to a socialist country.

Their ticket to power and *control* is a time tested 1-2-3 punch sequence which never changes: (1) convince anyone below median income that they are victims of the "rich" in a zero-sum game; (2) Convince the victims that they are *entitled* to that which they have been cheated out of by the "rich" in the rigged zero-sum game; and (3) their socialist advocates must be empowered to make this insufferable social injustice "right" by being elected to political office. In short, socialists peddle class warfare.

The way American politicians have ratcheted us toward socialism is insidious. When economic times are good, politicians are quick to give away public funds for costly new social programs, which is actually a redistribution of wealth. This played a major role in the housing bubble and sub-prime mortgage market collapse a decade ago.

When the economy takes its cyclic Democrat driven downturn, America is still stuck with the bill for a new social program which it cannot afford but will *never* go away. And throughout good economic times and bad, our national debt continues to climb at an unsustainable rate.

Politicians use the same tactic to raise taxes on gasoline when the price is low, only to have it reach new heights when the price cycle upswing returns...which it *always* does. The covert tactic leads to Bolshevik style government growth and a constant ratcheting towards socialism, which is the politician's objective.

We should momentarily digress to examine the concept of the "zero-sum game," which is key to the class warfare promoted by the left. It simply means the economy is now and forever static. It disregards completely the concept of any economic growth whatsoever. Under this liberal premise, the only potential source of economic improvement for the economically disadvantaged is to seize it from the wealthy. The seizure is justified by the common knowledge that every dollar possessed by a wealthy person was stolen from a poor person. This is, by definition, the "class warfare" the left is seeking.

But both the global economy and the American economy in particular are not *static*; in fact they are quite *dynamic*. This is easily demonstrable. The sum total of American wealth in 2018 does *not* equal the sum total of American wealth of 1968, 50 years ago. It changed dramatically with time. Nor does the American wealth of 1968 equal 1918, 100 years ago. It has increased immeasurably. A person in contemporary American "poverty" would be upper middle class a hundred years ago with a car, a flat screen TV, and a cell phone with the computing capacity of the entire federal government that *nobody* had then. This is the very definition of *dynamic*. This makes the entire concept of the left's zero-sum game as a basis for class warfare a fallacy.

American wealth is *dynamic* because of what I term *economic evolution*, which primarily includes technology and the catalyst for economic growth— capitalism. We work smarter now than in the last century, not harder. Moreover, without capitalism, there would be no technological advance. This is why the theft of intellectual property by communist nations is a growing international problem for America and the West. Communist societies are not capable of technological innovation; they can only mimic the innovation of capitalist societies for reasons that are discussed below and more extensively in Chapter 6.

Everyone benefits from *economic evolution*. *"A rising tide lifts all boats."* – John F. Kennedy. This *economic evolution* leading directly to economic growth, then, is the real source of economic improvement for *all* Americans. It is particularly impactful for the economically-disadvantaged because small gains are mathematically a greater percentage of their income.

So we learn the left's *"zero-sum game"* premise is not only wrong; it is 180° from the truth. It is the basis of their class-warfare propaganda. It is intentionally deceitful. This is true of virtually all liberal premises. *Never accept <u>any</u> liberal premise because the foundation of liberal premises is liberal logic, which does not exist.*

This brings us to a fundamental socio-economic dichotomy. Liberals advocate the redistribution of wealth in the interest of *fairness*. Crucial to their concept is that *they* are in *control* of the redistribution (minus overhead costs, a euphemism for graft). This ensures *fairness*. Conservatives advocate growth of wealth through free-market forces. This ensures *prosperity*.

We come to realize why capitalism is a target of liberals: *capitalism is the catalyst* in the economic growth reaction. It is in diametric opposition to the left's means to their end, class warfare. *"Prior to capitalism, the way people amassed great wealth was by looting, plundering, and enslaving their fellow man. Capitalism made it possible to become wealthy by <u>serving</u> your fellow man."* – Dr. Walter E. Williams. The left's plan, then, is to return us to the days of looting, plundering, and enslaving our fellow man, who are coincidentally the Americans who carried our great country to unequalled economic prosperity.

If "class warfare" can be accomplished at the ballot box, well and good. If not, we get the liberal Plan "B," which is what we have seen post the 2016 election: riots, a minority party legislative sitzkreig, and ridiculous judicial activism designed to manufacture a constitutional crisis.

Whatever its stated noble and idealistic intent may be, socialism has never worked effectively anywhere for very obvious reasons. It must be pointed out that the OCDL places a factor of 10 magnitude more importance on alleged intent *vis a vis* results. They are not result driven, but rather driven by their fallacious stated intent.

But results *do* matter. We are now a year and half into the Trump presidency. Trump represents prosperity for all as we now witness current record low unemployment for women and minorities. Obama represented government dependency for all as evidenced record low employment and record high food stamps across America. *This* is the dichotomy between capitalism and socialism. Ronald Reagan summed up very succinctly: *"I believe the best social program is a job."*

At some point I will submit my suggestion for a Trump 2020 campaign slogan: *"Donald J. Trump: Doing the Job Kenyans Just Won't Do!"* Admittedly, my slogan suggestion is a hind sighted non-starter, but I figure somebody will get a chuckle out of it.

As an example I cite the August 2016 visit by then candidate Trump to the severely flooded Baton Rouge area while Obama played golf on Martha's Vineyard. Let's not kid ourselves: as long as liberals control the MSM, there was never going to be a "Katrina moment" for Obama. But in truth he was shamed into dropping his golf clubs to take a plane ride to the historically flooded predominately white upscale community of Denham Springs, LA and doing his job.

Democrats seem to have settled on an "It's *not* the economy, stupid!" theme for 2020. By all appearances, they are not only *not* impressed by the highest employment, lowest unemployment for minorities and women, highest consumer confidence, stock market upward rampage, highest GDP growth data that anyone can remember, they are repulsed. That is because socialists understand economics. They vacillate among "It's not really happening," to "It's really the Obama economy delayed effect," and then to "It's irrelevant" alternate universes.

The things that really matter to the American people are "Russian meddling", the Stormy Daniels "scandal", the Don Jr. July 2016 20 minute meeting with a female Russian lawyer over adoption of Russian children ("COLLUSION!!!"), persecution of the jack booted ICE criminal enterprise (for actually enforcing the law), and the heinous breakup of illegal alien families at our Southern border. Yes, these *are* the compelling issues of our time. ***The MSM operates on the premise that "If we do NOT cover it, it is not news." I operate on the premise that if the MSM DOES cover it, it is by definition NOT news.***

In the meantime, the "Gong Show" tryouts for the next non-white male affirmative action party standard bearer are center stage and becoming ever more desperate. My money is *not* on Elizabeth F. Warren, Corey ("Spartacus") Booker and especially Alexandria Ocasio-Cortez. The earliest possible release date from federal stir for Ray Nagin is May 25, 2013 making him a non-starter in the "Next Messiah Sweepstakes". The world awaits with bait on our collective breath (not to be confused with bated breath) while the Democrats ruminate their next "take me to your leader" revelation.

Humans act in their own self-interest. The countercurrent nature of socialism is demonstrated with easily understood examples:

First, we have the case study of the university economics professor who decided to give his students a firsthand demonstration in the futility of socialism.

The professor asked for a show-of-hands question the first day of class: *"How many of you think socialism is a good idea?"* A modest majority of the students raised their hands.

The first couple of weeks of coursework were completed and then the students were tested. The test results were the usual Gaussian distribution array of A-F. Unilaterally, our comrade professor decided the grade distribution was unfair. He announced to his class that there would be a redistribution of grades in the interest of "fairness." The students who made Cs were OK, but there was too much inequity between the A students and the F students. The solution was all too obvious: lower the A students' test scores to C and raise the F students test scores also to C.

Naturally, the A students were livid while the F students were ecstatic. The intrepid professor absorbed the class feedback and announced his program of grade redistribution would continue throughout the semester.

The reaction of the students was to be expected based on human nature: the A students stopped studying because they knew their efforts would not be rewarded. The F students weren't studying anyway, so it made no difference to them. The C students stopped whatever studying they had been doing knowing that it would make no difference whatsoever to them.

So by the next exam there were no A's to redistribute. The A students backslid to C's, the C students backslid to D's and the F students held steady. By the time the test score distribution was finished, everyone in the class got a D.

This devolution continued throughout the semester on the same predictable trajectory. At the end of the semester everyone earned an F for the course. Socialists will quickly point to the virtue of grade equality and "fairness," which of course is their obsession.

To put a smiley face on the story we can imagine the professor concluded the course with a single final exam essay question: *"What did you learn this semester about socialism?"* and gave final grades for the course based on the essays alone.

Whether this story is a true or not is immaterial. The point is that it certainly plausible. It serves well to demonstrate the incompatibility of socialism with both human nature and prosperity, in this case test scores.

Another self-constructed example of fatally flawed socialism which illustrates its stifling impact on every aspect of human performance:

Imagine a group of young runners competing in a 100 meter dash. (At this point, the OCDL's mind wanders to the crucial identity- obsessed questions "Male or female runners?" and "Are transgenders allowed?") Everyone agrees that the race should be "fair." What is not agreed upon is the definition of "fair."

To a conservative, "fairness" means equality of *opportunity*. In this case, everyone *starts* the race at the same time when the starting gun is fired. Then the first one across the finish line is the winner. To the OCDL, "fairness" means equality of *outcome*. In this case, everyone crosses the *finish* line at the same time. In passing, this is also the genesis of the liberal infatuation with affirmative action.

Effectively by the OCDL definition no one is allowed to excel…excellence VERBOTEN! Everyone gets a participation trophy, the only trophy awarded. The result is there is no incentive for the children to make any effort at improvement, so they don't.

To the conservative, the lesson to be learned by this competition is how to deal with and overcome adversity in the real life situations yet to come. To compete and lose incentivizes the competitor to improve performance and become more competitive, a life lesson which becomes invaluable sooner rather than later. *Failure is the stepping stone to excellence.*

To the OCDL, no good can come from competition. It is the saboteur of self-esteem, which is the most important product of our education system. *"So what's the big deal? It's just a silly race that means nothing in the big picture,"* our liberal comrade would say...until the principal of non-performance is extrapolated to every socio-economic aspect of our lives. At that point we have descended to the mediocrity of Western Europe and beyond to the paragon of western hemisphere socialism, Venezuela. However, we will do so with exalted self-esteem.

There are multitudinous examples of the "virtues" of socialism that can be drawn from history, perhaps none as poignant as the Pilgrims who landed at Plymouth Rock in 1620. They braved a harrowing 43-day voyage across the Atlantic Ocean to find religious freedom, which eventually became the 1st Amendment of our constitution. They faced an uncertain future in America.

William Bradford was the leader of the new colony. Upon arrival in America, Bradford issued one share of common stock in the new "commonwealth" to each of the new settlers. Each of the Pilgrims was entitled to an equal share of the colony's collective production...without regard to contribution. To this day Massachusetts is known as a "commonwealth" in title.

The failure that followed was the same failure that has shadowed socialism throughout its history. It was particularly devastating to the Pilgrim community because there was zero backup. Food stamps, EBT cards, free Obamaphones, and Democrats were still a few centuries away. Starvation and freezing in the winter cold of New England ensued.

More than half of the new colonists perished in the first two years. The astute and observant Bradford realized major changes were needed if the new colony was to survive.

Bradford issued tracts of land ("private property") for the colonists to do with as they saw fit. Anything produced from the private property belonged to the individual property owner. From this point forward, the colony prospered from newly-incentivized production according to Bradford's "private property" idea.

Liberals will view the Pilgrims' experience as *selfish*. But Bradford understood the difference between *self-interest* and *selfish*. Even my cats get it. They act in their self-interest but they are not selfish. Yet again, liberals do not get it. They choose *not* to understand.

In the Pilgrims' case, acting in their own *self-interest* was more than virtuous. It was crucial to their survival. Liberals believe that there are ideals that are more important than survival, like "fairness." In truth, *dead people have no virtues.*

Excess production from the "private property" was used to barter for trapper furs, fish, and game. By the end of the first full growing season, the colony had made a 180° turnaround from starvation to prosperity. They held a feast of celebration with their friends, the Indians, who had taught them how to hunt, fish, and grow corn. The feast was called Thanksgiving.

De facto, Thanksgiving was a celebration of the first rejection of socialism in the new world, more than two centuries before Karl Marx and Friedrich Engels corroborated to produce *The Communist Manifesto*.

I recall a personal anecdote which is relevant to the point being made. A friend of mine named Larry came jogging past me in my yard one day in the early 90s. Larry had retired from a career in industrial procurement but post-retirement did overseas contract work in Russia. Larry told me he worked in Moscow. I asked him what it was like there. He told me that Chicago in the mid-40s was what he imagined.

A quick mental math exercise later led me to conclude that Russian economic progress under communism was about a third of American economic progress under capitalism during the same period. Follow the math: in the 75 *elapsed* years from the Bolshevik Revolution in 1917 to 1992 when Larry came jogging by, the Soviet Union had made 27 years of economic progress (1945-1917=27). Then 27/75 equals approximately one third. Although inexact and unscientific, I believe this exercise to be insightful in establishing an order of magnitude difference between the viability of the two economic systems.

We also note the Russian GDP *per capita* is about 13.7% of the USA. Perhaps my one-third guess was optimistically generous to Russian communism.

There are many possible comparisons between capitalism *vis a vis* socialism. At the top of our list has to be *per capita* income. For example, the United States has approximately twice the GDP of China and roughly one fifth the population of China. It does not take a Brainiac to then calculate that the United States has 10 times the *per capita* income of China.

Perhaps a more creative and illustrative examination of evidence would be the 1960s "Space Race" (which actually began in the late 50s) between the United States and the former Soviet Union. The Russians took an early lead in the "Space Race" with the successful launch and orbit of Sputnik 1 ("fellow traveler of earth") in October 1957. America's Explorer 1 followed about 4 months later. The Russians were first to orbit a man around the earth in 1961 in their Vostok 1 spacecraft. America did likewise about 10 months later when astronaut John Glenn orbited the earth in the Friendship 7 spacecraft.

By this time, President John F. Kennedy had announced America's intention to put a man on the moon by the end of the decade. But the real turning point in the race occurred when the Houston MLB franchise changed its name from the "Colt .45s" to the "Astros" at the end of the 1964 baseball season. It marked the relocation, expansion and focus of the NASA led space race effort to the Houston, TX area.

After a few years of experiments, test flights and training, the Apollo 11 spacecraft was launched on July 16, 1969. The journey to the moon included astronauts Neil Armstrong, Buzz Aldrin and Michael Collins and took three days. On July 20, Neil Armstrong stepped onto the moon's surface, said *"That's one small step for man, one giant leap for mankind,"* and then planted an American flag in moment of colossal political incorrectness.

Fortunately, there was no Justin Trudeau meandering about earth in 1969 to point out the error of hero astronaut Armstrong's insensitive commentary. The "Space Race" was over, America had won! And now, nearly a half century later, America remains the only nation to successfully land a man on the moon and return him to earth.

America's victory in the 1960s "Space Race" was more than just a triumph of capitalism over the diametrically opposed socialism. It was a triumph of the American spirit, ingenuity, creativity, imagination, individualism, entrepreneurial skill and determination focused into a gigantic team effort. *None* of this is allowed to exist under the 10 planks of the Communist Manifesto. This will be examined in greater detail later (Chapter 6 - What Makes America Great: Or Is It?)

American President Ronald Reagan defeated communism worldwide by the end of his second term. He did this by bankrupting the USSR in an arms race the Russians could not afford or win. It was a test of the two economic systems, capitalism and communism, to achieve and sustain military superiority. Communism lost, and effectively capitulated.

For a generation, the collectivist pestilence lay dormant and economies all over the globe made unprecedented progress under new free market force. Communism may have been critically wounded by the R^2 strategy, but liberal OCD was untouched. As long as there is an OCDL somewhere seeking to enslave people to satisfy their obsession for *control*, then communism has everything it needs to make a comeback. This may be the best explanation we ever get for America's misguided eight-year excursion into the twilight zone of "Obamunism" (Chapters 10 and 11).

Socialism has various names and is practiced in degrees. Collectivism, Marxism, communism, and socialism all represent the same basic failed idea: confiscation of the individual's work product for redistribution for the "greater good." The very idea is an open invitation to corruption, embezzlement, graft, bribery, extortion, coercion, blackmail, tax evasion, and a number of other RICO statute[1] crimes. Karl Marx somehow failed to mention this in his *opus magnum*. This by itself is enough to doom socialism. But the corruption aspect is inconsequential compared to the futility of the individual who is forced to work for nothing.

Whatever Karl Marx' "noble" intentions were for his 19th century *opus magnum* instantly devolved into a quagmire of corruption, evil, slavery and mass murder. It was the perpetual motion machine that crashed and burned on takeoff. It provided OCDLs the pretense and framework for the theft of worldwide wealth for the purpose of redistribution to the needy (themselves). The pestilence malingers on to this day despite its perfect global record of 0.000% success. In this sense it more deadly than the 14th century European Black Plague. It will remain a threat to socio-economy functionality as long as there are OCDLs seeking *control*.

Modern day collectivism has a spectrum of relative "success" depending on the level of commitment to redistribution of wealth. Liberals are quick to point to Western European "social democracies" such as France as a socialist "success" story. To be sure, France is not in poverty, but only because they utilize a hybrid economic system somewhere between socialism and free-market capitalism.

Their hybrid form affords them about 65% of the standard of living of the USA based on *per capita* income. Other forms of collectivism generally yield poorer results until we reach the extreme of Stalinist communism in North Korea, where outside the military, income is effectively zero. Tragically, collec-

---

[1] The 1970 **Racketeer Influenced and Corrupt Organizations Act**, commonly referred to as the **RICO Act** or simply **RICO**, is a <u>United States federal law</u> that provides for extended criminal penalties and a civil cause of action for acts performed as part of an ongoing criminal organization. The RICO Act focuses specifically on racketeering, and it allows the *leaders* of a syndicate to be tried for the crimes which they ordered others to do or assisted them in doing, closing a perceived loophole that allowed a person who instructed someone else to, for example, murder, to be exempt from the trial because they did not actually commit the crime personally.

tivism naturally gravitates toward the NorK extreme because of the selfishness of its corrupt leaders. *"The goal of socialism is communism."* – Vladimir Lenin.

As socialism metastasizes within a society, the GNP shrinks because the individual incentive to produce is destroyed. However, the *crucial* role of the government to redistribute the shrinking wealth is never destroyed. Because after all, "fairness" is the collectivist society's most valued virtue.

The number one priority of the socialist government is to perpetuate and grow itself. Government employees must "eat good" (for liberals, grammatically incorrect for effect) even if the rest of the nation is starving. How else is the crucial "fairness" going to be enforced? This is government priority *numero uno*. **"The government is a tick on the butt of America. It doesn't drive the economy; it sucks the blood out of the economy. "** – Dave Ramsey.

Government, then, requires an ever-increasing slice of the ever-decreasing socialist GNP pie. As the peons realize they are being squeezed at both ends by a government that has zero interest in their well-being, protests begin. The government which continues to "eat good" does not want to relinquish totalitarian power or *control*, and cracks down on the protestors. This could be called the Venezuelan (or "No Toilet Paper") stage.

Our socialist nation has now reached its moment of truth: if the people prevail, democracy survives. If the government prevails, the people are enslaved by a communist dictator. It will be interesting to watch ongoing events in Venezuela. They are now literally reaching starvation, eating the indigenous flamingo flocks for food. A mass exodus to western neighbor Columbia is currently underway.

There is no doubt about which side Obama would supporting if he were still in office.

If all this economic pinheaddery is true, why are the liberal underclasses attracted to socialism like groupies to a rock band? Ironically, they are attracted to socialism because of their insecurity. They want someone else to provide food, clothing, shelter, education, healthcare, free Obama-phones, etc. for them, to think for them, to give them a template to live their lives. Liberals are the tool for this job! ***"A government big enough to give you everything you want, is a government big enough to take away everything that you have."*** **– Thomas Jefferson.**

The liberal upper classes are attracted to socialism because impoverished people *need* government, i.e., they are more easily *controlled*. Thus we learn liberals' priorities, *control* vs. prosperity.

Because the socialist economic model is vastly inferior to its antithesis, capitalism, socialist regimes like North Korea must rely on aggression, extortion, and other felonious activity to approach economic parity because they cannot produce anything themselves. Petty gangsterism by a comical dwarf is never going to make up the gap between a failed ideology of socialism or its grotesque mutant overgrown bastard offspring communism and the successful capitalism. That is like peeing into the ocean and hollering *"Tidal wave!"*

But absent the common sense to convert to an economic system that actually works, petty gangsterism is all they have.

There are no entrepreneurs in socialist countries, for a number of reasons:

An entrepreneur is defined as a person who organizes and operates a business or businesses, taking on greater than normal financial risks in order to do so. Entrepreneurs are not only essential for a nation's economic success; they are a key piece of socio-economic evolution. New products like the incandescent light bulb, the telephone, the automobile assembly line, the air conditioning unit, the radio and television, the airplane, the personal computer, the cell phone, etc. are all the work products of entrepreneurs. We owe the entire industrial revolution to these individual pioneers of capitalism.

Socialism, however, does not recognize *individuals*. This means there are no rewards, financial or otherwise, for *individual* achievement. It means the incandescent light bulb could never have been invented in a socialist country.

There is no capital for the *individual* with a vision to venture in a socialist country because it all controlled by the state. **Destroy the wealth creators and no wealth will be created.** Try talking your average corrupt socialist bureaucrat into a loan to develop your aero-plane idea. Ain't gonna happen!

There is no "profit" in a socialist country. In other words, even if even if there was *individual* recognition and capital for your automobile assembly line idea, you would not be materially rewarded for your effort. Never mind, just take the day off!

Entrepreneurial talent and leadership is a *major* factor in making America the world's economic engine. (We will expand on this in Chapter 6.)

Socialists fall into five general categories:

(1) The lower or "Parasite" class. This class just wants "free stuff." They are obsessed with a sense of self- entitlement which they have been taught by liberalism. Their biggest problem with our growing $20T national debt is that it is not $200T, which would have resulted in more "free stuff" for them. It is safe to assume their least favorite Biblical quote is 2 Thessalonians 3:10....."*If a man will not work, he shall not eat.*"

This is by far the numerically largest class, and their continued support of getting "free stuff" is critical to the survival of socialism. This is an easy task for them. As noted playwright George Bernard Shaw so succinctly put it, "*A government which robs Peter to pay Paul can always depend on the support of Paul.*" The political fortune of the Democrat Party is *totally* dependent on parasites Paul and Paulina.

Within the context of this discussion, the terms parasite, liberal and Democrat are interchangeable. They suck up "free stuff" with the exuberance of a black hole.

Conservatives pay for the "free stuff" given away to parasites through ever increasing taxes. The resentment, contempt and raw hatred that parasites have for their conservative benefactors is palpable. If conservatives could be disarmed through gun *control*, they would be quickly purged from America by parasite mobs. The thought of "Who would pay for our 'free stuff' then?" does not occur to parasites...they will jump off *that* bridge when they get to it.

(2) The middle or "Magnanimous" class. This class perpetually seeks adoration for their "open mindedness." They are ostensibly obsessed with "fairness," but in reality are obsessed with the public display of their moral superiority which equates to their superiority as human beings. Of course their definition of "fairness" means an obsession with equality of *outcome*, not the *sane* definition: equality of *opportunity*. Metaphorically, this means everybody finishes the race tied for last, i.e., excellence is prohibited under socialism. They do not see themselves as impacted by the "fundamental transformation" to socialism because they have been propagandized that burden will fall upon only the "rich." Then once socialism is established, they learn too late that "rich" has been redefined downward to mean "anyone with a job," to increase the flow of revenue to the ever-expanding government. Ultimately they are swept away into the slave class by the socialist "bait and switch" ruse because the middle class is targeted for extinction by socialism.

The "Magnanimous" class are also commonly referred to as "useful idiots," dubbed so by the patron saint of collectivist chaos and anarchy, Saul Alinsky. "Useful" because they are early promoters of "the cause"; "idiots" because they never asked obvious questions like *Why are people universally trying to escape socialist countries TO the United States, and not vice versa?*

(3) A second middle or "Wayward" class. There are countless liberal Americans who are doing well enough under our current socio-economic system, but they are just plain bored. They are irrelevant outside of their own immediate sphere, for good reason. But this is not how they envision themselves.

Long on self-esteem and hubris with virtually zero critical thought skills, these people were prime targets for the 2008 Obama hopey changey "We are the ones we've been waiting for!" sloganeered campaign. They did not just buy the Obama nothing burger. They supersized it.

Now America is in the post "Obama Catastrophe" era, and these errant spirits are in search of another cause which will validate their relevance. Turns out the "historic first black American president" was not the answer they were looking for. However, even if they face up to this truth, it will not prevent them from defending the Obama legacy. To do otherwise would be an admission that they were duped by the Manchurian Teleprompter. **Liberals do not admit errors.**

To wit, socialism is a really cool "new" idea. In reality, Karl Marx died in the 19th century. But for the self-centered self-absorbed liberal, history begins the day they were born. Supporting Bernie Sanders, the ancient socialist refugee from the Muppet Show theater heckler-section balcony is even cooler than wearing a Che Guevara T-shirt.

So Crazy Bernie Sanders becomes the new standard-bearer for our street-variety liberal rebel without a clue.

What better way to establish a legacy of extreme relevance than to topple America's imagined evil capitalist economic system and replace it with an egalitarian utopia called socialism: a society in which increasing taxes on the "rich" will pay for everything imaginable?

These are not deep thinkers. They cannot do even simple math. They do not understand that socialism has never worked anywhere for obvious reasons. They do not understand that the socialist definition of "rich" is anyone with a job. They do not understand that slavery euphemistically called "redistribution" will lead swiftly and directly to an ever-declining GNP. They do not understand that the corrupt socialist government will require an ever increasing share of the ever-decreasing GNP to sustain and grow itself, which is its number one priority.

The egalitarian utopia they fantasize about is the solution to their problems. And of course, they are free to sabotage America in pursuit of their utopia, at least by non-violent means. They are right in their opinion, the only one that counts. They are afforded this freedom to subvert America by the 1st Amendment of our constitution which they seek to destroy. There is *no* such freedom in the collectivist utopia they seek. ***Irony is ALWAYS lost on the stupid.***

By the time they realize what has happened, the utopia they envisioned has metastasized into oppressive totalitarian communism. At this point, the game is over. There are no do-overs, no mulligans. It is a one-way street. The people who have seized *control* of the government are not going to voluntarily relinquish power or *control*. So it turns out our wayward liberal friend's "cure" was light years worse than the disease.

(4) The wealthy or "Patrician" class. These people have wealth and they want to keep it that way. They join the mob demanding redistribution of wealth to avoid becoming the target of the mob. They fit in about as well as the Frankenstein monster would carrying a pitchfork and torch to his own lynching.

Although they are free to redistribute their personal wealth at any time, they never do — because it is all for show, an act. All liberals are unaccomplished actors, you understand.

Instead of *their* wealth, they advocate the redistribution of *your* wealth. Because they are avowed socialists, their ludicrous populist hypocrisy will get copious airplay from the MSM. They are folk heroes to the liberal MSM.

We have all heard Warren Buffett publically lament that *his* tax rate was lower than his secretary's tax rate. This is because he is taxed on his *income*, not his *wealth*. He has a platoon of tax accountants looking for how best to hide his *income*.

Yet Mr. Buffett would have America believe he is begging to have his taxes raised. His tax accountants are probably in favor of a tax increase for Mr. Buffett as well for their own job security…more job security in finding yet another way to camouflage his income.

The correct answer to Mr. Buffett's crisis of conscience is *not* to *raise* his taxes, but instead to *lower* his secretary's taxes. This simple and obvious solution will *never* occur to a socialist.

Wealthy liberal American faux socialists are as common as flies at a garbage dump. The Kennedys, actor Matt Damon, the aforementioned Warren Buffett, John F. Kerry, Al Sharpton, and the Clintons are a few unsightly examples.

Wealthy liberal useful idiots will remain esteemed and untouchable right until it is time to confiscate *their* wealth. Will they then realize that they fanned the flames of socialist insanity that consumed *them*? Time will tell. In the interim, joining the socialist mob is the path of least resistance. Pathfinding this trail is something at which liberals are quite accomplished. It is as simple as molten lava finding its way down the side of a volcano.

(5) The upper or "Community Organizer" class. This class seeks one thing: the power to *control* the lower classes. They are obsessed with this because it is an overt display to all of their superiority. They do not care that socialism has never worked anywhere. That is *NOT* the point. They just want to be the ones who redistribute the wealth because this gives them the power of *control* that they obsess over, which *IS* the point. I doubt seriously that even they think they can spend your money more effectively than you can, any more than the bank robber planning his next heist. They are just pigs who want your money for themselves. ***Without redistribution of wealth, there is no opportunity for graft.***

This is why Barack Obama gushes with envy at dictatorships in Cuba, Venezuela, Russia, and China. It certainly is not the state of failing economies there. It is the *control* the dictators have over the proletariat. This is why Obama established diplomatic relations with Cuba. This is why Obama told Russian President Medvedev (03.26.12) in an infamous "hot mic" moment: *"This is my last election … After my election I have more flexibility."* Yet again we see the standard socialist mindset in the priority of *control* over prosperity.

Far left alleged comedian Bill Maher offered this gem of liberal insight on his HBO show on June 8, 2018: *"I hope for a recession to get rid of Trump. Sorry if that hurts people."* Allow me to decode the esteemed Mr. Maher's fantasy into consumption for common folk: "I am wealthy. I do not live paycheck to paycheck. I do not give a ____ (choose your own expletive) about people who do. I will gleefully throw as many of them under the bus as it takes to return my fellow radical leftist nut jobs back to power. Recession or not, I will still be eating chateaubriand and lobster in a Beverly Hills restaurant."

Mr. Maher's death wish for the American economy also gives us this insight into the liberal "mindset": the American economy doing well is synonymous with Trump doing well. This is because Trump is on the American people's side. The left is not. They are perfectly happy to trash the economic wellbeing of the American people to damage Trump. There is *no* ambiguity here.

Nor are Mr. Maher's ill wishes for America limited to the economy. We can safely speculate that he would equally delighted if terrorists successfully attacked an American population center with the caveat that he personally was not a casualty. Or a major hurricane made landfall at a U.S. population center. Or Kim Jong-un lobbed a missile into downtown Tokyo. Or Bashir al-Assad gassed thousands of his own people… again. Or the Chinese sunk an American aircraft carrier in the South China Sea. Or another Bernie Sanders supporter shot up a Republican baseball practice. Or a Russian jet buzzed the Statue of Liberty and knocked off her crown. Or Stormy Daniels claimed she aborted Trump's illegitimate child. Or Melania Trump wore a pair of mismatched shoes to the annual White House Easter egg roll.

Never before has such an eloquent declaration of liberal priorities been presented. No, Mr. Maher is *not* a comedian. He is a joke.

Maher's revelation is the same mindset that gave America the Mueller probe. The Russian collusion delusion/Mueller probe/FISAgate/FBI/DoJ treachery is a liberal manufactured crisis serving notice to America that if the left cannot have control of the government, there will be *no* government. The government will be abrogated via an FBI initiated *coup detat*. Metaphorically, it is the equivalent of tipping the chess board over one move before your opponent announces "Checkmate!"

Once America's faith in its own election process is sabotaged, political anarchy and chaos will quickly follow. But wait! Isn't that the goal of the George Soros piloted alt left all along?

Bill Maher's death wish for the American economy is merely a compartmentalized battle in the alt left's larger war against America.

Through hypnotic self-delusion liberals have convinced themselves that they are the saviors of humanity via "social justice," which is synonymous with redistribution of wealth. It is a delusion marinated in faux "moral superiority," which enables them to drone on with the sacred task of converting *greedy* America into the *fairness* and *equality* of North Korea. It is purely coincidental that universally the socialist leadership gets filthy rich in the redistribution process. Financing someone else's moral superiority through the socialist graft plan is *not* cheap.

It is of *zero* concern to this ruling class that the masses are living in abject poverty, if not starving. What peon wants to work making the wealthy ruling socialist class wealthier? The ruling class is in *control*, which is all that matters to them. The upper class has little concern that the national economic output is ever declining. The socialist ruling class could accurately be described as sociopathic without conscience...a luxury afforded by moral superiority. But after all, nobody's perfect.

Of course any redistribution that occurs goes *through* the ruling class *to* THEM FIRST. This is only appropriate because who better to be first in line but this superior class? There are many American examples of this: Congress exempting themselves from the laughable "Affordable Care Act," Congress voting itself a pay raise, Congress retirement on full pay, etc. No need to dwell on this all-too-obvious point. Incidentally, the "Community Organizer Class" focus is virtually entirely on Nazi-like socialist *control* (healthcare, gun *control*, energy, and the trajectory of the economy via the "climate change" hoax), so that once in power, it *stays* that way.

This obsession with *control* is why liberals cannot be bothered by external existential threats such as ISIS. Distractions like ISIS, Iran, North Korea, etc. are regarded as remote and no threat to the *control* they lust for. Instead they focus upon the perceived immediate threats to their power and *control*: Republicans, the TEA Party, and the NRA. *E.g.*, after the Orlando Pulse gay nightclub massacre in June 2016, liberals had no comment about the shooter because they do not perceive radical Islamic terrorism to be a threat to them. Their criticism was instead directed at the NRA, which had *nothing* to do with the heinous Pulse massacre.

Synopsis: All of these socialists have two common characteristics regardless of class: (1) They don't give a _____ (roll your own metaphor here) about anybody but themselves; and (2) they all have the personality disorder called "Obsessive Compulsive Disorder" (OCD).

American liberals like Hillary Clinton have now deemed themselves "progressives." They consider the transformation from capitalism to socialism to communism to be "progress." In fact, from your perspective, it is progress from freedom to slavery, from prosperity to poverty. But from their sociopathic perspective, it is progress toward the *control* over which they obsess. Within my personal vernacular, I define the term "progressive" as insidiously incremental evil.

5. SIGNALS FROM THE KOREAN PENINSULA:
THE PATH IS CLEAR

"One picture is worth a thousand words." – **Tess Flanders.**

As an eagle scout in the Boy Scouts of America (BSA), I learned Morse code.

Morse code can be transmitted a couple of different ways: by telegraph with audio dots and dashes (dit-dah sounds); or by line of sight with flags, called "semaphore" (commonly called "wig wag").

In the context of the previous discussion of socialism, there could be no clearer message to humanity about the "virtues" of collectivism than that "wig wagged" by the Korean Peninsula nightly.

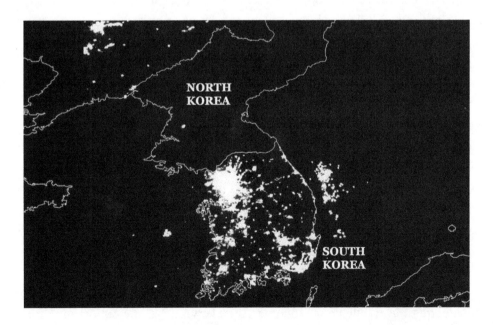

There is undisputed truth clearly visible to anyone who would take the time to look at a satellite image of the Korean Peninsula at night. No amount of words could provide clearer contrast of capitalism with Stalinist communism…the results <u>cannot</u> be disguised. It is an indelible object lesson in the abject failure of collectivism.

The southern portion of the peninsula is South Korea, a *capitalist* nation of 38 million people. From the satellite image, it could easily pass for a densely-populated area of the United States, Western Europe, or Japan. In South Korea, there is light.

The northern portion of the peninsula is North Korea, a *communist* nation of 22 million people. It could easily pass for the Gobi Desert. In North Korea, there is <u>*no*</u> light.

Of course, reactions of conservatives (from Earth) and liberals (from Uranus) to this image are complete polar opposites. The initial reaction of the liberal is that the image has been photo- shopped, because they have never seen it before. It is fake, and North Korea is actually doing just fine. They think this because that is what *they* would do to make their bogus point.

Once the authenticity obstacle is cleared, the liberal takes a closer look at South Korea and sees "inequity," "unfairness," and "greed." There are South Koreans earning 10 times (or more) than others. Giant red flag, this is intolerable! It should be noted here that liberals are mercurial to conflate "self-interest" with "greed," or anything else that will make their convoluted point (e.g., conflating "war on radical Islam" with "war on Islam, or "illegal immigrants" with "immigrants", or conflating *all* Americans with illegal immigrants with the *uber* conflation "We are *all* immigrants.").

The most recent addition to the parade of liberal illogical conflation is to equate revoking the security clearance of departed Obama rogue saboteur CIA Director John Brennan with an attack on Brennan's 1st Amendment right. I have *never* had a government top secret clearance but I have *always* had a 1st Amendment right. Still wondering how that is possible.

Perhaps most astonishing about the ever absurd liberal conflation to produce an illogical "conclusion" is the hubris to think Americans are stupid enough to be persuaded by such shallow specious rhetoric. It only works on fellow liberals.

Then our liberal comrade looks at North Korea and sees equality and "fairness"; everyone's income is equal (at zero). Egalitarian in every sense of the word. Big gold star! Moreover, there are no evil capitalist corporations polluting the environment to sell power to citizens for a profit. Another gold star!! The socio-economic environment is very ordered and completely *controlled* by the government. Also, there are no stray dogs or cats in North Korea (go figure). Yet another gold star!!!

Our conservative friend sees the image quite differently. In South Korea, he sees prosperity. Although there is income inequity, everyone has an income. And everyone has the opportunity to pursue higher income and a higher standard of living, limited only by circumstances largely within their control. In South Korea there is a power company that sells power (for profit). As a result, there is light at night.

The conservative also sees North Korea differently. He sees a ruthless dictator who is a parody of himself, an absurdly oversized military, and *gulags* full of dissenters, providing the "order" and *control* our liberal comrade lauds.

We think back to our example of the 100 meter race and the template it provided for a nation's socio-economic structure. South Korea is modeled upon the conservative concept of equal *opportunity*. In the race, everyone is free to run as fast as they can once the starting gun has been fired. In the capitalist "race," everyone is free to pursue a brighter economic future for themselves.

North Korea is modeled upon the liberal concept of equality of *outcome*. In the 100 meter race, everyone finishes tied for last place. In the communist economic "race," everyone is tied at zero income.

The satellite image is also instructive for other reasons: the lone speck of light in the sea of North Korean darkness is not a mystery either. It is the capitol city of Pyongyang. And this is as it should be in a country whose primary source of income is counterfeiting other nation's currencies, kidnapping, extortion, and panhandling welfare from its big brother, communist China. The extortion figures to take center stage on a world scale after the NorKs demonstrate a ballistic missile that doesn't blow up on the launch pad.

The Supreme Leader of this paradise on earth is deserving of nothing less than the very best for the sacrifice he has made for his people: the multi-billionaire (with a "B") Kim Jong-un has his own private island where he is entertained by his own harem of handpicked showgirls in drunken orgies. Anyone who disagrees with the amenities Dear Leader affords himself will be staring down the barrel end of a firing squad, a hangman's noose, or a life sentence in a *gulag*.

The long-term solution to the communist insanity of North Korea is unification of the north and south. The economic system and prosperity of the south would instantly overtake the north and both countries would be immensely better off, particularly the north. This is what happened in Germany a quarter century ago.

Of course, circumstances were somewhat different in Germany, or more specifically, in Berlin, which was the epicenter of the German phenomenon. Berlin is a city of approximately 4 million people. At the conclusion of World War II, it was divided among four allied occupying nations.

Russia controlled the eastern half of the city. The western half was divided into three sectors controlled by the United States, Great Britain, and France. Eventually the new post-WW2 Soviet- puppet nation of East Germany took control of East Berlin while the new nation of West Germany took control of West Berlin.

The communists erected a wall between East and West Berlin in 1961 to stop defection to the west. Of course, their claim was that the wall was built to stop illegal immigration FROM the west. Never mind the countless East Germans who were killed trying to scale the barbed wire topped wall to freedom. Their dead bodies were merely capitalist propaganda.

What resulted in Berlin was a side-by-side fishbowl comparison of the two competing economic systems, capitalism vs. communism. As luck would have it, the contrast was stark, just like the two Koreas, for precisely the same reason.

West Berlin thrived while East Berlin struggled. Manfred in East Berlin peddled around on a broken-down bicycle among building ruins shelled out in WW2. Decades pass and Manfred notices high-rise skyscrapers going up within view on the other side of the wall. He cannot help but notice his cousin Siegfried in West Berlin is driving a brand new BMW to his penthouse apartment. Manfred senses something is wrong here.

By this time, the technical improvement in global communication has reached a point where the truth can no longer be hidden from Manfred in East Berlin.

It is now the late 80s and Ronald Reagan is nearing the end of his second term. He has bankrupted the East German puppet master, the Soviet Union, with an arms race the Soviets could not afford. As the

Soviet Union crumbles economically, its satellite block of Eastern European communist nations concurrently follow suit.

On June 12, 1987, Ronald Reagan delivers his famous "Mr. Gorbachev, tear down the wall!" speech at the Brandenburg gate in West Berlin.

Within a few years, East and West Germany are unified into the *capitalist* economic powerhouse of Europe called "Germany."

This is a result which liberals are unwilling to accept or recognize even now, three decades later. When pressed about the outcome of the Reagan years, liberals will acknowledge *no* Reagan success and instead credit Russian president Gorbachev for ending the Cold War. In fact, in the American left's self-delusional theater-of-the-absurd Orwellian revisionist history, the 1980s never happened. There was no Jimmy Carter mess for Reagan to clean up. The unfortunate collapse of the totalitarian Soviet-controlled empire was actually engineered by their Russian communist comrades. Yeah, right!

Liberals are revisionists out of necessity. It is their mechanism for covering up their ongoing parade of monumental failures. E.g., Hillary Clinton did not fail in her 2016 presidential bid. She was defrauded by Vladimir Putin and the Russians in "collusion" with the Trump campaign. This is revisionist history, because in reality the Russians had nothing to do with her loss.

Similarly, liberals view the United States Constitution as a living document. This means they are authorized to imagine any interpretation they want to the document. It is a form of revisionism. They are in *control*. Based upon this logic, they are able to contort the Constitution into whatever they need based on the liberal obsessive compulsive whim *de jour*.

The timing of the East German crisis should not be a mystery. By the time the Berlin wall was demolished in November 1989, seventy-two years had elapsed since the Russian Bolshevik Revolution of November 1917. The World War II "baby boomers" now in charge were two generations (WW1 and WW2) removed from the global communist movement of the World War I era.

They inherited a thoroughly dysfunctional socio-economic system from their forefathers. They recognized the ever-widening standard of living gap between themselves and the free world. They had zero personal credibility invested in this truly bad idea which had cost their forefathers decades of economic progress and 100+ million lives. They had "no skin" in the disastrous communist game. East Berliners could not be isolated from the advances in communication technology which brought the truth to them. In the fishbowl of Berlin, the truth was all too apparent. Time for drastic change.

The North Korean people are far more isolated than were the East Berliners: communist China to the north, the Sea of Japan to the east, the Yellow Sea to the west and a 2.5 mile wide de-militarized zone (DMZ) to the south segregating it from South Korea. Unlike Berlin, you cannot look over a 2.5 mile wide DMZ and observe the results of capitalism. The country is so poor and so poorly run that communication technology has no chance of reaching it, which is a very good thing for its leaders.

There are four primary obstacles to the happy unification conclusion on the Korean peninsula: (1) the Dear Leader is fine with the way things are. He is (literally) "fat and happy"; (2) North Koreans are far more effectively isolated from the truth about communism than East Berlin was; (3) oversized NorK military is oversized and well fed for this very reason, to crush any overthrow attempt; (4) The Chinese Communists do not want another successful capitalist nation literally on their doorstep, another Japan. That would threaten their leadership, who are also happy with the *status quo*. So they subsidize North Korea with welfare, which by some estimates comprises 80% of North Korea's effective income, to maintain the *status quo*.

The future of the Korean peninsula then is in the hands of China. I am not holding my breath waiting for them to do what is best for anyone but themselves.

The island nation of Cuba presents another interesting case study of capitalism juxtaposed by communism. The satellite image of Cuba at night is not quite as bleak as North Korea, because of the American dollars that flow to Cuba from Cuban refugees in Florida to the relatives they left behind.

Cuba is the satellite of the United States of America, the global epicenter of capitalism, and benefits greatly from proximity. North Korea, on the other hand, is the satellite of communist China. Table scraps from communist China are quite meager.

SYNOPSIS: The night time satellite image of the Korean peninsula is the perfect metaphor contrasting capitalism with communism.

6. WHAT MAKES AMERICA GREAT: OR IS IT?

"And let us resolve they will say of our day and our generation that we did keep faith with our God, that we did act 'worthy of ourselves'; that we did protect and pass on lovingly that shining city on a hill." – **Ronald Reagan.**

My regard for President Reagan remains immense. For more than three decades I considered him the greatest American president of my lifetime. Recently he has been displaced in that intrapersonal survey.

I can think of no better preamble to the discussion of America's greatness than the opening scene of the HBO television series *"Newsroom."* It is easily found on the internet with almost any search engine for anyone who has not yet seen it.

The setting for the scene is an auditorium full of college-age students. The students appear eager to fill their vacuous minds with wisdom from a panel of talking-headed pundits on the stage in front of them. The panel moderator has posed the question to the panel *What makes America the greatest country on earth?* It is time for the series star panelist to opine.

Our star is reluctant to answer the question and uncomfortably attempts to deflect it with some "How 'bout them Braves?" style generic banter. Meanwhile, a female student in the back of the auditorium begins flashing him with over-sized idiot cards. The card messages reject the premise of the question. Our star panelist is pressed to respond until he finally blurts out what can best be described as scripted impassioned pontification.

Like the *"big bosomed lady with the Dutch accent"* in a Rod Stewart song, his ad-libbed lines were well rehearsed. He sprays derogatory comments about the USA around the auditorium like a cornered skunk. No one is spared.

Our intrepid pundit cites statistics on crime and education to make his point that America is on a decidedly downward trajectory. He kicks his word gumbo up a notch with a few "f-bombs"…impressive indeed, particularly for this audience demographic.

The tirade concludes with a fervent plea for America to return to the glory days *"when you could leave your front door unlocked, when people had compassion and respect for one another, and a return to our once world- class manufacturing base when Americans actually 'made' things."* Mr. Newsroom's grand finale: *"America is no longer the greatest nation on earth…but we could be,"* in synchronous harmony with the card flasher at the back of the auditorium. It was remarkably prescient of the liberal *"Newsroom"* screenwriters to come up with Donald Trump's 2016 *"Make America Great Again"* campaign theme in this 2012 episode four years before its time. Perhaps they hind-sighted the early Obama years 2009-2012 and extrapolated that failure out exponentially to where it actually ended up. *"Tell Vladimir this is my last election … After my election I have more flexibility."* – Barack Obama (03.26.12). In any event, the scene clip I saw truncated at this point.

Music to the liberal ear indeed! Mr. Newsroom attacked America as no longer the greatest country on earth while cleverly sidestepping the very key issues of income and standard of living which attract the overwhelming majority of immigrants to our country. The simple fact that the United States of America *is* the economic engine of the entire planet escapes our *wunderkind* pundit completely, or perhaps it is just irrelevant. ***"It's the economy, stupid."* – James Carville (1992)**

That clip was enough for me. A liberal show, liberal actors in a liberal setting, liberal writers on a liberal "premium" cable network…never mind!

I should note here that the actor's bedazzling outburst with rapid-fire recital of cherry-picked negative statistics was good theater for liberals who universally choose form over substance. This is all the liberal mind can process; intellectual content requires a skill set that the typical liberal does *not* possess. After all, the *"Yes we can* (what?)!" and *"Hope and change* (to what?)" read off a teleprompter by *"…the first mainstream African-American who is articulate and bright and clean and a nice-looking guy…"* – Joe Biden (02.08.08), the human avuncular gaffe in search of an place to happen, was an easy sell to the 2008 "Coalition of the Gullible." This classic "form over substance" campaign was all it took to get Obama elected in 2008. To be clear, the *"Yes we can…"* was the form, the missing (…to what?) was the substance; the *"Hope and change…"* was the form, the missing (…to what?) was the substance. Get the idea? The substance remains MIA to this day. ***"Our biggest mission in life is to avoid being fools."*** – Dr. Wilhelm Schumann ("Ship of Fools" - 1965).

Although I have no idea what happened after that 5-minute scene clip, you can bet it was *not* the logical sequitur: "If America is not the greatest country on earth, who is? And why?" "Why are illegal immigrants pouring across our southern border by the tens of thousands; what do they know about America that this liberal master of teleprompter elocution does not know?" would not be a good bet either. And

"Why do liberals encourage open borders and unlimited invasion into a decrepit and declining racist bigoted county like America?" never occurred to the screenwriters either. Finally, "America provides virtually everyone not only the freedom but the *means* to leave and go anywhere else on the planet they wish to go anytime they are ready to do so. If America is the cesspool of racism, unjust incarceration, and social injustice that liberals so frequently lament, why don't they just leave?" didn't make it into the script either.

Why weren't these highly relevant questions included in this scene? Why isn't Mr. Newsroom down at the southern border "enlightening" the illegal invaders to go back, they're better off where they came from? Why did he not point out that the USA is the economic engine of the entire planet? And because of that, the USA *per capita* income and standard of living are the envy of every other country on the planet.

I will respond to my own questions: because (1) he is a liberal, the group responsible for 100.000% of the negative statistics he cited; and (2) *I* didn't write the script.

So what *does* make America the greatest country on earth? Abundant natural and human resources is a trite answer, but are nonetheless major factors in the overall American success story. No country on earth has greater natural resources than the United States of America. Sadly, many of these natural resources are out of reach due to the obstruction by liberals in the faux name of "environmentalism." The true motive for the obstructionism is convoluted, but has little, if anything, to do with the environment. Rather, it is rooted in a sense of global redistribution of wealth, which is a primal OCDL obsession.

Allowing America to more fully utilize its abundant natural resources will only widen America's income gap with the rest of the world. This *cannot* be tolerated by liberals. And because liberals have no desire or concept how to create wealth, their only remedy to the income inequality they so loathly observe is to lower the income of wealth creators, who provide virtually all job growth in America. A poorer America is more government-dependent, which equals government growth and *control* over the lives of Americans, also a primal OCDL obsession. Of course, the ultimate burden of this global income redistribution *from* America that results from liberal environmental scams falls disproportionately on the American poor, a heavy price to pay for someone else's obsession. OCDLs do not care; their self-prescribed psychological well-being and therapeutic redistribution easily overrides any job for some poor redneck schlub in Dothan, AL., or sodbuster in Grand Island, NE.

The Paris Climate Accord is a classic case study of wealth redistribution from the United States to the rest of the world under the masquerade of "environmentalism." Americans' standard of living, jobs, and production of American energy reserves would be sacrificed for decades while the rest of the planet carries on without restriction, all for liberal's imaginary environmental obsession. The *real* goal here is global redistribution of wealth, not environmental protection. And every dollar that is redistributed will flow through the hands of liberal politicians like Al Gore, who will impose his (or her, in the case of Hillary Clinton) personal fee on the "transaction." The common name for this is "graft."

On a global basis, America is a very young nation. America's natural resources are easily eclipsed by our human resources: three hundred and twenty million people predominately descended from *legal* immigrants who were spirited enough to take a chance on an unknown land and an unknown future, all for the promise of a new start in a land of worldwide reputed liberty and economic opportunity.

That spirit survives today in a "can do" entrepreneurial attitude. It is the same spirit that won two world wars in the 20th century, overcame the Great Depression, defeated communism worldwide, and put men on the moon, then returned them safely to earth.

In addition to our natural and human resources, America is a large nation roughly the size of Europe with a *single* language, culture and sovereign borders. Europeans speak multiple languages because they have to. The English language unites America and gives us a communication advantage that Europe can only envy. In addition, we have a single currency and we are free to travel and trade unencumbered from sea to shining sea.

"A *country is defined by its borders, language*, and *culture*." – Dr. Michael Savage. Of course, if given the choice between speaking a single language in America or 57 different languages in each state (by the Obama 2008 state count), the intellectually superior liberal will take the 57 different languages. It is European mimicry and indicative of "cultural inclusion" and "diversity", which are America's most important products second only to self-esteem. The unwashed and uneducated conservative on the other hand only sees dysfunction and division in American Balkanization of our communication medium, our language.

None of this is *simpatico* with the liberal mindset. Under the disguise of "multi-culturalism", "diversity," and "inclusiveness," liberals seek to divide America into enough minority victim groups that they can co-opt into a 50% plus one governing majority. This is their "Big Tent" strategy, or more appropriately their "Victims-R-Us" strategy.

Radical liberal Democrats (the only kind left) would import as many illegal non-citizens into the U.S. as possible, preferably through a wide-open southern border. They find it necessary to do this to reestablish the voting majority they have lost to decades of abortion, largely what would have been their base. Their "lost (aborted) Democrat generation" needs to be replaced.

Non-assimilation of the new arrivals is a key component of the liberal Democrat strategy. It is far easier to convince the *non-assimilated* illegal immigrant that he (she or it) is the victim of white America and that he is owed citizenship including the right to vote, education, healthcare, and welfare. *Assimilated* immigrants are by definition legal and self-sufficient, in no need of the Democrat handout-for-vote *quid pro quo*, you understand. The lone requirement for all of this government *gratis* is protest, which they will also have the right to do once in America, then vote Democrat. From the liberal politician perspective, the only thing that really matters is that the victim groups continue to vote for them. *"I weep for you," the Walrus said: "I deeply sympathize. With sobs and tears he sorted out those of the largest size"* – Lewis Carroll (*Alice through the Looking Glass*)

So we see that the liberal Democrat's faux compassion is nothing more than pandering for votes, which they must first import by any means necessary. This is a major reason they never achieve any positive results for their constituent minority victim groups. However, we must remember that it is the intent and the struggle that count, *not* the result. After all, *"What difference at this point does it make?"* – Hillary Clinton before the U.S. House Oversight Committee hearing (May 8, 2013).

Natural and human resources, a vast land with uniform language, culture, currency, and secure borders are key ingredients in the American success story, but there are other even more critical ingredients in our unprecedented national prosperity. The foundation of our great nation is a conceptual foundational tripod which I call the "Three Cs of American Exceptionalism." These are in no particular order of importance c̲apitalism, C̲hristianity and our c̲onstitution.

The summary version of the role these Three Cs play in America's success story is that capitalism provides us with our superior standard of living; Christianity provides us with our morality and compassion; and the Constitution provides protection from an intrusive executive-order-style government which would quickly seek to enslave us. I would hypothesize that it is the confluence of these three pillars which allow for the successful utilization of American natural and human resources. This is the foundation of America's unprecedented exceptionalism.

It is no coincidence that all three of these structural pillars are perpetually under assault by the left. Obama has attacked them all with the viciousness of a 6-pack of starving hyenas.

The left rejects the freedom you and I enjoy as Americans because it is the freedom to remove *them* from the *control* over which they obsess. America has steadily removed Democrats from public office in national, state and local elections since the inauguration of our historic first affirmative-action president on January 20, 2009. This has only amplified their disdain for American freedom.

The assault on America's freedom from the left has been unmistakable, undeniable, and relentless for many decades. Like virtually everything else they do, it is driven by their OCD madness.

Capitalism has several key components which make it successful. It is private ownership and operation of business, which means that the business participants have a vested interest in its success.

The goal of the business with few exceptions is *profit*, which is shared among ownership, management, employees and business equity holders (*e.g.*, stockholders). Profits feed all of these business participants, which means they all have a vested interest in efficiency.

Another key component of capitalism is capital accumulation, which gives businesses mass production economy of scale. Capital accumulation is also an industry in and of itself: banking and loan.

The feature that allows capitalism to succeed where socialism fails is that individuals are working in their own self-interest through various forms of profit sharing. This incentive does not exist within socialism. In all socialist ventures it is someone else's money at risk of loss or gain. Within the socialist economy we have lethargic feckless business participation leading to unsatisfactory results. It is the same reason that US federal government spending is abysmally inefficient: it's someone else's money. Same reason Medicare/Medicaid spending are out of control: the patient decisions are not based on economics.

Capitalism is the enemy of the OCDL in a fight to the death for several reasons. Capital produces income. Where there is income, there is without exception income inequality, which violates every liberal obsessive instinct of "fairness" and equality of outcome.

Moreover, poor people are more dependent on government and therefore easier for government to *control*. A prosperous proletariat is a Bolshevik's worst nightmare. A self-sufficient working class has little need of government interloping: corruption, graft, bribery, embezzlement, coercion, extortion, blackmail and all the other felonious pastimes with which socialist regimes routinely amuse themselves.

The socialist regime is the "middleman" between the people and their wealth. Remember the nighttime satellite image of North Korea? The only speck of visible light in the entire country was Pyongyang, the capitol. The power grid is intact and fully functioning in Pyongyang, where the government "middlemen" hang out. So the destruction of capitalism is crucial to the survival of socialism.

Obama's assault on capitalism was mostly nickel-dimer smash-and-grab heists from the federal treasury aimed at *quid-pro-quo* retirement of his campaign debt. The debt was run up on the accounts of campaign donors, bundlers, teachers unions, the SEIU, ACORN, Solyndra, etc., all of whom got their fill at the trough of taxpayer dollars from Obama's trillion-dollar stimulus (aka "porkulus") package, originally reputed to be for "infrastructure rebuild." In truth, no infrastructure was ever rebuilt, nor was there ever any intention to do so. The Frito Bandito* was more subtle.

[* "Politically incorrect" and "Racist!" reference? Or lighthearted metaphoric use of a 1960s advertising icon demonstrating American 1st Amendment freedom of speech?? Snowflake or patriot??? Earth or Uranus????]

The eight years of Obama socialism juxtaposed by the several of months of Trump capitalism since are a case study in economic results. If you were seeking employment in the Obama economy you were standing in the unemployment and food stamp line. If you are seeking employment in the Trump economy employers are standing in *your* line. It is as simple as that. No amount of pretending about Obama's skin color is going to change that.

Like capitalism, Christianity stands in diametric opposition to socialism. The Ten Commandments establish the framework of Christian morality and allegiance to God.

For reference, we list the Ten Commandments:

(1) Thou shalt have no other gods before me.

(2) Thou shalt not make unto thee any graven image.

(3) Thou shalt not take the name of the Lord thy God in vain.

(4) Remember the Sabbath day, to keep it holy.

(5) Honor thy father and thy mother.

(6) Thou shalt not kill.

(7) Thou shalt not commit adultery.

(8) Thou shalt not steal.

(9) Thou shalt not bear false witness against thy neighbor.

(10) Thou shalt not covet.

Liberals hate the 10 Commandments, fundamental to Christianity. To a liberal, the 10 Commandments are judgmental and personally oppressive: *"Who are you to sit in judgment of me!?!?!"*

Liberals have the same contempt for the American legal and court system. To be sure, they are tolerant of the law when they receive a favorable ruling. When the law rules against them, they feel no obligation to comply because they are always "right" in their obsessively-compulsively-disordered opinion. And so we add schizophrenia to the standard liberal resume of psychological disorders.

Barack Obama's refusal to enforce immigration law during his entire eight-year term is compelling evidence of his contempt for the law. *"America's immigration system is broken"* was his classic rhetorical one liner. No, in truth *the presidency* was broken. It was repaired on November 8, 2016, by vote of the American people.

Obama fancied himself an expert on the Constitution because he had an *alleged* degree in Constitutional Law from Harvard. His academic records remain sealed, so it is unlikely that this will *ever* be verified by anyone who can be trusted.

Regardless, it was obvious that he had little knowledge and even less respect for the American Constitution, which protects the American citizenry from would-be dictators. The absence of respect is further evidenced by his *"I've got a pen and a phone…"* comment after the American people took the

House majority away from him in the 2010 midterm election. The clear implication of this comment was that he would unilaterally make *fiat law* now *without* Congress, a procedure diametrically opposite to what America's founding fathers had designed.

The Obama regime weaponized the federal bureaucracy (IRS, DoJ, the FBI, the Bureau of Land Management and the EPA) to harass his political opponents. The DoJ interfered in *local* (*not* federal) criminal matters (e.g., Michael Brown in Ferguson, Freddie Gray in Baltimore, and Trayvon Martin in Orlando). Obama personally engaged in a never-ending relentless rhetorical assault on the 1st and 2nd Amendments. His unilateral participation in international agreements which rightfully required congressional ratification (e.g., The Paris Climate Accord, the Iranian Nuclear Treaty, the U.N. Small Arms Treaty) are some of the lowlights of his disrespect for our constitution.

The Obama Department of Justice's litigation-winning percentage (45%) was the worst in modern presidential history. It is a record that might qualify him for a seat on the 9th Circuit Clown Car of Appeals in San Francisco, but definitely not a McJob. I would expect a 50% winning percentage from *"the deaf, dumb, and blind kid"* in *"Pinball Wizard"* (*The Who* song -1969) flipping a coin.

In contrast to the 10 Commandments, the ten planks of *The Communist Manifesto* authored by Karl Marx and Fredrick Engels in 1848 established an amoral allegiance to a soulless state government. It is a case study in the liberal OCD obsession with *control*. It is an outline for slavery.

For reference, we list the *Ten Planks of the Communist Manifesto:*

(1) Abolition of private property in land and application of all rents of land to public purpose.

(2) A heavy progressive or graduated income tax.

(3) Abolition of all rights of inheritance.

(4) Confiscation of the property of all emigrants and rebels.

(5) Centralization of credit in the hands of the state, by means of a national bank with state capital and an exclusive monopoly.

(6) Centralization of the means of communication and transportation in the hands of the state.

(7) Extension of factories and instruments of production owned by the state; the bringing into cultivation of waste lands, and the improvement of the soil generally in accordance with a common plan.

(8) Equal obligation of all to work. Establishment of Industrial armies, especially for agriculture.

(9) Combination of agriculture with manufacturing industries; gradual abolition of the distinction between town and country by a more equable distribution of the population over the country.

(10) Free education for all children in government schools. Abolition of children's factory labor in its present form. Combination of education with industrial production, etc. etc.

These ten planks effectively abolish the individual by omission. All ten planks of *The Communist Manifesto* address allegiance to a totalitarian central *state*. There is no consideration or even recognition of the *individual* whatsoever. There is no private property (Plank #1); there is a heavy "progressive" income tax (Plank #2); and there is no inheritance (Plank #3). Plank #4 advocates government confiscation of all personal property of emigrants and "rebels" (translation: anyone who did not vote for the communist regime). Planks 5-9 advocate the centralization of communication, transportation, production, education, etc. and every other aspect of the population's lives. Finally Plank #10 advocates free education for all children in public schools which are in truth indoctrination sites. The ten planks are exemplary guidelines for an ant farm.

The abolition of the *individual* eradicates *individual* responsibility, *individual* contribution, *individual* creativeness, *individual* recognition of accomplishment and the drive for the *individual* to excel at *anything*.

Also, we may contrast the two ideological doctrines (10 Commandments and Communist Manifesto) as to the origin of individual rights. To our Christian brothers and sisters, our rights come from God and are eternal. To our communist comrade, rights come from government and are dependent on oligarch fiat.

If we inventory our planet for these two economic systems, we find many more socialist-controlled countries than those capitalist in nature, because their leaders rather enjoy slavery. We can imagine that ruling slaves beats work and can be quite lucrative.

Without question, these two sets of ideals are in direct conflict and competition with one another. All religion is the enemy of communism. Typically communism is seeded in civil unrest, which depends upon a breakdown of respect for authority and morality (e.g., the February 01, 2017 post-election Berkeley riots). Civil unrest oftentimes leads to a revolution where the proletariat throws off the yoke of an overbearing oligarch, only to find out too late that they have traded it for the yoke of oppressive totalitarian communist slavery…and they now wallow in abject poverty…witness the transformation of Cuba within my lifetime.

But more significantly, it is the direct competition for allegiance that puts communism at odds with religion. In point of fact, the first five Commandments address allegiance to God and the Faith. All ten of God's Commandments serve to enrich the mind, spirit, and soul of the *individual* Christian, both in reverence and in deed.

The ever-ongoing struggle between the socialist ideology of Marx and its mortal enemies Christianity and capitalism may be viewed as a battle for the soul of the individual. Marx' ideology would destroy the individual soul, while Christianity would provide guidance and growth for the soul. The dichotomy of choice could hardly be any starker.

The socialist agenda begins with the key plank #10: *"Free education for all children in government schools."* Sounds quite innocuous, huh? I mean, who's gonna argue with free stuff? We know education is a good thing to have, and it is not cheap. What a deal!

What we already know is reinforced yet again: *"If it seems too good to be true, it probably is."* – Gary Adler. The "free education" in the Communist Manifesto means *state-controlled* education. Communist "education" means inculcation of the youth with a failed and toxic ideology from the genesis of their formative intellectual development. The influence of corrupt liberal educators on student formative ideology cannot be underestimated. The defeat of the "Common Core" curriculum movement was crucial to maintaining education at the local level, as opposed to a central federally-controlled education system easily targeted and *hijacked* by ill-intended leftists.

The television series *The Americans* is a long-running favorite of mine since the first season aired in 2013: well-scripted, well-acted, with a suspenseful situational storyline.

Storyline: two Russian national spies (*Mikhail* and *Nadezhda*) come to the United States as young adults and assume the identity of a married couple named Philip and Elizabeth Jennings. They have two teenage kids (naturally) and live in the suburbs of Washington DC. Their cover is that they are owner/operators of a mom-and-pop travel agency. In reality they are Russian espionage agents working for the KGB. Living across the street from a counter-espionage FBI agent who doesn't know what they are up to kicks the plot up a notch. The timeframe setting is the early 80s during Reagan's first term.

Occasionally the episode storyline flashes Philip and Elizabeth back to their youth in Russia. Without exception, their memories of the homeland are of miserable poverty and inequity.

Philip tells a Russian joke: "A woman enters a store and asks the owner for some ground meat. The owner replies '*We are the store that has no fish. The store that has no meat is across the street.*'" Now they are living the upper-middle-class life in DC: never in need of food, nice home, car, quality schools for children, money left over for recreation, etc.

As the seasons roll by and their clandestine adventures continue, one question lingers on in my mind without an answer: these two have lived in both Russia and America long enough to know that Russia is dysfunctional and America is highly functional. How is it that these seemingly intelligent-enough-not-to-get-caught-at-what- they-are-doing super spies never ask themselves why America works and Russia doesn't?

Then in Season 5, the husband-wife team are assigned the task of infiltrating a research project in mid-America which the KGB thinks is attempting to develop plague to wipe out the Russian wheat crop. While on location in Kansas, Philip surveys a bountiful wheat field as far as the eye can see. He asks himself *"Wait a minute. We have just as much land as they do. We can't even feed ourselves. Why can't we grow crops like this?"*

That *is* the key question, isn't it? And of course, the answer is quite simple. It is the difference between communism and capitalism. But that answer will never occur to Philip because of his *educational* background in Russia. Even more fundamental to the discussion at hand is *"Why did it take Philip his entire adulthood to reach the point of asking this question?"*

Philip and Elizabeth have lived their entire adult lives in the United States. Why can't they see that the United States is the land of plenty for anyone willing to work for it, and the Soviet Union is the land of nothing no matter how hard you try? Do they dismiss what they see as an anomaly, an isolated aberration of what they have been taught in school? But it is *not* isolated; it is in fact ubiquitous.

The answer is *"Education."* In the case of Philip and Elizabeth, *"education"* means being force-fed communist propaganda K-12 and beyond. It is a testimonial to the effectiveness of the grade school propaganda in the Soviet Union that any prosperity Philip and Elizabeth observe in the United States is interpreted as evil exploitation of colonized victims. They were taught that capitalism is evil and the United States is the epicenter of the global capitalist menace. This is *no* different from the class warfare that American liberals are peddling to American voters through Occupy Wall Street (OWS). Philip and Elizabeth are the misguided products of the *"Free education for all children in government schools"* described in Plank #10 of the Communist Manifesto.

Just to briefly clean up *The Americans* Season 5 storyline, Philip and Elizabeth kill a wheat research project worker who catches them intruding on classified project grounds. Philip and Elizabeth then learn later from a credible source that the project is *not* about destroying wheat crops, but instead it is about developing a genetically superior wheat crop that is resistant to blight and crop failure. Once developed, the goal of the project becomes to share the "super wheat" technology with the world to mitigate global hunger. This revelation drives true believer Philip, particularly, to self-doubt about the virtue of his career. End of Season 5.

Our liberal comrade shrieks *"It's only a television show!"* True, in a few isolated cases liberals have actually mastered the obvious, *e.g.*, they can spot a television show when watching a television. But the plot was entirely plausible, which is why the series now runs on into a 6th season. Although only a fictional television series plot, it is the clearest possible demonstration of the *intent* of Plank #10 of the Communist Manifesto.

When the Communist Manifesto abolishes the individual, it also abolishes *entrepreneurial* talent. I consider the American entrepreneurial phenomenon to be unique on this planet.

Lost in strict socialist statist allegiance is the entrepreneurial spirit that was crucial in making America the economic engine of the planet. "Entrepreneur" – "*A person who organizes and operates a business or businesses, taking on far greater than normal financial risks in order to do so.*" I would define an entrepreneur as an individual who has developed a successful business venture from concept to completion including personal financial risk.

Of course this definition is quick to bring war whoops from Elizabeth F. Warren (Yes, I know, "*Racist!*"), plus an I-can-hardly-contain-myself-from-laughing-out-loud "*You didn't build that!*" read by the community organizer-in-chief off his teleprompter. It was rather amazing to watch the 2008 campaign slogan "*Yes we can!*" morph its way into the "*You didn't build that!*" of 2012. This line was composed with the full hubris of a liberal speechwriter who has never had a real job in his life.

An entrepreneur does not function in a vacuum, nor does anyone else. What he does is identify a business need for a service or product, and then coordinates the resources required to bring his idea to market *profitably*, a word long since excommunicated from the liberal vocabulary.

America does not have a monopoly on entrepreneurial skill. However, there is little doubt about who is the world leader in this vital economic skill set. America is a new land, settled and developed within the last 300 years, largely by first, second, and third generation *legal* immigrants who were necessarily risk takers. They left the security, certainty, and oppressive conformity of their origin to take a chance on a better life in America. Risk-taking is an attribute which also defines contemporary Americans, and continues to be a major part of what makes us the greatest nation on earth. The "can-do" mentality (not to be confused with the sloganeered meaningless Obama campaign bumper sticker "Yes we can"), the self-reliance, the self-confidence, the self-challenged, ingenuity, determination, innovation, self-motivation, and non-conformity are all American long suits in the global "Monopoly" game of international economics. "Sameness" is not in our DNA.

The intangible that sets Americans apart is the understanding that **90% of the game is attitude...which is 100% within YOUR control,** *that* it is your attitude that ultimately determines your altitude.

Liberals are totally intolerant of risk. In their *Utopia*, risk cannot exist. Planning of the central state has taken all risk completely out of the picture. This is a manifestation of their detachment from reality. Without risk, there is no reward. So the risk-free mindset is simultaneously a precursor *and* a product of socialist poverty. The liberal aversion to risk leads to the one trick pony solution of all socialists like Obama to confiscate the people's money and throw at every problem they see...yet another expressway to socialist failure.

How well does the American entrepreneurial profile align itself with the ten planks of *"The Communist Manifesto"*? A square peg in a round hole would be an understatement. A giant anteater unleashed upon our happy little Marxist ant farm might be a more appropriate metaphor.

In contrast to American entrepreneurial skill, communist China's long suit is slave labor. The ant farm guidelines of *The Communist Manifesto* ten planks are a perfect fit for China. The 50-60 million non-conformist Chinese citizens who were murdered during the Mao Zedong era will hardly be missed in a nation of over a billion population. *"If you want to make an omelet, you must be willing to break a few eggs."* — Vladimir Lenin.

Nor will the hundreds (thousands?) of Chinese civilians massacred in Tiananmen Square by the Chinese military on June 04, 1989. Any liberal would agree that this is an insignificant price to pay for the conformity, allegiance, and *control* demanded by Marxism.

Theft of American intellectual property by China is now a major component of the Chinese economy. Theft of Chinese intellectual property by America (or anyone else) is *not* a problem because there *is* no Chinese intellectual property. The Chinese people cannot create because creativity is a product of the individual, who is not allowed to exist within the communism system. Creativity requires independent thought which will *not* be tolerated. Independent thought carries with it the potential threat of mutiny and revolution, both capital offenses…this makes independent thought a capital offense. Critical thought is the biggest threat to our model socialist ant farm.

The Chinese can use an i-phone. They can assemble an i-phone. But the Chinese will never *create* an i-phone. They cannot *create*; they can only mimic. *America* is the home of creativity.

This is why China will *never* displace America from the top rung of the global economic latter. China may be able to assemble a cell phone more cheaply than their American counterparts, but they cannot *conceptualize*, innovate, and otherwise develop a cell phone. Slave-priced robotic labor is the only competitive economic advantage the Chinese have.

From time to time I pick up tremors that the economy of China has surpassed the American economy. This is not true. The United States GDP exceeds the Chinese GDP by approximately 60%. When we acknowledge that the population of China is 4-5 times that of the United States, we see that the Chinese income per capita is only 14% of its American counterpart. This does not mean that they are not gaining. The remedy for this is quite simply "Make America Great Again!"

The American entrepreneurial and individual phenomena are not limited to economics. Art, music, literature, performing arts, etc. all require individual creativity which is moribund under socialism. Who was the last great North Korean composer? What was the last great Cuban novel? Name a great Chinese painter? ***"Art is the daughter of freedom."* – Friedrich Schiller.**

Liberals will point to athletics, figure skating, ballet, etc. in counter argument. These examples hardly count as proof of socialist *exceptionalism* over *individualism*. All of these are state-subsidized to form a basis for socialist propaganda. It is the only way for the vast majority of performers to upgrade their standard of living relative to the proletariat. It is more a testimonial to capitalism than socialism, of performers pursuing their own economic self-interest through participation in state-subsidized sport.

Without question, the entrepreneur is a key component of what we think of as "American exceptionalism," which any liberal will deny exists at all. *"I believe in American exceptionalism, just as I suspect that the Brits believe in British exceptionalism and the Greeks believe in Greek exceptionalism."* – Barack Obama World Apology Tour (04.03.09).

At this point, it is timely to acknowledge that the OCDL's obsession with "fairness" (equals sameness) is second only to his (her, its) obsession with *control* (equals power). This obsession with "fairness," which we have previously defined as equality of outcome and *not* equality of opportunity, has global reach. It has no borders, which drives the OCDL to advocate open borders. It drives our historic first Marxist president to totally dismiss America's unique exceptionalism.

The OCDL's obsession with sameness is ubiquitous. It drives a great deal of our current news cycle, confounding normal conservative Americans in the process. Costly Obamacare one-size-fits-all health-care coverage (wherein men get badly-needed pregnancy benefits), transgender bathrooms, newly designated "cisgenders" so that transgenders won't feel "ostracized," genderless birth certificates, gay Ken dolls, fraudulent rape cases (UVA and Duke) designed to indict all males for the felony of being males (now cleverly labeled "toxic masculinity" by liberals), Femi Nazism, and the general wussification of America are all the products of the liberal obsession with "sameness."

Have we uncovered the reason liberals are in the hopeless minority in America? Liberals are a small mentally-disordered subset of the American population who demand the total conformity outlined in the ten planks of *The Communist Manifesto*. They have no problem with someone in central authority telling them what to think and do; independent thought takes effort. Their utopia lies within George Orwell's *1984*.

Also lost in the single-minded allegiance to the state are all remnants of personal accountability and responsibility, leading directly to classic droppings of "liberal logic" such as "The gun did it. Let's ban guns." Or "It's society's fault. Let's ban capital punishment." It is also the genesis of Obama-era word-smithing pinheadery such as "man-caused disasters," "overseas contingency operations," and "work-place violence" designed to avoid identification of the radical Islamic perpetrators, the ultimate *taboo* for our historic first Muslim-descended president.

In classic "form over substance" character, liberals (who now self-identify as "progressives") devote much effort into disguising reality with faux semantics and pseudonyms (e.g., "The Affordable Care Act," the "Fairness Doctrine," "Net Neutrality," the "DREAM Act," etc.). They are accomplished in meaningless simple-minded propaganda sometimes called "sloganeering:" "Black lives matter," "Win the future" (aka "W.T.F."), "Pigs in a Blanket, fry 'em like bacon," "I'm with Her," "F—- the police from Oakland to Greece," etc.

Liberals have learned this craft of propaganda from their European forerunners, the Nazis. The word "Nazi" is an abbreviation for the word "*Nationalsozialist,*" or National *socialist*. The Nazis literally wrote the book on propaganda.

The German Minister of Propaganda during the 3ʳᵈ Reich era was Dr. Joseph Goebbels. He committed suicide during the 1945 collapse of the 3ʳᵈ Reich. The following principles of propaganda were transcribed from Goebbels's personal diary after his death:

- Avoid abstract ideas - appeal to the emotions.

- Constantly repeat just a few ideas. Use stereotyped phrases.

- Keep it simple.

- Give only one side of the argument.

- Continuously criticize your opponents.

- Pick out one special "enemy" for special vilification.

Sound familiar? *This* is the format for the liberal/Democrat message. Saul Alinsky later rewrote these same principles into his 1971 primer for the modern-day radical liberal malcontent called *Rules for Radicals*. His book serves today as a behavioral guide and instructional operating manual for 21ˢᵗ century anarchists, liberals and Democrats.

The personal accountability crisis reached epidemic proportions during the eight-year tenure of Obama, who led by example: "*(Fill in the Blank) is Bush's fault!*" This is no mystery. Personal responsibility is the antithesis of the victimhood that liberals in general, and Obama in particular, peddle to America for a living.

The no-growth economy and all things failed domestically were "Bush's fault." Obama's ongoing international problems were America's fault, and the appropriate remedy was a world apology tour… after which the America's problems worsened substantially.

The OCDL is driven by a mental disorder. The American patriot is driven by the love of freedom gifted him by his forefathers. Can the liberals force the square peg into the round hole? Certainly not by any reasonable estimate of the American population. By "reasonable estimate," I do not mean your typical NYT/CNN poll of the first 100 people they meet on the campus of Columbia University. I mean the 2016 presidential election, the 2014 mid-term election and the 2010 mid-term election, which were the *real* polls. The 2008 and 2012 presidential election were exceptions decided by the racial component, *not* on conservatism vs. liberalism. More on this assertion later.

If all of this is true, where does it leave America? Let us take inventory. Americans are approximately 4% of the global human population. It is in fact quite the privilege to live here in a nation with the highest *per capita* income (equals standard of living) on the planet. We have the right to freedom of speech, to worship as we see fit, to assemble, to defend ourselves, the right to choose our leaders, freedom from unreasonable search and seizure, plus many other rights and privileges afforded by our constitution and laws. These are just a few of the reasons foreigners show up by the thousands at our borders wanting in.

And yet there are those living here who hate America, who would destroy all they see if given the chance. As eternal victim Michelle Obama informed America in July 26, 2016 speech at the DNC "I wake up every morning in a house that was built by slaves." This just in: YOU ARE FREE TO LEAVE because THIS IS AMERICA! But rather than leave, the brotherhood of malcontents remain to make life miserable for the Americans who are happy to live here. They are called "liberals".

For eight years we had a "leader" who gleefully managed the decline of America, starting with a worldwide apology tour. "The new normal," "strategic patience," "leading from behind," "man-caused disasters," "work place violence," and "undocumented immigrants" were sadly crammed into the American lexicon. And at the end of the eight year reign of mismanagement, scandals, absurd interloping and egregious corruption (Chapters 10 and 11), our outgoing president demanded an 18% *increase* in retirement pay. For reference, this approximately twice the pay raise our military received during the Obama presidential era. You don't know whether to laugh or cry.

We also note that his successor Donald J. Trump, who was tasked with cleaning up Obama's global mess, declined to take *any* salary as president.

It is possible to manufacture the illusion that liberals are in the majority only by hijacking key components of our society: our education system, the media, public opinion polls, the entertainment industry, the legal (judiciary) system, Internet search engines, social media and the government bureaucratic "deep state," *et. al.* Only through control of these crucial forums of communication, culture, and government can this mentally disordered, constantly enraged vocal minority project itself as the majority. The public narrative is then controlled with liberal propaganda. ***Minority noise equals the illusion of the "majority."***

SYNOPSIS: In the end, America's choice is simple and stark: God, the morality of His Ten Commandments, the freedom of self-determination and a prospering economic environment; or Karl Marx, the non-morality of *The Communist Manifesto,* and the slavery of corrupt and bankrupt socialism. America's motto is "In God We Trust." The liberal motto is "In Government We Trust."

The OCDL has no problem making this choice for herself *and* you, empowered to do so by virtue of her delusionary self-imagined superior intellect.

7. THE SWAMP: EVEN WORSE THAN WE THOUGHT?

It is no longer Democrats vs. Republicans...it is Washington D.C. and the Main Stream Media vs. America.

There is no recession in Washington DC. There is no unemployment in Washington DC. The construction industry there is flourishing and property values are soaring there — all of this prosperity in a city that produces absolutely nothing but red tape, regulation, and enforcement misery upon the rest of our nation.

Meanwhile, in America's heartland, coal mines are being abandoned, factories are being closed, banks and lending institutions are drowning in red tape (manufactured by Washington DC), small businesses are closing due to the strangulation of Obamacare, etc. Is it any wonder there is a nationwide opiate epidemic in America? It has been inflicted by Washington DC.

What's wrong with this picture? The same thing that was wrong with the satellite image of North Korea at night (Chapter 5). The only speck of light in North Korea came from the capital city of Pyongyang. It is the same story for the same reason in America, but on a much grander scale. In both countries, the "ruling class" is looking out for itself and no one else. The pigs from George Orwell's *Animal Farm* run Washington DC.

"Based on what evidence?" retorts Congresswoman Maxine F. Headroom (D – CA) in her most pompously defiant "innocent until proven guilty" Viola Davis performance. Based on the fact that 5 of the top 6 *per capita* income counties in the United States are contiguous with the Washington DC city limits. For reference, they are listed below:

Rank	County	State	Median Household Income
1	**Loudoun County**	Virginia	$117,876
2	**Fairfax County**	Virginia	$112,436
3	**Howard County**	Maryland	$108,844
4	**Hunterdon County**	New Jersey	$105,186
5	**Arlington County**	Virginia	$100,474
6	**Stafford County**	Virginia	$97,606

*Data provided by the 2012 American Community Survey prepared by the U.S. Census Bureau.

It is also based on the fact that the federal government is budgeted according to a baseline of current spending *times* an inflation factor, then *times* a population-growth factor. This is known as "baseline budgeting," designed to keep federal spending growing while reporting it as zero budget growth to the ignorant American voter. My budget does not work that way, does yours?

This scam was set up by the *Congressional Budget Act of 1974*. It means that a 3% inflation rate plus a 4% population growth will result in a 7% federal budget increase, but will be *reported* to the American people as *zero* budget growth. Likewise, a 5% increase in the federal budget will be *reported* as 2% *cut*. It is legalized fraud designed to feed Washington DC's ever-increasing government spending addiction. With that comes an ever- increasing accrual of power in Washington DC. Meanwhile, the purchasing power of the average American paycheck has not increased since well back into the 20th century.

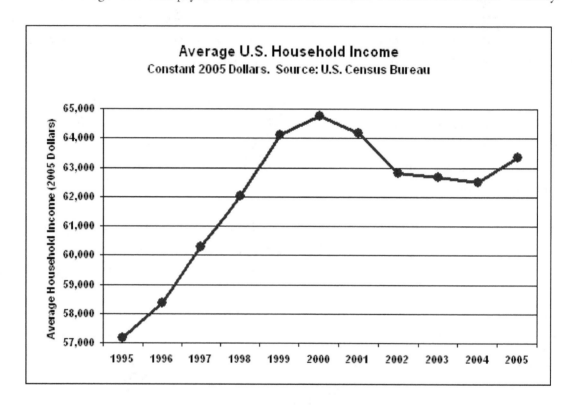

Translation: your paycheck is frozen in time so that the federal government may grow into the $4+ trillion per year out-of-control Leviathan before us today. Is this why the federal budget never balances and the current national debt is closing in on $20 trillion?

"That's *not* fair!" rebuts Senator Phil A. Buster (R-KS). Precisely! It is not fair that you may lose your seat in an election or retire and continue to draw the same paycheck you draw now for the rest of your natural life. No, it is not fair that you dumped this pathetic socialist nightmare called "Obamacare" on the American people, then voted to exempt yourself, your family, *and* your staff from it. No, it is not fair that you have pilfered Social Security funds for decades to get yourself reelected, and now we learn the biggest Ponzi scheme in the history of our planet that we have been forced to pay into our entire lives is flat broke. Is this why *over* half the current members of Congress are millionaires?

We see why the Washington DC swamp likes the *status quo*. They are dug into the federal government money mainline like a tick on an Alabama hound. Approximately 300,000 federal employees in Washington DC making on *average over* $100K per year. Do the math. That is a $30 billion a year payroll for people who produce precisely *nothing*. And *nothing* would be bad enough, but in most cases what our federal government produces is substantially *less* than nothing. I base this last comment on my personal experience with the IRS, who cannot even read or understand their own forms.

Why would anyone with a career in the Swamp want any deviation from the *status quo*? Obviously, this rhetorical question needs no response.

But the gravy train does not stop with the decadent $30 billion Washington DC payroll. Who is it that administers the $4+ trillion United States government budget? Who granted the half-billion dollar loan to the scam green energy company Solyndra, owned and operated by an Obama campaign bundler? Who "misplaced and lost" $6 billion in state department funds, primarily under the watch of Hillary Clinton while the Clinton Foundation was thriving? Who loaded the cargo plane with $1.7 billion of cold untraceable foreign cash for Iran's nuke development? The answer to all of the above is our $30 billion-a-year-payroll federal government employees in Washington DC. And why did Slick Willy Sutton rob banks? *"Because that's where the money is."*

No, the state of the Swamp is just fine and holding...until June 16, 2015, when Donald J. Trump came down the escalator at Trump Tower and announced his candidacy for president. Among his primary stated goals from the outset were to "Make America great again," and to "Drain the swamp." Trump's announcement was the biggest joke in the Swamp since Democrats named Obamacare "The Affordable Care Act."

Without reliving the 2016 presidential campaign in detail, let's just summarize it by saying it was a swamp creature's worst nightmare. Trump went from national joke in the MSM to Republican presidential nominee to president quicker than an Everglades Burmese python can swallow a raccoon.

On election night, media experts, learned scholars, professional observers and pundits shrieked in horror as Hillary's Midwest firewall was torched to the ground. Hillary was toast.

The Swamp and the media did not take their defeat well, nor did the next would-be godmother of the Swamp. From the post-election cocktail hangover of depression, self-delusion, paranoid schizophrenia, pathological narcissism and the like came the phenomenon known as Russian "collusion delusion." It is a swamp gumbo of 100% FBI/DoJ/media propaganda designed to reinforce the media wet dream that they remain in charge of the public political narrative and the narrative outcome.

The "collusion delusion" media campaign was based upon a daily 4pm quote from an unnamed source alleging that someone inside the Trump sphere was observed in a compromised position with a Russian "agent," e.g., having a Smirnoff vodka martini, putting *Wish Bone* Russian salad dressing on his salad, watching Boris and Natasha on "moose-and-squirrel" cartoon show, and other assorted high crimes and misdemeanors. Whether or not any of these anonymous sources actually existed is doubtful. But Trump is the enemy of the Swamp. Therefore the MSM proceeded merrily along, utilizing the lofty "Guilty until proven innocent" side of its double standard.

America is currently undergoing a rebirth of McCarthyism, which is defined as the practice of making accusations of subversion or treason without proper regard for evidence. The original McCarthy (WI senator) led Soviet red scare era occurred during the early 1950s. It was a shameful chapter in American history characterized by reckless and absurd accusations and slanderous innuendo designed to destroy professional careers and personal reputations.

Of course, that *is* the goal of the current resurgence of liberal McCarthyism. This time the target is the president of the United States. Just as McCarthyism made its current miraculous comeback on demand from the MSM, I am convinced that if I stand here long enough in my polyester suit and platform heels, they too will return into style and I will be lauded as a 21st century fashionista.

The simple truth is that the left will not abandon the Russian collusion delusion illusion while they still need an excuse for their catastrophic 2016 election loss. It will play on as long as Democrats imagine propaganda usefulness, i.e., until they reach the dreaded reality that their ludicrous farce is doing them more harm than good. The steady decline in Robert Mueller's approval ratings indicates that point has already been reached.

The Mueller probe needs an infusion of adrenalin. May I suggest no longer "indicting" Boris, Natasha and their assorted bot comrades? Instead indict the root of all international evil, Vladimir Putin himself for election "meddling". Then Chuck E. Cheesehead Schumer, who has assumed the role of God Almighty by virtue of an election-yet-to-come mandate, can issue a new public demand for President Trump: travel to Moscow and arrest Putin to stand trial in the United States in the *modus operandi* of Dog the Bounty Hunter. Not picturing the Schumer-Trump dynamic yet? Imagine God handing the 10 Commandments down to Moses.

I personally have zero interest in being force fed this anal extrudate burger by the deranged syndrome inflicted American MSM. I will become interested when the *real* Russian related crimes are investigated: the manufacture, finance and subsequent government misuse of the Russian "dirty dossier", the UraniumOne/Clinton Family Foundation bribery, the Bill Clinton $500K Russian "speech", et. al. Likewise, an announcement of a special prosecutor to investigate the Mueller investigation would be of interest.

What the Swamp-based MSM is actually in charge of now is their non-existent credibility, which currently sits at minus 6 (and falling rapidly) on a scale of 1 to 10. In most public opinion polls, the "journalist profession" rates at the bottom with generic lawyers, below Congress and substantially below Charles Manson. Obviously, credibility and even ratings are no longer a priority to the MSM. What could matter more than this to a "journalist"?

Let me venture a guess. Could it be remaining in favor with those who control the money? Could it be remaining a "swamp thang" in good standing, welcome at cocktail parties, dinners and wienie roasts? And when I need a favor, I will just go visit *The Godfather* on his daughter's wedding day.

The American people and what they think does not matter to "journalists." Outside of the Swamp, ordinary Americans are unwashed and uneducated flat-earthers, bitter clingers, and rubes who actually take the Constitution and the law literally. "*...the rabblement hooted and clapped their chapped hands and threw up their sweaty nightcaps and uttered such a deal of stinking breath...And for mine own part, I durst not laugh for fear of opening my lips and receiving the bad air.*" — Senator Casca (from *Julius Caesar* by William Shakespeare). The American rabblement are so gullible they actually think they elected Trump president on November 8, 2016.

The rabblement must be made to understand that electing the president was *never* their job. Their job is to pay taxes so that wealth may be redistributed by the Swamp to people who will vote to keep them in power, and to sign up for Obamacare for the same reason. The IQ-intensive task of selecting our nation's leader must be left up to the pigs of *Animal Farm*, the rocket surgeon (intentionally mixed metaphor for panicked liberals) "J" school graduates.

"The pigs, the smartest animals, soon start directing the other animals' work." – **George Orwell** *Animal Farm.*

And the proletariat also must be punished for ignoring the direction given them by the MSM. So the media doubles down on the fake news that saturated the campaign trail. It didn't work then, but this is all they know. Superficially, they are attacking Trump. In reality, they are attacking his voters.

The election reaction by the Democrats and their apparatchiks in the MSM has been quite predictable. Their rejection of the "illegitimate" 2016 Trump victory followed the template of the illegitimate 2000 Bush victory, all the way down to the Rep. John Lewis (D-GA) boycott of the inauguration ceremony.

They expected to be in power in the White House for another eight years when the American people abruptly said "NO! NO mas!!!" The fireworks extravaganza on the Hudson celebrating Hillary's victory had to be cancelled. The nationwide liberal rave celebrating the death of America as it was founded was also postponed indefinitely. The grand final chapter to the Clinton cleptocracy saga was aborted. The "America for Sale CHEAP! Call 1-800-CLINTON" sign remains in Hillary's garage.

And the White House silverware, which was purloined when Hillary vacated the premises in 2001, remains safe for at least one more presidential term.

The plan was for the Clintons to get filthy rich off of the Hillary presidency. They got halfway there. They covered the "filthy" part nicely.

And let us be clear about what the Democrat/media cartel grow more terrified of each day, because it is *nothing* they can speak of. It is not that Trump will launch missiles at an ally in a fit of egotistical rage. It is not that Trump will dismantle their *magnum opus*, Obamacare. No, those are merely talking points for public consumption, a façade of deceit which masks the truth. ***Liberals lie about their motives 100.000% of the time.***

The sum of all liberal fears is that Trump will *succeed* and belie everything they stand for. It is that they will be confronted with explaining a Trump-success-follows-Obama-failure narrative the same way that 30 years ago they were confronted with the humiliating task of explaining the babbling fool Carter, who facilitated the ayatollahs' takeover of Iran, followed by Reagan, who defeated communism. They fear the similarity of economic ideas between Trump and Reagan, which will undoubtedly yield similar results. They fear that they will have to spend 3 more decades manufacturing revisionist history which unsuccessfully flails away at discrediting the next Ronald Reagan just as they were forced to do with the original.

The primary weapon of the left in day to day combat with the American public is the corrupt MSM, which they control. The tactics of propaganda the MSM utilizes are tried and tested from the days of the Third Reich. They flood the airwaves with hypocrisy laced faux outrage at their conservative targets. Their acting brilliance will easily persuade the cretin American public. America will be *Grubered* (Chapter 10) yet again.

We must acknowledge also the investment the MSM had in Obama during the 2008 campaign: women fainting in the aisles during the campaign as Obama coolly and competently directed first-responder aid, the "Obama girl" ads, the media cover-up of his association with felons, gangsters, thugs, terrorists, and malcontents, the Styrofoam Greek columns, the God-like reverb of *"This was the moment when the rise of the oceans began to slow and our planet began to heal,"* etc. Trump success will be particularly painful juxtaposed by the *uber* failure of their now-departed Messiah. This is the real source of the liberal psychotic desperation America is now witnessing.

Republican swamp-critter reaction has been somewhat more subtle. They cannot react with the open defiance of the rest of the Swamp. Unlike the Democrat side of the Swamp, the Republican side of the Swamp is littered with failed presidential candidates. They all appear to be quite bitter. Watching a DC outsider waltz into the White House doesn't make *them* feel any better.

Republican masterminds like Karl Rove, George Will, Bill Kristol, Charles Krauthammer and other titans of "group think" reminded us daily before the election that "This isn't how it is supposed to work." And "You can't tweet your way into the White House." I thought Rove's "high floor, low ceiling" analysis of Trump's nomination chances was particularly insightful...not of Trump, but of Rove. Perhaps the American people wanted a break from the "conventional wisdom" that has gotten us $20 trillion in debt.

Between the liberal Democrat hatred and the moderate Republican resentment, it is obvious that legislative victories are going to be scarce for President Trump. We witnessed seven years of Republicans campaigning on repeal and replace the Obamacare cluster. Then, when it was time in 2017 for action, the Republican "Washington Generals" choked. (The Washington Generals were the team of crash-test-dummy perpetual loser opponents of the Harlem Globetrotter basketball team.)

The motives of the Democrats and their MSM comrades are clear enough. Their choice is the Obama legacy plus a massive multi-trillion dollar government entitlement program which further grows the federal government versus an infeasible financial burden on the American people, whom they care absolutely *nothing* about. And if Obamacare is expunged from the American consciousness, what is left of their precious Obama legacy? Benghazi? Fast and Furious? The scorned 2009 Stimulus (aka "Por-kulus")? The Arab Spring? An Iranian nuke? The IRS scandal? Perhaps we can close our eyes, click our heels three times and pretend Obama actually ordered the Osama Bin Laden (OBL) raid? They all have a vested interest in salvaging a legacy that is as devoid of positive accomplishment as the resume Obama brought to his candidacy eight years earlier. Liberal revisionist historians have a monumental task before them putting lipstick on this pig!

For the Swamp-dwelling congressional Republicans, the choice is between giving Trump and all the Americans who voted for him "the finger" versus keeping their campaign promises to the American people, whom they also care *nothing* about.

Two things both sides of Congress and the MSM have in common as the political chicanery plays on are (1) their total contempt for the American people; and (2) they *all* dwell in the Swamp together. The key differences between the two parties is that Democrats always *overplay* their hand for two reasons: (1) they have *carte blanche* backing by the MSM; and (2) they are insane. Contrast that with Republicans who always *underplay* their hand because: (1) they are viciously criticized by the MSM; and (2) they are cowardly. Our current dysfunctional two-party system has completely failed America.

Meanwhile, Trump sits at his desk in the Oval Office "with pen in hand" awaiting legislation which gives the American people relief from the Obamacare nightmare. But there is none forthcoming. Who gets "credit" for this legislative sitzkrieg?

The Democrats 2018 midterm election strategy will surely be one for the history books. They unilaterally made the Obamacare mess, then refused to make any effort whatsoever to clean it up. Meanwhile, the billion-dollar Obamacare website fizzled like a North Korean ICBM, insurers left the Obamacare exchanges, and both premiums and deductibles skyrocketed, rendering the "insurance" worthless from the Day 1 inception.

Their pitch to the American people will be what, exactly? "We gave you Obamacare, then successfully obstructed Republicans' efforts to mitigate the damage. ELECT US AGAIN!!!!" The next election cycle should produce some interesting bumper stickers. Or maybe the Democrats will just revert to a battle-tested winner from their Rolodex grooveyard of forgotten oldies like *"Hope and Change!"* and *"Yes We Can!"*

Pelosi and Schumer are currently tossing around *"Drain the Swamp!"* rhetoric in an epiphany of marketing genius probably best characterized by "Monkey see, monkey do." Apparently no one has told them that this *Republican* slogan is what lost Democrats the 2016 election. Can *"Make America Great Again!"* be far behind? *Liberals are too stupid to be embarrassed.*

I submitted *my* campaign slogan suggestion to the DNC recently under the pseudonym "Big Blue Wave Kahuna":

I have not yet gotten a reply.

Democrats have clearly demonstrated that they cannot lead. They refuse to follow (*#Resist!*). And they cannot afford to get out of the way because the spectacular Trump success is humiliating them on a daily basis. This leaves them praying for an American *catastrophe* aloud (e.g., Bill Maher) instead of praying for America.

Hopefully the point of this protracted narrative is clear. We began this chapter with this quote: *"It is no longer Democrats vs. Republicans…it is Washington D.C. and the main stream media vs. America."* I know of no better way to bear witness to this quote than with the rejection by both parties' establishment of the American people's elected president Donald J. Trump, who ran on the campaign slogan *"Drain the Swamp!"*

We could also bear witness to the Swamp *vs.* America claim with a quick review of the immigration issue, which is high on the priority list of the American people. Donald Trump ran for president on the promise that he would build a wall on our southern border. How effective a physical wall will be is debatable. I do know that it has been successful for many centuries in China. It was highly effective in stopping Palestinian homicide bombings of Israel originating in the West Bank. The West Bank Wall was hysterically decried by leftists, Muslims, and Islamophiles worldwide when the project was announced in 2002. The virtual perfect record of success of the wall since has been ignored. Walls at San Quintin, Joliet, Leavenworth, etc. seem to have worked quite well. Likewise the wall around Vatican City in Rome separating the Pope and his posse from the Roman rabble outside gets a 5-star consumer rating.

We were once so magnanimously informed by a Pope Francis (01.24.14) reality check from behind the 20+ foot Vatican walls, *"Build bridges, not walls."* Yet again we observe that ***"Irony is ALWAYS lost on the stupid."***

When the White House experienced a rash of security breaches during Obama's second term, they raised the wall surrounding the White House grounds. When Obama left the White House for his new Washington DC residence in 2017, they built a wall around the new residence. ***"You don't need a physical wall, ex-President Obama; just have a 'virtual fence.'"*** It is unclear if Mexico will pay for Obama's personal new wall. The Berlin wall worked well from 1961 until it was torn down due to "popular demand" in 1989.

Liberals oppose a border wall because they *know* it will work. This is the same reason they oppose the Trump tax cuts. They assume that they eventually return to power. If/when they return to power, they do not want to be forced to abandon or tear down a southern border wall to restore the illegal immigration that serves to keep them in power. That would be too obvious to the American voter. It would suicidal in the court of American public opinion on the grand scale that Obamacare was.

Their hope is that if a border wall is *never* built, America will eventually elect another Obama who will refuse to enforce immigration law by citing the fallacious *"America's immigration system is broken!"* excuse, and the next border stampede will resume.

Liberals (Obama, Hillary, Biden, Schumer, Pelosi, etc.) supported a border fence in 2006. However, they now understand that they *must* have the illegal alien vote to restore themselves to power and steal from the taxpayer fed treasury again.

The other reason liberals oppose a southern border wall is that it will *forever* be a monument to Trump success and Democrat defeat. Trump vigorously campaigned on the wall. Democrats opposed both Trump and the wall. To successfully obstruct the wall would be a re-creation of the 2016 election with a happy ending for Democrats this time. This makes stopping the wall critical to the psychological well-being of your basic issue Democrat. The safety of the American people and the sovereignty of our nation, not so much. Liberal priorities all too clear.

Miraculously, America's *"broken immigration system"* repaired itself on Jan. 20, 2017. This gets Donald Trump halfway to sainthood, which requires two certifiable miracles for canonization.

Liberals claim their opposition to southern border wall construction is based on their newfound concern over national debt control, which was MIA in the 10-year stretch before Trump took office. A brief look at America's national debt:

Jan. 20, 2009 BHO **takes** office $10,699,805,000,000

Jan. 20, 2017 BHO **leaves** office $19,573,445,000,000

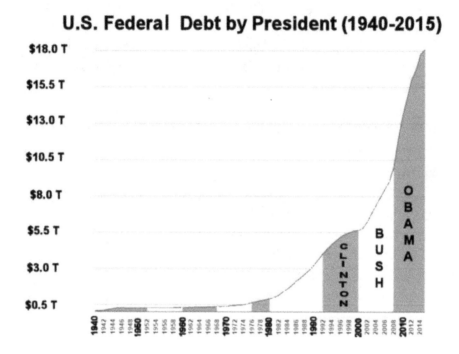

U.S. Federal Debt by President (1940-2015)

So the same liberals who nearly doubled our national debt over the last eight years are now opposed to a $20 Billion border wall, which barely shows up in the national debt round off. The wall expenditure equals approximately 0.5% of America's $4 Trillion annual budget.

Either Democrats are even worse at math than anybody realized, or they are hoping *you* will get lost in the million, billion, and trillion redwood forest. Or maybe they are just lying yet again to the American people.

The truth is that there are precisely *zero* moderate Democrats who care about a balanced budget. They are interested in pilfering cash from the American people and yet unborn generations of Americans so that they can live it up now.

But the wall is only a piece of the larger immigration issue. The Democrat's position is easily understood. They want an open southern border and instant citizenship for anyone who can walk, drive, fly, swim, or float across the Rio Grande River.

This would accomplish a number of high priority objectives for the Democrats: (1) it would establish a new permanent underclass of low-educated, low-skilled voters in need of big government and welfare bribery; (2) it would replenish their base which they have been aborting for decades; (3) it would give them a permanent voting majority nationwide just like the 1986 amnesty-for-border-security hoax (called the *Immigration Reform and Control Act of 1986)* gave them a permanent voting majority in California.

Obliterating America's southern border is completely compatible with the liberal globalist purview of wealth redistribution from America to the rest of the world and equality of outcome. Ultimately our liberal comrade will witness America's standard of living declining to that of the rest of the hemisphere ("the new normal") and the liberal obsession of outcome equality will result. Everyone will be in the same sinking boat. The "shining city on a hill" that Ronald Reagan imagined becomes strewn with hypodermic needles, garbage and human feces like San Francisco.

A country without a border is not a country. Liberals understand this. However, this consequence is not a problem for liberals, who hate America anyway. But to destroy an *existing* southern border wall would expose the truth to the American people.

Democrats have chosen to take their stand against the border wall in the *Deferred Action for Childhood Arrivals* (DACA). Under DACA, the approximately 800K minors who were brought into the United States without legal status would be allowed to stay on a deferred deportation basis. The DACA executive branch policy (*not* law) was established in 2012 by Obama. DACA is in fact another example of Obama's refusal to enforce existing immigration while simultaneously whining *"America's immigration system is broken."* America's immigration system has *never* been broken; only the enforcement was broken.

America now (2018) observes the one-year anniversary of Donald J. Trump entering the White House. We look back in awe at the "winning": the unprecedented economic turnaround, enforcement of immigration laws at our southern border, defeat of ISIS, massive rollback of crippling Bolshevik regulation strangulation, abolition of the Obamacare mandate, etc.

Liberals protested this progress on Nov. 8 (anniversary of the presidential election) by screaming at the sun. Democrat legislators protest the Trump first anniversary by shutting down the government in the name of the 800K DACA "dreamers." This is the Congressional Democrat's version of "screaming at the sun." The desperation to hijack the news cycle away from Trump's magnificent year of accomplishment on its anniversary is nothing short of psychotic self-delusion. Democrats are perfectly willing to sabotage any and all Trump success if there is any chance of manufacturing the illusion of Trump failure. *Nothing* is off the table. The MSM will be more than happy to be complicit in focusing on the government shutdown red herring rather than the Trump record of accomplishment.

Obama's DACA strategy was completely transparent: once established in the U.S., it would be "cruel and inhuman" to deport the 800K future Democrat voters. So now the Democrats threaten to shut down the U.S. government unless the 800K so called *"dreamers"* are given legal status to remain in the

U.S. Let's be clear: there are *no "dreamers."* The DREAM Act was a *failed* piece of 2001 legislation. The name *"dreamer"* lives on only because it comports with the liberal fantasy land mindset of rainbows, unicorns, purple penguins, and their imaginary Marxist egalitarian utopia, where "Kum bah yah" is the global anthem.

The Democrats have a mandate to naturalize the *"dreamers"* by virtue of their imagined sweeping 2018 mid-term election victory, which will be predicated by two years of their hatred and contempt for Donald Trump. They count heavily on the mirage of the generic ballot poll, which gives them a huge lead in West Hollywood, Harlem, and the Haight Ashbury district in San Francisco...the same poll that had Hillary Clinton sweeping to victory in 2016.

The campaign for *"dreamer"* voting rights will begin in approximately one New York nano-second after their legal status is established. Senator "Chucky Doll" Schumer (D-NY) will be all over that like sugar on frosted flakes.

But one step at a time. First, in parable speak, the camel peeks its nose into the tent. By the numbers (1) the illegal aliens enter the country; (2) Obama refuses to deport them via his unilateral highly official sounding illegal DACA decree, which is actually a *refusal* to enforce existing immigration law; (3) the DACA illegals remain as long as Obama is in the White House, and are now interwoven into the *barrio* fabric; (4) they get legal status via their Democrat co-dependents, who must have a new voter base influx to replace the domestic voter base they are aborting; (5) how far behind can citizenship and the right to vote be? (6) It is inhuman to break up families! All family, friends and acquaintances must now be imported for humanitarian reasons; (7) repeat steps (4) – (6) wash/rinse/spin cycle for even more vote imports. Voila! The new Democrat *voter* base is established...and throughout the entire process, America marvels at what truly compassionate people Democrats are!

The lone bright spot in a government shutdown scenario is that Congress will miss *no* paychecks for not doing their job. Yes, they *were* able to pass *that* law. "NumChucks" Schumer and "Dickless" Durbin will miss no meals.

And make no mistake, Democrats could *not* care less about the DACA *people* either. They care ONLY about the future DACA *votes*. Or more succinctly, they care *only* about keeping *themselves* in power, and the DACA *illegal immigrants* are a means to that end. The DACA *illegals* will become their new voter base. But wait! There's more!!! They also will serve as landing strips for the invasion of their illegal alien relatives. That makes each of the 800K *illegal aliens* a multiplier that can be parlayed into *millions* of new Democrat voters. Obama's idea was that DACA will metastasize into a permanent Democrat voting majority via chain migration...effectively America will degrade itself into what California has already become.

This is *not* compassion; this is *greed*. Perhaps one day Democrats will show the same interest in American citizens. At the rate potential American citizens are being aborted by the government-funded Planned Parenthood, I seriously doubt it...they cannot afford to. Democrats must mitigate their abortion voter loss by getting illegal aliens into the United States *now*. They have no time for American citizens, least of all our military, for whom they have total contempt. Their DACA strategy is *crucial* to their return to power *now*.

My guess on the latest Democrat strategy is DACA amnesty (now) in exchange for the promise of a border wall (later). Then they block the border wall when they take back the House in 2018…or worst case scenario, when Oprah *("The Next O!")* wins the presidency in 2020. In the Democrat playbook, this is the Ted Kennedy ("the Lyin' of Chappaquiddick") "okey doke" which he pulled in the 1986 amnesty for border security deal. In cartoon vernacular, Lucy holds the football for Charlie Brown.

As "global citizens" *first*, Democrats find the concept of *"making America great again"* repulsive. This takes collectivism to the OCDL global extreme. It is the true meaning of the radical *"#Resist."* The lowest unemployment numbers (including *women* and minorities) this century due to the new Trump economy should have every American joining in a protest march, liberals rationalize.

This is how these people think. Thankfully, not all Americans suffer from debilitating myopic OCD. If that were the case, America would already be North Korea.

It should be pointed out that here again, the liberal prefers rhetoric over results...form over substance. House Minority Leader Nancy Pelosi (D-CA) so eloquently announced to America that the bonuses, pay raises, and announced American business expansions that resulted from the Trump tax cuts are *"crumbs"* and *"doggie do."* Ms. Pelosi has a net worth estimated at $200 M. She does not live paycheck to paycheck. She thinks flyover state Americans are *"out of touch."*

Democrat border security motives are purely sinister self-interest, but *not* clandestine. On the other hand, the Republicans' motives are *both* sinister *and* clandestine.

The sinister component of the Republican motive is that they act in their own self-interest, not in the interest of the American people. The clandestine component is that they are motivated by pursuit of money from the K Street (Washington DC) lobby, who want increased immigration for cheap corporate unskilled labor.

Both parties find motivational common ground in one hideous thought: within the Beltway, we can *all* get filthy rich by selling what is not ours to sell...America. In every transaction there are winners and losers. It is obvious who the winners are here. The losers are the American people who are over run by the invading horde of illegal immigrants.

The invading illegal aliens do not seek to assimilate themselves into America. If that were the case, they would have entered the country legally through existing American law. Instead their first act upon American soil was to defy American law by breaking it.

They are immediately propagandized with a simultaneous sense of entitlement and resentment by liberals who strive for a factional America that can be manipulated and *controlled* as voting blocks. America owes the invading illegal immigrant masses more than education, healthcare and welfare for the magnanimous gift of their presence.

The invaders seek to *"fundamentally transform"* America into the same socialist latrine they just left because they know no other way. American liberals, who are embarrassed, ashamed and disgusted by America's greatness, have no problem with that. They understand that *"a nation is its borders, its language and its culture"* – Dr. Michael Savage. This makes the illegal immigration invasion at our southern border the liberal "hat trick*". Their euphemism for this wanton assault on America is "diversity".

*Sports term for triple score most often used in ice hockey.

The K Street lobby-driven immigration caper is a rerun of a truly deplorable 19th century movie. The characters have changed but the plot has not. In the 19th century original, a bunch of white southern plantation owners decided they would import cheap unskilled labor from Africa to improve their plantation (corporate) bottom line.

From their perspective, they would consider their slavery tactic to be an unqualified success. But how did that work out for *you* two centuries later, America?

Let us recap the unintended consequences of the 19th century "cheap labor" grand idea: in the 1860s, America fought a gruesome civil war in which 600,000+ brave Americans died to end slavery. Then in the 1960s, America went through another massive upheaval called the "Civil Rights Movement" to guarantee *all* Americans equal rights under the law regardless of *"race, creed, color, gender, or national origin."* The era included many inner-city (Detroit, Newark, Watts, etc.) riots in which entire city blocks were burned to the ground and stores were looted.

A half-century later, America suffered through the worst presidency in our nation's history in another futile attempt to end all residual racial acrimony from the 19th century slavery blunder. Racial relations declined significantly, which should be no surprise with a "community organizer" in the White House...that is what "community organizers" do.

And now in the post-Obama era America is confronted with radical anarchist billionaire George Soros-funded leftists who want to destroy every Confederate monument and statue ostensibly in an effort to drag America back to the 19th century civil war mindset.

This just in: destroying our historical monuments is *not* a cure for your OCD or the all-consuming hatred that mestasizes from it. However, we do know that the assault will not end as long as there is a race hustler industry that profits from it. It will not end as long as there are liberals who are obsessed with reliving the civil rights movement of the 1960s to showcase their faux moral superiority. It will not end as long as there are politicians who can peddle victimhood to get themselves (re)elected. It will not end as long as there are people who are diseased with OCD looking for an external piñata to relieve their omnipresent oppressive mental anguish. It will not end as long as there are Democrats.

Now back to Washington DC. Let's face the cold, hard truth. Republicans don't really want to govern anyway. They are perfectly happy being in their lifelong role of the Washington Generals. They govern with the confidence of a second story burglar who is double parked in front of the Capitol building. Democrats, who are out of power and likely to remain that way, act with the hubris of Walt Kowalski in the movie "Gran Torino": *"Get off my lawn!"* This just in: it ain't *your* lawn.

To govern means working to fulfill campaign promises to America. It requires more effort than cowardly and feckless Republicans are willing to expend. Besides, with any success comes criticism from the MSM; *i.e.*, with actual progress comes MSM-manufactured perception of Republican failure as America now witnesses daily with Trump.

It has become ever-increasingly apparent that Republicans would rather face the guillotine than be targeted with negative commentary from the *Washington Post* or the *New York Times*. This is why they run for cover annually at any hint of confrontation over federal budget restraint. The MSM bellows like the Wizard of Oz and the Republicans cringe like the cowardly lion during this annual farce. This is why America is now nearly $20 trillion in debt. An Academy Award for both the MSM and the Republicans for the annual rerun of *"Groundhog Day"* DC budget style.

The American people do not want an open southern border; that was a huge determinate in the election of Donald Trump. The proponents "immigration reform" (equals amnesty) are virtually all inside the DC beltway. So within the issue of immigration that again see the opening quote to this chapter repeated: *"It is no longer Democrats vs. Republicans...it is Washington D.C. and the main stream media vs. America."*

Nor do the American people want a $20 trillion national debt so that food stamps and other government bribery can be exchanged for Democrat election victories *quid pro quo*. Sadly, more than half of that debt can be chalked up to our historic first "affirmative action" president. *"Obama so loved the poor he created millions more of them."* – Anonymous.

And what of other major issues on the Trump agenda which require legislation? Will Trump and America again get the same Abbott and Costello "Who's on First" routine from the Republican-controlled Senate (aka, the Washington Generals) again? My guess is yes, because the survival of the Swamp is at stake.

Legislation is not the only battleground of the Swamp vs. America. Liberal judicial activism has been substantially exacerbated by Barack Obama. Altering the Senate confirmation process for lifetime-appointed federal judges from 60 votes to 51 votes on November 21, 2013, allowed Obama to stack the District of Columbia Circuit of Appeals in Washington DC with liberal activist judges. The move was a major step in his planned takeover of the American judiciary, which is a one-third equal branch of our government.

Of course, liberals had no way of knowing this bold myopic visionary maneuver would backfire four years later to confirm conservative Neil Gorsuch to the Supreme Court (SCOTUS). ***"What goes around comes around."***

One of Trump's first acts as president was to sign an executive order banning travel to the United States from seven lawless or openly hostile Middle Eastern nations. The seven nations had been identified earlier by the Obama regime as problematic potential sources of terrorists.

The hysteria, hyperventilation, and outrage performance by the left was again Oscar-worthy. Here was a most favored victim group being aggrieved by the Russian-backed white boorish buffoon, Donald Trump. The whole scenario was a race-obsessed liberal's worst nightmare.

The standard liberal retaliation in a situation like this is to use the judiciary to accomplish what they cannot accomplish at the ballot box. In this way, the minority can continue to rule the majority, and thus maintain the *control* they lust for.

The game plan to block the Trump travel ban is all too obvious: "judge shop" to find a left-coast liberal judge who provides the desired ruling. The absurd ruling will then be appealed to the ultra-liberal 9th Circuit Court of Appeals in San Francisco, which will uphold the absurd ruling of the original liberal judge. Of course the 9th Circus, which is overturned 80+% of the time, is just a rest stop on the way to the SCOTUS. There the liberals envision a 4-4 deadlock which will effectively uphold the 9th Circus decision.

Voila! *This* is it!! *This* is how liberals stop Trump and overthrow the 2016 election result!!! Never mind the constitutional crisis that follows. The left has never had anything but total contempt for the American Constitution anyway. Perhaps *this* is the way to get rid of it!

So the state of Washington files suit against Trump's executive order because of all the revenue that will be lost by the state universities, which will be deprived of revenue from the vital tuition from students from these travel-banned countries.

The Department of Justice (DoJ) cited the Law, 8 U.S. Code § 1182 – "Inadmissible aliens" (f) as authority for Trump's executive order:

"Whenever the President finds that the entry of any aliens or of any class of aliens into the United States would be detrimental to the interests of the United States, he may by proclamation, and for such period as he shall deem necessary, suspend the entry of all aliens or any class of aliens as immigrants or nonimmigrants, or impose on the entry of aliens any restrictions he may deem to be appropriate."

Based on my limited layman's understanding of the law, the Court has two requirements to rule in a lawsuit: (1) that the litigants have "standing" in the court, i.e., that they "have skin in the game." The court will not entertain hypotheticals. And (2) that the "four corners" legal principle be applied, i.e., that the legal meaning of a document is contained solely within the text of that document. In this case it means that the legal statute cited by the DoJ is to be taken literally as written.

Without question President Trump and his legal representative, the DoJ, had standing in the matter. Washington state Attorney General Bob Ferguson suing on behalf of unnamed Middle Eastern families and universities who were going to suffer *"immediate and irreversible"* harm from Trump's order was clearly an interloper and political grandstander, a local liberal opportunist with larger political aspirations.

As for the "four corners" aspect of the case, the statute is clear and unambiguous as to the power entrusted to the president. It has to be that way because the president sees highly classified intelligence which is crucial to evaluating the threat to the homeland. Federal judges do not.

However, I remind readers that liberals do not function based on logic and therefore have no need of the facts and information contained in an intelligence report, briefing or anything else. This is what intellectual hubris does for liberals. Besides, the judge himself is not likely to be the victim of a psychotic Yemeni terrorist; he most likely lives in a gated community.

A sixth grader with dyslexia could have correctly interpreted this statute (*"suspend the entry of all aliens or any class of aliens...he may deem to be appropriate."*) and ruled properly in the suit against Trump's executive order. James Robart, a liberal left- coast federal judge could not because the law is secondary to his obsessive compulsion to advertise to the world his self-imagined *superior morality*...which in truth is infidelity to the law and monumental stupidity. Robart is a liberal first...being a judge is an infrequent occasional afterthought. ***Willful ignorance equals stupidity.***

So Judge Robart ruled in favor of the state of Washington in the case and instated a nationwide halt to enforcement of the travel ban, citing <u>not</u> the relevant legal statute 8 U.S. Code § 1182 (f) or the executive order text but rather on an imaginary *"religious ban"* based on Trump campaign rhetoric. If campaign rhetoric was fact, then half of Trump's supporters would be "deplorable" according to Hillary Clinton: *"you could put half of Trump's supporters into what I call the basket of deplorables. Right?"* Clinton said at Sep. 9, 2016, fundraiser in NYC. *"The racist, sexist, homophobic, xenophobic, Islamaphobic—you name it. And unfortunately there are people like that. And he has lifted them up."* No doubt Judge Robart would accept this as evidence in any legal before his court matter also.

The judge's ruling was punctuated with typical meaningless liberal happy talk: *"The President's order was un-American and unconstitutional"*; and *"No one is above the law…not even the President."* Obviously Judge Robart never met the Clintons. He left off his personal punch line: *"No one is above the law…except me!"*

Spearheading (a decidedly "racist'" term which should be banned) the bellicose hyperbole for the left was Washington Democrat Governor Jay Inslee, who declared Trump's order *"inhumane."* *"This is un-American; it is wrong, and it will not stand."* said Gov. Inslee. *"The clear intent of this executive order is to discriminate against one faith amongst all God's children."* I personally take his remark to be an insult to Allah.

So here we have an executive order which does not include within its text the words "Islam" or "Muslim," yet somehow discriminates *exclusively* against them. How is this possible? And how is it possible that a travel ban which <u>ex</u>cludes the seven most populous Muslim nations on earth (in order they are Indonesia, China, India, Pakistan, Bangladesh, Nigeria, and Egypt) be a Muslim ban? ***"Never let the facts get in the way of a good story." – Nucky Thompson (Boardwalk Empire).***

There is a perfectly logical explanation for all of this: liberals are incapable of logic, which is a direct symptom of their OCD. They are masters at conflating non-equivalents to produce a specious conclusion. In this instance, *any* Muslims or *some* Muslims equals *all* Muslims.

We have seen this movie before. For example, to denounce *radical* Islam for the 911 attack in America or the Charlie Hebdo attack in Paris is to denounce *all* Islam, and therefore must be condemned as *"Racist!"* Never mind that Islam is an *alleged religion*, not a race. Classic liberal conflation on full display. Of course, the reason liberals incorrectly refer to the *alleged religion* of Islam as a "race" is to assault any opposition with the exclusively American radioactive invective "Racist!" which is a prime obsession, designed to incite the liberal mob with its Pavlovian "red meat". It is the same reason liberals incorrectly refer to ethnicity of Hispanic as a "race".

Another example of liberal conflation is that denouncing the miscreants who ran the Obama FBI/DoJ thugocracy equals a "declaration of war on the *entire* FBI." No, America only wants to weed out the felons.

The other factor which enters the Judge Robart ruling is *bullying*. Here we see that in its classic liberal form: one unelected federal judge overturning the will of the American majority as manifested in the 2016 presidential election result. The American people clearly voted for national security. Liberal judge Robart's retort via his obviously errant ruling: "NO!"

So the lawsuit against President Trump's seven-nation (Yemen, Somalia, Libya, Iran, Sudan, Iraq and Syria) travel-ban marches onward and "upward" to the 9th Circus with the 100% predictable outcome there. They rarely get anything right as evidenced by their 80+% overturn history. Last stop for the executive order lawsuit is the SCOTUS.

There the justices voted 9-0 to reinstate Trump's executive order travel ban with modest exceptions (the statute authorizing Trump's order has _no_ provision for exceptions, so this too is judicial overreach), overturning Judge Robart _and_ the 9th Circus. Obviously, even the usually-errant four liberal SCOTUS justices have the reading and comprehension skills of our dyslexic sixth grader. And as it turned out, _"No one is above the law."_ Not even Judge Robart.

In terms of constitutional law, the Washington state lawsuit was an uber-dangerous gambit by the left to circumvent the Constitutional concept of _separation of powers_: in this instance, the judicial branch usurps the executive branch's authority to implement national security policy. It is discouraging that this egregious attempt at manufacturing a constitutional crisis by the left got as far as the SCOTUS because half the justices are more often than not overwhelmed by liberal ideology, same as Judge Robart.

What is the net result of all of these legal machinations? An executive order which was signed by President Trump on January 27, 2017, should have been in force the same day. Instead, it was delayed by the activist liberal judicial swamp until the SCOTUS ruled in the federal government's favor on June 26, 2017. During this period, America was exposed to the threat of terrorist(s) entering for nefarious purposes from seven lawless nations. And because there was no major terror attack on American soil during that 5-month period does not mean it was not incubating.

Is anyone on the left humiliated or even embarrassed by this SCOTUS outcome? Quite to the contrary, they are giddy that they could game the judicial system all the way to the SCOTUS with liberal buffoonery.

The judges along the way who couldn't interpret the simplest of legal statutes correctly are lifetime appointees. I cannot imagine bringing a case before any of them knowing full well that they have zero fidelity to the law. What is even scarier is that this kind of judicial malpractice is exactly what Barack Obama or Hillary Clinton is seeking to promote to the SCOTUS.

Perhaps we should be encouraged by the 9-0 whitewash (oops... "racist" again!). Was this a "No More Buffoonery!" stop sign to the left coast Nano-wits who manufactured this monumental waste of time, effort, and money? Probably not. Do stupid people know they are stupid? Same answer.

Has the swamp corruption gravitated elsewhere into America's court system? The Trump "Dirty Dossier" case history is telling.

In a never-ending spiral downward into the depths of corruption, the 2016 Clinton campaign financed a $12 M "dossier" alleging Trump sexual misconduct while on a Moscow business trip. We should acknowledge that no one who worked on the Clinton campaign has ever had a real job, they have nothing better to do than sit around and dream up felonious political Nixonian hijinks.

The details of the "dossier" are far beyond salacious. The author was a former British MI6 agent Christopher Steele ostensibly in *collusion* with Russian contacts. The idea was that Trump would be a target for Russian blackmail if elected.

Immediately prior to the election (classic "October surprise!"), Steele fed his nearly completed *opus magnum* to American intelligence agencies. When the FBI did not take the bait, Steele leaked his handiwork into the MSM. All the MSM media needs to make a front page above the fold story is the words "Trump" and "Russia" together regardless of context. This is Journalism 101.

The "dirty dossier'" failed to produce the desired media dumpstorm. Trump was successful in branding the entire excursion into "The Twilight Zone" of dirty tricks as "fake news" and won the election. With zero collaboration whatsoever, the entire "dossier" was properly discredited.

The post-election financing of the "dossier" continued through an organization called Fusion GPS. Steele's "dossier" was eventually completed after the election and passed on to FBI with an assist from the bitter interloping maverick Senator John McCain. It was then on the basis of this discredited "dirty dossier" that the FBI went to the United States Foreign Intelligence Surveillance (FISA) Court with requests to wiretap Trump's campaign associates, which were approved.

The FISA Court was established under the Foreign Intelligence Surveillance Act of 1978 (FISA) to oversee requests for surveillance warrants against foreign spies inside the United States by federal law enforcement and intelligence agencies.

So President-Elect Trump's campaign associates were given "foreign spy" status by the FBI under Director James Comey and the FISA Court. I have it from the same unnamed source who told Harry Reid that Mitt Romney *"hasn't paid any taxes for ten years"* the "dirty dossier" was actually based on a Bill Clinton misadventure. The dossier author just whited out Clinton's name and typed in "Donald Trump" to make a payday.

The Swamp gumbo roux thickens. If Watergate was a bathtub, "FISAgate" is the Pacific Ocean. The "FISAgate" plot could easily be the sequel to *"Enemy of the State"* (1998 movie). But let's not kid ourselves. By the time Hollywood is finished mutilating the storyline, FBI conspirators Peter Strzok (the disgraced FBI miscreant, *not* to be confused with the Polish porn star) and Lisa Paige will be courageous virtuous freedom-fighters in the style of Che Guevara, attempting to save America from Donald Trump and his cretin *racist* neo-Nazi horde from flyover country. "Mother" Strzok (pronounced "Struck") can best be caricaturized as Eddie Haskell ("Leave it to Beaver" juvenile delinquent) graduates to *mafia capo*. Matt Damon and Scarlett Johansson would be perfect in the hero and heroine roles.

Think about this: the FBI are the federal police. They went to the FISA court with a *known* fraudulent justification for wiretap surveillance of American citizens and later a President-Elect of the United States. They did not disclose the source of the dossier which ultimately was the Hillary campaign to the FISA court. The "dirty dossier" story was leaked to the MSM who printed stories on it. The FBI then used the MSM stories as circular corroboration for the warrant requests. An analogy would be if a cop leaked a story that you had committed a bank robbery to the press, then requested a warrant for your arrest based on the newspaper story. Our liberal comrade protests *"No newspaper would do that!"* Of course they *all* would do that if our hypothetical "bank robber" was Donald Trump during the 2016 election cycle...and beyond after Trump *won* the election!

The FISA *Court* then approved the request...not once, but <u>*four*</u> times on the required quarterly warrant renewals! So a year later, the renewing FISA judge still couldn't tell the "dirty dossier" was Hillary campaign-financed fictional tabloid trash because the FBI didn't tell them? Are they that gullible? Are they complicit? Did they make campaign donations? If so, to whom? What happens if the FBI shows up with same warrant request based on the same justification *today*? Is the surveillance shut down *yet*? This puts the FISA judges who approved the warrants into the middle of the web.

This is the epicenter of the *Swamp*! It has slimed its way into our federal police force and our courts!! Apparently it does not want to be drained any more than Al Capone wanted to be sent to Alcatraz!!!

Had Hillary Clinton been elected, Obama's *"fundamental transformation of America"* into a banana republic would have been completed. The "FISAgate" corruption would have never seen the light of day.

All of this legal system d!p$h!ttery occurred before the January 20, 2017, inauguration of Donald Trump, while *alleged* "constitutional lawyer" and micromanager *emeritus* Barack Obama was still in command of the federal bureaucracy. It is precisely the genre of white- collar crime caper the self-imagined lawyer would participate in as evidenced by "FISAgate" FBI conspirator Lisa Paige declassified text messages.

This is what a thugocracy looks like. And make no mistake, the corruption gravitates downward from the very top. **"$h!t rolls downhill. Bureaucracy rolls faster." – David Wellington.**

The 4th Amendment of the United States Constitution protects its citizens from *"unreasonable search and seizure."* The pathetic abuse of power in the Trump "dirty dossier" caper by all involved gives us insight into liberals' contempt for the law and the Constitution in general, and Obama's contempt in particular.

The Obama thugocracy graduated from the minor league IRS high jinx of the 2012 campaign to the 2016 "Big Show": manipulation of the FISA court by the FBI-gone-*Stasi* (East German secret police), led by James Comey. The 2012 IRS shenanigans were just a *"Saturday in the Park"* (1972 Chicago song) walk-through for the abuse of government power we now know happened in 2016. I think the FBI and DoJ conspirators took their cue from the IRS thugs four years earlier, i.e. there were zero consequences for the IRS perps then. They were covered with full immunity by Obama's reply to the Bill O'Reilly question of corruption within the IRS during the Feb. 2, 2014 televised pre-Super Bowl interview: *"Not even mass corruption — not even a smidgen of corruption."* This was Obama's "Hands off!" dog whistle to the DoJ regarding potential IRS criminality. It was also his green light signal to the IRS to keep on keepin' on. And from Obama's "investigation" of his own IRS, we may conclude Obama is no "Sam Spade" ("The Maltese Falcon" 1941).

We can only hope as Americans that the full extent of the felonious "dirty dossier"/FBI/FICA misadventure gets full public exposure, and those responsible are punished appropriately, including prison time. No, I am not alluding to any Mueller-indicted Russians who will *never* see an American courtroom. The Mueller "investigation" will remain a permanent fixture on the DC scene, a guilty verdict in search of a crime until either (1) the Macarena makes a comeback; or (2) Jeff Sessions actually starts doing his job. It is taxpayer financed ($20+M) opposition research for the Democrats in 2020 against Trump. It is a political, financial and personal colonoscopy.

Without question the FISAgate lawyerly conspiracy goes all the way to the <u>TOP</u>. As the layers of the conspiracy onion are peeled, look for the *allyl methyl sulfide*-induced Democrat tears to fall.

The first onion layer the Democrat Beltway conspirators were counting on was a Hillary Clinton election victory. This would have made all their bureaucratic felonious misdeeds disappear like flatulence in the wind. The second onion layer is the standard "missing evidence" trick. Minimal lawbreaker time and investment is required.

It worked adequately for Lois Lerner (IRS thug) and later for Hillary Clinton (Democrat presidential nominee thug). The problem with this maneuver from page 1 of the "Liberal Legal Evasion Playbook" is that Obama no longer has his hands on the federal bureaucracy, and specifically the DoJ, control levers. The third onion layer is conspirator "plausible deniability." This means that some middle management schlub must fall on the sword and do the time to protect the Messiah. Meanwhile, the Messiah does another replay of his best Sgt. Shultz impersonation which he perfected back in his first term: *"I know nothing…NOTHING!"*

The final layer of the onion will be standard liberal *"Racist!"* accusation. This will clear Obama of any and all wrongdoing that occurred on his watch. It is his perpetual "Get Out of Jail Free" card.

When the gun is empty, *"Racist!"* is what liberals always fling at their opponents.

Of course, any pursuit of criminality against Obama regime miscreants is contingent upon having a real Attorney General. Jeff Sessions has been MIA since Day 1 in office based on his recusal from all Swamp drainage matters. At a time when it is crucial to have a competent patriot in the A. G. position to flush the Obama Justice Department corruption down the toilet, Sessions surrenders to "The Swamp". The Sessions' appointment was easily Trump's worst decision as president.

Do not expect Deputy A. G. Rod Rosenstein, who is actually Barney Fife in wire rimmed glasses, to do anything but sandbag a Drain-the-Swamp effort.

"Barney" Rosenstein, who grew up on airplane food, is a career swamp thang. He is a lifelong practitioner of Clintonesque corruption as witnessed by his signature on the last phony FISA Trump surveillance warrant application, long after it became common knowledge that the entire Russian collusion epistle was a sleazy Hillary financed hoax. Subsequently we learn there were *no* hearings during any of the FISA warrant processing. This is definitely banana republic territory.

Barack Obama (01.21.09) via memo: *"My Administration is committed to creating an unprecedented level of openness in Government. We will work together to ensure the public trust and establish a system of transparency, public participation, and collaboration. Openness will strengthen our democracy and promote efficiency and ef-*

fectiveness in Government." In other news, O.J. Simpson has resumed the search for Nicole's murderer after being paroled for his armed robbery conviction from Nevada State Prison.

As for Comey and his merry band of FBI miscreants, there are *hard* times ahead.

They bet on the wrong horse and lost. Now they pay the price. Likewise for their DoJ co-conspirators.

But wait, there's more! Now America learns on the eve of the Inspector's General (IG) report on the Hillary Clinton email investigation that at least one FBI informant was imbedded in the Trump campaign. This information was leaked by the DoJ in an effort to get out ahead of the IG report with their own spin.

Former Obama CIA director turned CNN "commentator" James Clapper (aka "the Clap") enlightens America that *"It is a very good thing that there was a (paid) FBI informant in the FBI campaign."* Yes, a Trump campaign which is not properly *secretly* monitored by the FBI reporting to outgoing president Barack Obama is a menace beyond all comprehension and will surely destroy the America Obama has so carefully "transformed". There *should* be a taxpayer financed spy in every Republican campaign reporting directly to Obama. *THIS* is precisely how I want my taxpayer dollars spent, along with interference in Israeli national elections, running assault weaponry to the Mexican drug cartels, arming the Muslim Brotherhood in Egypt with F-16 fighter jets and tanks, and financing Iranian terrorism including a nuclear weapon. Any similarities between the Watergate break-in that ended the Nixon presidency in 1974 and the abuse of the federal bureaucracy at the end of the Obama eight year reign of buffoonery (I mercifully bypass the word "evil") are purely imaginary.

"Who the hell thinks this cr@p up???" we may ask rhetorically. My response? A "community organizer" who has never had a real job in his life, who cannot even identify a real problem (much less solve it), and who harbors a seething hatred for the country which made him its president. It is all baked into to the price of "affirmative action". Next question.

CNN's entire viewership, which includes all the people asleep at airport terminals, grunts doing cardio at the gym and the hospital waiting room walking dead, becomes the focus group for this liberal group-think manufactured pile of happy horse cr@p. CNN is a perpetual loser in the cable news rating war and the political propaganda war they started with Trump because they cannot distinguish their biased convoluted opinion from "breaking news". This is unlikely to change without a wholesale flush of current management down the porcelain receptacle.

Other trial balloon "explanations" surface ahead of the IG report: the FBI plant was there in the Trump campaign to protect America against *Russian* election interference, *not* to surveil the Trump campaign. The fact that no Russians were ever found is irrelevant. No such spy was necessary for the Clinton campaign. Again, the Clinton involvement in the UraniumOne sale and accompanying quid pro quo Russian donations to the Clinton Family Foundation, and direct large ($500K) cash payments to Bill Clinton for "speeches" delivered in Russia are also irrelevant.

Yes, the informant was planted in the Trump campaign to "protect it"? Forget questions like "From what?", "Why wasn't the Trump campaign made aware of this 'guardian angel'?", and "Can you name one Russian who was actually involved in any of this?" *None* of this is going to pass the smell test under the nose of the American people.

The one thing that all of the corrupt election *meddling* federal agencies (IRS, FBI, CIA, DoJ) have in common is that they all reported to Barack Obama. Obama supersized the uber-corrupt "Chicago way" into a nationwide pestilence. Yet again the Kenyan menace has done America a "solid"...or as pre-school children would call it, a "number two". In Pelosi-speak, the 2016 election interloping by the Obama posse is the cherry on top of the eight year pile of "doggie do". Thank you, Charlie Fox-trot...*this* will be your legacy.

In eight short years, Americans no longer trust *any* part of the federal bureaucracy or the federal election process. Now every election that Democrats lose will be condemned with the imaginary paranoid stench of "Russian collusion". Moreover, they have just demonstrated they can do it based on *zero* evidence, exclusively on media propaganda.

Scarier yet is the realization that none of the participants in the biggest conspiracy in American election history think they did anything wrong. This is a direct result of the "the end justifies the means" OCD liberal creed. It remains to be seen if a jury of their peers will agree with them.

The irony is off the charts: in the 2012 election debates, Obama mocked Romney for heralding the Russian threat. The 180° Russian turnaround whiplash from 2012 to 2016 can most kindly be described as Orwellian: ***"The past was alterable. The past never had been altered. Oceania was at war with Eastasia. Oceania had always been at war with Eastasia." – George Orwell ("1984").*** It can most accurately described as schizophrenic opportunism completely devoid of conscience, which is a liberal pre-requisite. During the 2016 election campaign, Obama announced to America that (1) he told Putin to "cut it out" after being informed by the intelligence community of Russian election interference; (2) that it was impossible to interfere with the American election because it was so geographically diverse; (3) he advised Trump to "stop whining" about an election result that had not yet happened, and "go out and start making a case for votes"; and (4) joined in the chorus of boos with Hillary and the MSM when Trump refused to blindly accept every possible 2016 election during a presidential debate. A year and a half later all liberals continue to reject the 2016 election result based on no evidence whatsoever. *"Liberals project themselves onto their political opponents."*

Democrats hope to obfuscate the Trump dubbed "Spygate" debacle with semantics: The Trump campaign was surveilled by a *confidential informant*, not a spy. My online dictionary defines a *spy* as *"a person who secretly collects and reports information on the activities, movements, and plans of an enemy or competitor."* Yes, yet again clearly *"It depends on what the meaning of the word 'is' is."* -Bill Clinton (Sep 13, 1998). Let's see how many months we can watch the swamp dwellers debate the crucially important semantics "issue". At this point it is useful to define *red herring*: *"something that misleads or distracts from a relevant or important issue."* Desperate people do desperate things.

The conduct of the entire executive branch of the federal government during the 2016 election cycle may be summed up in one choice military term: "FUBAR". This grand finale was eight years in the making.

I forecast judicial buffoonery for the foreseeable future. The skunk cannot change his stripe. Liberals cannot be cured of OCD. Their disorder must be fed with the destruction of America constantly. The *status quo* is *never* acceptable to the obsessively-compulsively- disordered liberal.

Liberals have lost the executive and legislative branches of our government, which makes the judicial branch their last stand…and they are not going to capitulate to common sense, logic or reason, none of which exist in the liberal playbook. It has not happened in my lifetime, and the past is still our best indicator of the future.

Elsewhere in the Swamp, classified leaks became a pivotal battleground in the Trump vs. Swamp war the day after Inauguration Day. Just like the Kim Jong-un central government in Pyongyang, the number 1 objective of the federal government in Washington DC is its own survival. The number 2 objective is its own growth. The well-being of the American people is nowhere on their radar.

Swamp creatures (federal government employees) are natural leftists.

Now enters Donald J. Trump, a *highly* successful businessman, as President of the United States. Trump has spent his entire half century+ career finding ways to profitably do more with less. Inside the DC Beltway, this very concept is nauseating blasphemy. It is a complete contradiction of the last eight Obama years of government over-regulation, overreach, and expansion wherein taxpayer money is no object.

So Trump vs. career government employees (the "Deep State") is the mongoose vs. the cobra: death for one or the other. Thousands of six-figure government jobs are at stake.

Having failed to defeat Trump in the 2016 election, the "Deep State" has revised its target to the 2020 presidential election. They now are single-mindedly focused on their next objective: damage Trump by any and all means to damage his reelection bid. Their comrades in the MSM have the same objective and are all-too-willing accomplices.

This is the backdrop to the tactic of leaking *classified* information to embarrass, discredit, sabotage, and otherwise delegitimize the Trump presidency. The same tactic failed to damage the Trump candidacy, but it's all they got (colloquial grammar).

To the extent the leaks are real (e.g., leaking a transcript of a telephone conversation between President Trump and another head of state), they range from felonious to treasonous. The threat to national security is *real*. But it is also of no consequence to the leakers. Survival of the Swamp (and their 6-digit salaries) and obsessive-compulsive-disordered hatred of Trump come *first*.

Most of the alleged "leaks" insinuating turmoil and chaos within the Trump administration are total fabrications of the MSM, according to *my* reliable sources. See how easy conforming "news" to match *your* agenda becomes when you lower your "journalism" standards to zero?

Let me posit a scenario. Reporter "A" calls Reporter "B" in the next cubicle with an anonymous tip that former Trump campaign staffer Harry Porker was seen with known Russian operatives Boris and Natasha Snowski in early 2016. "There is an image of the three of them floating around the internet," says Reporter "A."

It's noon and Reporter "B" submits his "bombshell" story to his editor who approves it in the time it takes to say "OK!" By midafternoon, Reporter "B's" exclusive is ready to print and he has posted the message onto Twitter in half the 140 characters ration. Twitter is the electronic tom-tom (highly racist term offensive to Native Americans like Elizabeth F. Warren) of the 21st century and the entire MSM is linked in. Trump's sordid sabotage of American democracy is spread across the media by the *real* saboteur like hot peanut butter across a slice of Wonder Bread.

From there it spends 3 days minimum in the cable news headlines until it is revealed to be specious, like the Trump's post-inauguration alleged disposal of the White House MLK bust story.

By this time the next "October surprise *de jour*" is warmed up and ready for delivery. This time it is Reporter "A" who gets the anonymous call from Reporter "B." All this according to my unnamed sources in the MSM.

Of course, this may be totally inaccurate. There may not be a second anonymous reporter at all. It may be that Reporter "A" came up with the whole hoax *de jour* himself (or herself). ***"Journalism": where the parallel universes of liberal fantasy and conservative reality become one.***

DC regulatory agencies are necessarily populated with government advocates who naturally align themselves with the 10 planks of the Communist Manifesto. Big government is what puts bread on their table; it is job security. The self-avowed Marxist Obama, who would gleefully grow the federal government at the expense of the private sector, was the answer to any federal bureaucrat's prayer.

With the right leadership at the top, the entire federal government could be transformed into the Veteran's Administration (VA). Expansion of the federal government means pay raises, bonuses, promotion opportunities, etc. for federal bureaucrats. Also, disciplinary action or termination for non-performance of job requirements is disallowed. Tragically, in the case of the VA, it did *not* mean any improvement in veterans' healthcare.

Government healthcare was never about healthcare. It was about government. The Obamacare website, which should have cost a few million dollars to craft, cost over a half billion dollars...not a problem in the government of zero accountability, zero responsibility, and printing press for when the funding runs low.

The first act of the government after Obamacare was passed into law was to hire 15,000 more IRS agents. How much impact were these 15,000 agents on the quality of healthcare in America?

It became painfully apparent to Americans *after* the 2012 presidential election that the IRS had been used by the incumbent Obama regime to harass conservative political action committees (PACs) over their tax-exempt status in the period 2010-2012 *before* the election. The new IRS manpower from the Affordable Care Act (Obamacare) was obviously put to good use. Obama's personal guarantee that *"There was not a smidgen of corruption in the IRS"* was confirmation that the conspiracy went all the way to the top just like *"I will sign a universal health care bill into law by the end of my first term as president that will cover every American and cut the cost of a typical family's premium by up to $2,500 a year"* actually meant that a typical family's annual premiums would *increase* by $2,500 a year.

Lois Lerner headed the IRS group responsible for tax-exemption status during Obama's first term. She was called upon to testify before Congress after the 2012 election as to why groups with the terms "patriot" and "Tea Party" tax-exempt statuses were universally denied or delayed during the 2010-2012 pre-election time range.

She declared in her opening statement to Congress that she was not guilty of any and all wrongdoing in the matter, and then exempted herself from any cross examination by taking the 5th Amendment… a unique defense strategy to be sure.

Ms. Lerner was placed on administrative leave (at full salary) and later resigned. She was found in contempt of Congress in a bipartisan vote of its members. However, the Obama Department of Justice (DoJ) refused to prosecute her on contempt charges because the Swamp *meister* looks out for his own.

What FBI investigation into the IRS abuse scandal that was done concluded that although the conservative PAC tax exempt statuses were handled with "poor judgment, mismanagement, and institutional inertia," there was no evidence of criminal wrongdoing. Therefore, the DoJ recommended no criminal prosecution. The fact that *zero* liberal PACs were subjected to the same "institutional inertia" is irrelevant, nothing to see here, move on.

Perhaps the most discouraging aspect of this entire pathetic abuse of power is that no one ever gets fired for it. This is what allows thugocrats like Lois Lerner and IRS Director John Koskinen to sit down in front of Congressional investigators and refuse to answer questions about IRS harassment of conservatives wearing his signature "jerk-with-a-smirk" grin. They know there is no consequence and no deterrent keeping them from doing it again. This green-lights future corruption.

The lack of personal responsibility was particularly acute during the Obama years, where defiant behavior was condoned if not encouraged.

All attempts to subpoena Ms. Lerner's email prior to the election were unsuccessful: the *"hard drive crashed,"* and the backup tapes were erased after they had been subpoenaed due to a *"communication error."* If you believe that, you probably fell for the Nigerian prince email scam, too.

So dozens of conservative PACs were disenfranchised from participation in the 2012 election process. The example of the FBI investigation of criminal email activity was established for the Hillary Clinton scandals in the next election cycle. Ms. Lerner is now retired on full government pension. Al Capone laments from wherever the hell he is that he did not first hijack the DoJ at the beginning of his career.

Obama could not suspend the 1st Amendment rights of his political opponents. The closest thing he could do was the 2012 IRS harassment. Then in 2016 a far more sinister conspiracy was executed by the "usual suspects": the Obama regime, the MSM, the DoJ, the FBI, the DNC and the Hillary campaign…FISAgate. On the bright side, America was able to repulse Obama's gun control obsession, which is his political "final solution".

Never before Obama has the federal bureaucracy been so egregiously weaponized against the American people. In this particular episode, it was the IRS, the DoJ, and the FBI. And the Swamp beat goes on.

SYNOPSIS: Every branch of our federal government (executive, legislative and judicial) reeks with corruption. So does the MSM. It has all served to make Washington DC the wealthiest city in America, the mirror to what Pyongyang is to North Korea.

By the election of Donald Trump in 2016, America has declared itself a "swamp free" zone.

8. VICTIMOLOGY 101:
CORE CURRICULUM FOR THE OCD LIBERAL M.A.B.S.

"Victimhood and a 'can't' do spirit is mostly what the Democrat Party has mostly been about since the Great Depression." –Cal Thomas.

Selling victimhood to a minority class is an easy sale. It takes no skill whatsoever, because what you are selling is an excuse for failure, or more precisely that your failure is somebody else's fault.

At some point in our lives everyone has failed. People who can learn from mistakes and failure will move on and eventually excel. People who cannot will remain failures for life. *"It's not how many times you get knocked down. It's how many times you get back up."* – Vince Lombardi

Victimhood is always the easy way out because it requires zero effort. Liberal leaders, called "community organizers," are in search of people who want to take the easy way out. This is how they make their living. Sadly in America we have an education system that encourages failure with socialist purple penguin participation trophies and the like. It is through this education system that the seeds of failure are sown to eventually produce the current "snowflake" generation. Barack Obama is a product of America's contemporary education system.

By now it is all-too-common knowledge that Democrats peddle victimhood for votes. Their strategy is no secret. Import enough immigrants into the United States to make this a majority minority country, then give them full citizenship, full voting rights, and full welfare benefits. So consumed are liberals with their obsession for control that they are perfectly willing to give our country away to third world invaders to reinstate themselves in power. It is the Cloward-Pivin[2] strategy gone global. It has become necessary to do this because the liberals' ghoulish obsession with abortion has depleted their indigenous voting base.

They really don't care how they do this, but it needs to happen quickly to return them to elected power quickly. *Controlling* America is their number one priority. They are not interested in the assimilation of immigrants into American society or culture. They camouflage their intent with poll-tested mis-directives like "diversity" and "multiculturalism." These are liberal "dog whistles" for disunity, sometimes referred to as "Balkanization," which is key to liberal electoral strategy. *Liberals lie about their motives 100.000% of the time.*

The disunity is a precursor to civil unrest, the wet dream of every "community organizer". Manufacturing unrest is how they make their living. *"There is a certain class of race problem- solvers who do not*

---

[2] a political strategy outlined in 1966 by Columbia University sociologist professors and political activists Richard Cloward and Frances Fox Piven that called for overloading the U.S. public welfare system in order to manufacture civil unrest and eventually anarchy.

want the patient to get well because as long as the disease holds out they have a medium through which to make themselves prominent before the public." – Booker T. Washington

Anyone who disagrees with Liberals or recognizes their true intent is labeled a "xenophobe." Liberals are heavily invested in labels because it is easier than thinking. Labels simplify relationships greatly for the liberal who *must* have simplification to cope.

They label wide swaths of "oppressed" minorities because they do not acknowledge or even see individuals, a byproduct of Marxist inculcation. Minorities are subdivided according to race, gender, religion, and sexual orientation. They see blacks, women, Muslims, gays, Hispanics, etc., never as individuals. **Liberals evaluate based on *identity*, conservatives evaluate based on *ideas*.** These groups are the victims of white-male-supremacist America.

For example, liberals do not see Dr. Ben Carson as an accomplished world-class neurosurgeon. They see a "black." As a "black," *Mr.* Carson is entitled to certain benefits such as food stamps, a free Obama phone, HUD housing (of which ironically he is now the Department Secretary), affirmative-action boost through the education system, etc. in exchange for his total support of the Democrat agenda. Turns out *Dr.* Carson needed none of that.

There is NO possible deviation from the monochromatic liberal template. What they are actually seeking is *control* over Dr. Carson's life, because *control* is what OCD is all about. All it takes is the Faustian sale of your soul to the Democrat Party for *quid pro quo* government handouts. This codependency becomes generational; it is by now a way of life for millions of Americans.

But Dr. Carson is more than an anomaly in the data. He is a threat. He is a myth-buster. He is not only a high-profile Republican, he was also a candidate for the 2016 Republican presidential nomination.

How can this be if Republicans hate all minorities, particularly blacks? This myth has been established by decades of liberal propaganda, just like "global warming" (or its latter day iteration, "climate change") or more recently "Russian collusion" and *"Hands up, don't shoot!"*

It is unacceptable to liberals that Dr. Carson campaigned across America in direct contradiction to the liberal paradigm "Republicans hate blacks." The spectacle of Dr. Carson campaigning *as* a Republican destroys any imagined liberal credibility faster than a Godzilla rampage through downtown Tokyo.

Clearly Dr. Carson is defective! Yes, that's it!! This must be exposed by the MSM!!! He must be made an example of what happens to minorities who have ideas of escaping the Democrat plantation, birthplace of the Ku Klux Klan (KKK). If one escapes, others will follow. It is fortunate for Dr. Carson that he was only one of sixteen Republican presidential candidates in the 2016 primary season. The MSM attack on Dr. Carson was diluted by concurrent attacks on the fifteen other candidates, particularly the front runners like Donald Trump.

America has seen this movie before. In 1990, Clarence Thomas was nominated by President George H. W. Bush for Supreme Court Justice. Dr. Thomas was subjected to a protracted Senate confirmation hearing after former EEOC employee Anita Hill leveled uncorroborated allegations of sexual misconduct at Thomas.

Thomas commented of the hearing process: *"This is a circus. It's a national disgrace. And from my standpoint, as a black American, it is a high-tech lynching for uppity blacks who in any way deign to think for themselves, to do for themselves, to have different ideas, and it is a message that unless you kowtow to an old order, this is what will happen to you. You will be lynched, destroyed, caricatured by a committee of the U.S. Senate rather than hung from a tree."*

Dr. Thomas' *crime* had nothing to do with sexual misconduct. His *crime* was that he was a black who escaped the Democrat plantation. The final Senate vote was 52-48 in favor of confirmation. Justice Thomas has now successfully served on the SCOTUS for 27 years with honor and distinction.

Alaska governor Sarah Palin stepped into the national spotlight in 2008 when she became the first Republican female candidate for Vice President running with Sen. John McCain. She is a devout Christian, conservative, ruggedly self-reliant, self-confident, principled, and attractive mother of four. Because of her conservative views, she was savagely attacked, mocked, and ridiculed by the OCD Left during the 2008 campaign and since.

We find similar case histories for Alberto Gonzalez, the first Hispanic Attorney General and Condoleezza Rice, the first female black Secretary of State, both appointed by George W. Bush.

The salient point here is that the only interest liberals have in minorities is to advance the cause of liberalism. Minorities who escape the Democrat plantation will be dealt with just like their 19th century counterparts, as we saw with Justice Thomas.

Liberals (who weren't even born then) are obsessed with reliving the 1960s. After the *control* obsession, they are obsessed with both race and their own moral superiority, which has now been deemed "virtue signaling." The rhetorical device liberals utilize to simultaneously demonstrate *both* is to call you "RACIST!" Liberals seek to turn every debate into whether or not *you* are a "RACIST!" because they cannot win *any* debate on the merit of their ideas. The "RACIST!" strategy levels the playing field away from logical debate where they have no chance at winning and into an "Animal House" (1978 movie) food fight at which they excel.

It is the purpose and *destiny* in life of liberal *superheroes* to put an end to this rampant bigotry. And where this bigotry does not exist, they will imagine or manufacture it to show off their super powers and superior morality.

Without this battle, there is no performance stage for these incredibly morally-superior-to-you Pecksniffian liberal social justice warriors.

Not all minorities are created equal in the eyes of liberals. The "most favored minority" status is based on race. We would expect nothing else from the race- obsessed liberal.

Muslims move to the head of the minority class because not only are they predominately dark-skinned Middle Easterners, but they are by definition non-Christian. Liberals will fail to notice I did not pen *anti*-Christian, because that is what Liberals want to see, i.e., a divisive racist remark.

Skin color plus non-Christian is the liberal daily double. *"The enemy of my enemy is my friend"* – **Unknown.** Liberalism and Christianity do not mix. There can be no clearer demonstration of this axiom than when God was booed at the 2012 Democrat national convention in Charlotte.

What a moment of pride that must have been for Barack Hussein Obama! Allahu Akbar!!!

Over 80% of America is Christian. Liberals feel surrounded, outnumbered, overwhelmed. It is a short leap from the universal liberal OCD to paranoia. They believe that Christians sit in judgment of liberal social practices, and they feel threatened.

Whatever faint spiritual commitment liberals have is to government, which serves as their *creator*. Christianity is in direct conflict with the communist philosophy as defined by Marks' *Communist Manifesto* (Chapter 5: "10 Commandments vs. 10 Planks of the *Communist Manifesto*"). Again, any enemy of Christianity is a friend to the liberal.

The OCDL is by nature offensive-minded, because to them, the *status quo* is unacceptable, intolerable, and insufferable. It is due to the mental disorder, *not* the socio-economic environment which they seek to adulterate as therapeutic relief.

Embracing Islam is consistent with their attack mentality. It is a means by which they can confuse, confound, and undercut Christianity *vis a vis* their intolerable and unjust American socio-economic environment.

One of the most perplexing issues confronting conservatives, patriots, and American loyalists is this convoluted attraction of liberals to Muslims, which I call "Islamophilia." Although superficially confusing to most logical Americans, it is easily understood by anyone who recognizes what liberalism is: a symptom of acute Obsessive Compulsive Disorder (OCD). What liberals obsess over is (1) *CONTROL*; (2) their own faux MORAL SUPERIORITY; (3) RACE; (4) "FAIRNESS"; and (5) hatred of Christianity. Islam is a culture which simultaneously encompasses religion *and* all branches of government. Islamophilia, which is an unnatural irrational emotional attraction to the culture of Islam, provides temporary relief for liberal obsessions. It is in effect the Scrabble equivalent to a quintuple word score; or, even better, the weathercaster mentioning "New Orleans" and "Category 5" in the same sentence.

Liberals are envious of the elitist ayatollahian *control* of Islam. They are gleeful at the anti-constitutional nature of a religion that would simultaneously give them totalitarian control of all three branches of government and the economy. Liberals fantasize about the societal and economic (dis)order they could create with this *control*: the perfect egalitarian Marxist utopia complete with social justice and political correctness would instantaneously emerge if they possessed Islamic *control* of all speech, actions and thought in America. This is the same reason liberals gush with overt admiration of communist dictators like Fidel Castro, Mao Zedong, Hugo Chavez, et al. as they pretend these dictators rule over their liberal imagined utopia.

Liberals are also envious of the Muslim right, no the *duty*, to eliminate "infidels", *i.e.*, to murder anyone who disagrees with them. Imagine what Maxine Waters would do with that!

And thus, *Islamophelia* is born. OCDLs are synonymous with Islamophiles, who are the antithesis of the alleged Islamophobic strawmen they loathe. Islamophelia is a blend of liberal "virtual signaling", egomania, misguided values and the perpetual liberal need for a scapegoat, a villain, a strawman to condemn for their own mental disorder.

The visceral display of *moral superiority* is critical to the liberal's concept of self-worth, which in reality is near zero. It is their opportunity to shower themselves with relevant hubris in a lifetime of mediocracy. To reinforce this latter point, Hillary Clinton is a lifelong high-profile liberal, yet in the 2016 presidential campaign, not one of her supporters could cite a single accomplishment. That is still true today.

Liberals are universally attracted like Barack Obama to a teleprompter to socio-economic "transgressions" wherein a class of victims can be established. Note that within the liberal vernacular, "victim" means everyone but white males. (Denouncing their own race and gender is a prerequisite for liberal certification of *any* white male.) It is then through "victim" advocacy that the liberal's *moral superiority* is established. Moreover, "victim" advocacy provides the liberal a means to create minority rule, which is the ultimate display of the *control* they obsess over. Minority rule allows them to bully their political opponents, which is a key opiate of liberalism.

A prominent recent example of this is the absurd liberal crusade for "transgender bathroom equality," which in reality means anybody-in-any-bathroom-at-any-time in order to accommodate a guestimated 0.3% of the American population (at the expense of the embarrassment, humiliation and women/child safety of the other 99.7% of our population). It is duly noted that liberals are magnanimous to a fault (failing?!?!?) with other people's money, rights, security, and safety as in the case of "transgender bathroom equality." These are trivial indeed in the quest to run their *moral superiority* up the flagpole for all to see. And besides, what could possibly go wrong with nationwide unisex bathrooms? This is but another essential step along the pathway to their egalitarian utopia.

Liberals hit the liberal OCD "daily double" by demonstrating their "tail-wags-dog" *control* of forcing the 99.7% majority to make the absurd concession of genderless bathrooms to the 0.3% minority…*plus* the *moral superiority* of rescuing America's suddenly "helpless" and discriminated-against transgender population. What these people have been doing for bathroom facilities for, say, the last century or so is not relevant to the liberal who demands *fairness* for this oppressed class NOW! It is no coincidence that this "issue" suddenly became white-hot in the final year of our historic first metro-sexual president.

If transgender advocacy is the liberal OCD daily double, then Islamophilia is the double trifecta because it brings with it incrementally the liberal obsessions of race *and* fairness. As a bromide for liberal OCD, Islamophelia is the right tool for the job.

Liberals see everything through the prism of *race* first. It is a symptom of "white guilt" by people who condemn their own imaginary "white privilege." "Racism!" is the universal liberal cry for anything that does not conform to their pre-conceived utopian outcome…e.g., Obama's failed presidency was due to opposition by "racists" (no explanation required for why he was elected in 2008 and re-elected in 2012 because that subverts the narrative). Also, Donald J. Trump's election in 2016 has been attributed to "white supremacists;" (had the also white Hillary Clinton won, no such explanation required.)

In the Middle East we have approximately 7 million predominately white Israelis in a nation the size of New Jersey (U.S. fifth smallest state). They are surrounded by 100+ million predominately dark-skinned Muslims occupying several million square miles of land. The Israelis live in relative prosperity while the Muslims live in poverty and squalor. It is instantly apparent to any liberal that this inequity is due to *racial* injustice, and that victimhood status must be assigned to Muslims. Our liberal superhero now becomes an advocate for the Muslim "race."

It is also apparent that "the playing field must be leveled" and this egregious Middle Eastern socio-economic injustice must be corrected. In the interest of *fairness*, wealth must be redistributed and Israelis must be punished for their crimes of greed...for in the "zero sum game" liberal mindset, every dollar of wealth possessed by a white-skinned Israeli is solely because it was stolen from their regional neighbor dark-skinned Muslim. Islamophelia no more complicated than that.

Remember, to the *fairness*-obsessed liberal, *fairness* does not mean equality of <u>opportunity</u>; it means equality of <u>outcome</u>. It does not mean that everyone lines up at the 100 meter dash <u>starting</u> line equally... it means that everyone crosses the <u>finish</u> line simultaneously...and this becomes the *fairness* obsession. Effectively it means that no one may run faster than the slowest runner, and that <u>no one is allowed to excel</u>. It is this obsession with sameness that gives socialism its historical 100.000% failure rate.

That the root cause of the Israeli economic success is anything other than *race* would *never* occur to the *race*- obsessed liberal. In reality, Israeli children receive a Western-standard quality education. Juxtapose this with the Muslim culture which places zero value on education. If they read at all, it is only one book, the Quran. Their idea of education is teaching their children how to strap on a suicide vest, field strip an AK-47, behead an infidel, and inculcating them with videos filled with hatred toward Israel, America, Western Europe, and any religion other than their own.

It is my steadfast assertion that until the millennium+ old Middle Eastern Muslim culture reforms itself to embrace the education standards of the rest of mankind irrespective of skin color, there will continue to be envy, jealousy, hatred, strife, and mayhem there. They will continue to fail in the global market place of ideas. A century ago their education deficit could be camouflaged in their little corner of the world. This is no longer possible on a globe which shrinks each day from improvements in travel and communication technology. And as the world shrinks and its inhabitants are metaphorically compressed together, Muslims take no responsibility for falling behind the rest of the civilized world, *vis a vis*, their education deficit...any more than Hillary Clinton will take responsibility for her 2016 election defeat.

They will continue to seek out and perpetrate murder and mayhem on "infidels" like Israel who are the imagined cause (scapegoat) of their failure. They will look about the world as they are now able to do and covet the possessions that result from the economy of an educated people. They will not understand why they cannot keep up. The envy turns to resentment, hatred, and violence toward the West. Meanwhile, just like Hillary Clinton, the real scapegoat is staring them in the mirror daily.

Is there anyone who believes that if Israel ceased to exist as a nation tomorrow that the Palestinians wouldn't overrun the land turn it instantly into the poverty, squalor and despair of Gaza? Is there anyone who thinks that the Palestinians wouldn't then automatically create a new strawman who is the cause of their failure and seek to violently destroy them?

Summed up in a single sentence, education is the anecdote for radical Islam. They must be driven by the hope of a brighter economic future, not hatred of non-conformity to Islam.

And precisely what are the chances this embrace of world-scale education standards by Muslims will ever happen? That a centuries old culture which doesn't advocate education for females *at all* will reverse itself? That the mentality that *success* equals murdering your neighbor and stealing his property will reverse itself? There are two chances: slim and none...and Slim just left town.

In the Middle East, persecution of homosexuals, Christians, and women is common Muslim practice. Of course, the mayhem is no longer confined to the Middle East, but is spreading like a California wildfire to the West. The radical Islamic global strategy appears to be invade and infect the West with the anti-education culture, dragging Western culture backward by a millennium+ in the process.

It must be pointed out here that race outranks gender, sexual orientation, and surely religion (particularly when the religion is Christianity) on the liberal totem pole of victimhood. This is why the Muslim persecution of homosexuals, Christians, and women does not rise even to the classification of "collateral damage" within the liberal mindset.

The liberal tolerance of Muslim persecution of homosexuals is a barometer for liberal hatred of Christianity, which liberals view as a clear and present danger to their very paranoid existence. They are perfectly willing to tolerate Muslims pushing suspected homosexuals off the top of buildings in the Middle East as a show of support for Islam, the enemy of Christianity. Just look the other way and pretend it never happened.

So now the invasion and non-assimilation of Muslims threatens civilization itself in Western Europe. Massacres like Berlin, Charlie Hebdo, and Champs-Elysees Avenue in Paris, Barcelona, Brussels, Nice, the World Trade Center and Pentagon, Ft. Hood, Boston, Orlando, San Bernardino, Chattanooga, *et al.* are becoming all too increasingly commonplace in the West. The lone European country which has not been overrun by the Middle Eastern violent crime wave is Poland, which has not allowed *any* Middle Eastern immigration.

After each attack in America, Obama went to excruciating lengths to warn Americans of an imaginary imminent "Muslim backlash" that has *never* happened. Astonishingly, he showed zero empathy toward the Westerners who were the victims of mass murder and mayhem that *actually* occurred. Simultaneously, he found the imaginary backlash by imaginary American "bitter clingers" reprehensible. "That's not who we are as Americans!" he repeatedly scolded the American citizenry. We recall the National Prayer Breakfast (02.05.15) where Obama told his audience *"Humanity has been grappling with these questions throughout human history,"* speaking of the murderous acts generic religion can inspire. *"And lest we get on our high horse and think this is unique to some other place, remember that during the Crusades and the Inquisition, people committed terrible deeds in the name of Christ. In our home country, slavery and Jim Crow all too often was justified in the name of Christ."* Can the omnipresent *"That's not who we are!"* be far behind?

This *"teachable moment"* (an Obama-patented specialty) was less than one month after the *Charlie Hebdo* massacre in Paris. Two radical Islamic terrorists forced their way into the offices of the French satirical weekly newspaper *Charlie Hebdo* in Paris. Armed with rifles and other weapons, they murdered 12 people and wounded 11 others. The terrorists identified themselves as Al Qaida-Yemen. In Obamaspeak, this was *not* terrorism, it was *"workplace violence"* based upon his Ft. Hood, TX, massacre precedent. *"Teachable moment"* is liberal dog whistle-ese for a red herring to divert the news cycle away from the truth, in this instance the latest outbreak of radical Islamic atrocities.

Throughout it all, Obama never once uttered the words "radical Islamic terrorist." It was almost as though he was a covert Muslim.

None of this provides any clue to the liberal as to the terrorist attacks and anarchy that is in store for the U. S. should we remain on this path of the Obama-led uncontrolled invasion by Middle Eastern

Muslims. Liberals are uniquely able to will this tsunami of evidence "into the cornfield" (reference to 1961 "The Twilight Zone" episode) just like the imaginary "*Hands up, don't shoot!*" the imaginary "Russian collusion," or the imaginary "Benghazi was caused by a crappy YouTube video." They choose instead to "focus" on their unspoken obsessions, and Obama's obsession to "*fundamentally transform America...*" into a minority white country by any means necessary. The Middle Eastern invasion is a key component of the Obama transformation.

Those who would voice opposition to the liberal obsession I call Islamophilia are sanctimoniously decried as "*Racist!*", "*Xenophobe!*" and "Islamophobe!"....to which I respond with "*Islamophile!*" This term also accurately describes the left coast Nano-wit Federal Judge Robart with no common sense, no access to government intelligence, no touch with reality and no respect for the law. Robart ruled against President Trump's hostile state targeted travel-ban in early 2017. They effectively ruled *for* the continued Obama Middle Eastern invasion from the most lawless of countries hostile to America. Their moral hubris was underwhelming. Apparently the SCOTUS wasn't impressed, either.

Blacks obviously qualify for the liberals' "favored minority status" under the racial exemption. However they earn liberal demerits for being predominately Christian and being largely already assimilated into American culture. Also, the black population growth has stagnated due to liberal abortion policy, meaning there is no growth potential in the voting booth.

Liberals have patronized blacks for over half a century. Many blacks now realize their votes have been bought for overpriced promises and under-delivered results. ***"Poor people have been voting Democrat for 50 years...and they're still poor."* – Charles Barclay.** I will attach this inferred adder to Mr. Barclay's observation: "*...and Democrats intend to keep them there forever.*"

Liberals have destroyed the black family unit in exchange for a minimal welfare check. This decades-old practice has caused immeasurable grief, misery, hardship, loss of human potential, and generational poverty within the black community. It was a conscious decision on the part of the Democrat party in the 1960s to buy black votes with government welfare checks and displace black fathers from the black family unit.

Perhaps Dr. Thomas Sowell may be best quoted on this issue which is so crucial to the well-being of America: ***"The assumption that spending more of the taxpayer's money will make things better has survived all kinds of evidence that it has made things worse. The black family, which survived slavery, discrimination, poverty, wars and depressions, began to come apart as the federal government moved in with its well-financed programs to 'help'."*** I think it is now obvious that the federal government was not seeking to help the black family, Dr. Sowell, but instead enslave it as laid out in the 1960s LBJ plan.

We fast-forward to the 21st century and now 72% of black children grow up without a father. This is particularly devastating for young black males. By the time they are teenagers, their mothers can no longer control them. They get no discipline in the public school because liberal policy has removed it, along with all traces of faith, religion, and God. It should be no surprise that 80% of male inmates come from single parent homes.

What then are the influences on the teenage black male's direction? If he is fortunate, athletics. A good coach will teach him that performance and results count, as well as self-discipline, work ethic, team-work, and team comradery. A good coach will become the youngsters' role model and mentor.

If not athletics, the default father guidance comes from fellow black teenagers in the street. Black NFL players protest the disproportionately high black incarceration rate. This is where a young male without the guidance of a father winds up, regardless of skin color.

The predominately black (75%) NFL players think the problem is with the judicial system, and specifically police departments. It is not. The problem is the destruction of the black family by the Democrat Party and fatherless black families.

One of the fundamental guiding principles of economics is that you incentivize activity by subsidizing it. Conversely, you discourage activity by taxing it.

Of course this image is *"Racist!"* because the bear is black. Perhaps a polar bear would have been more politically correct.

Democrat politicians understood this principle when they gave welfare checks to single black mothers. Their faux compassion has created chaos in the black community in exchange for their own re-election.

A monthly government check *cannot* replace a father. This is exponentially more important for teenage males. I know this to be the case based on personal experience.

I was a teenage male in the 1960s. I played some sports, did well academically, and was an Eagle Scout. There was plenty of opportunity to get into trouble, but it was nothing compared to the hazards facing teenage boys today. I was fortunate enough to have my father's sound guidance through my teenage years. He died when I was 20. Up until his death, he was the beacon of light that showed me the way. It was priceless.

Early on, doing the right thing may have been out of fear of punishment. Early on it may have been "because I said so," or "Do as I say, not as I do." But as I aged even after his death, I have come to understand you do the right thing because it is the right thing to do. You must be motivated for the right reasons: God, family, and country above all else, the emphasis always on right over wrong. ***All motivation is intrapersonal.***

Part of doing the right thing involves respect: for others, their rights, and their pursuit of life, liberty, and happiness; respect for *authority* in the home, school and public venues. If these ideas did not come from my father, he certainly reinforced them.

Authority in public means the police. The police are the only thing that stands between the general public and anarchy. Without enforcement of the law, there is no law.

Former San Francisco Forty Niners quarterback Colin Kaepernick started the NFL "tradition" of "taking a knee" during the pregame national anthem. He once wore a pair of socks which depicted the police as pigs during a game. I can imagine a home invasion robbery at the Kaepernick mansion in San Jose, CA. Who's he gonna call? Ghostbusters???

No, he calls 9-1-1...

Kaepernick to 9-1-1: "They're shooting at me!"

9-1-1 to Kaepernick: "Join the (Insert your own expletive) club!!! <Click>

I personally admire what the police do in exchange for very low pay and much personal risk. My father taught me this code of conduct when interfacing with a police officer: (1) Keep your mouth shut unless spoken to. (2) Respond to questions with *"Yes, sir"* or *"No, sir."* (3) ALWAYS obey the officer's commands in a spirit of cooperation.

My father's instruction did not include hysterical outbursts like "Pigs in a blanket, fry 'em like bacon!" or "What do we want? Dead cops! When do we want 'em? Now!" designed to escalate acrimony.

Where does this attitude come from? It does *not* come from a father who knows better. It comes from an ill-conceived fantasy of street machismo formed in the *absence* of a father. It comes from professional race hustlers, "community organizers," and Democrat politicians who peddle victimhood, disunity and even anarchy for a living. They are all not only peddling an excuse for failure, they are peddling failure itself. They are peddling despair and hopelessness. They are peddling hatred, anger, and class warfare because "Your problems are someone else's fault."

It comes from a fatherless hood and streets that are saturated with the macho-belligerent victimhood mentality because of decades of relentless liberal propaganda. And they are peddling generational indentured servitude on the Democrat plantation.

America witnessed that mentality for eight years while Barack Obama was in the White House. He peddled victimhood to himself first long ago. Then he inseminated America with it.

Racial acrimony in America has decreased significantly since Obama left office. This is not a coincidence. Whereas Obama supported the anarchist group Black Lives Matter (BLM), Trump has shown no tolerance. This sets the tone for the entire massive government apparatus.

In addition to Trump's step-change shift in the enforcement of the rule of civil law, there has been a similar attitudinal shift within our federal government on border enforcement. Illegal border crossings are down 70% since Trump took office. The shift in U.S. government attitude toward ISIS has produced similar positive results. ISIS territorial control and revenue have declined 70-80% in 2017. The Dow Jones Industrial Average (DJIA) is up 28% since Trump's election victory. Economic growth for 2Q2017 (Trump's first full quarter in office) was 2.6% compared to the 2016 average of 1.6% under Obama. This growth is *before* any tax reform or tax cuts are legislated.

Individually, these performance results highlight Obama's ineptitude. Collectively, they form the basis for Trump's impeachment, according to Congressional drama queens Maxine Waters (D-CA), Al Green (D-TX) and Frederica Wilson (D-FL), who have the collective IQ of a blight-infested tumbleweed.

As these barometers of presidential performance soar upward beyond all expectations, the drumbeat of impeachment quickens its pace. Donald Trump is exposing Barack Obama as a Marxist street-clown, which is both "Racist!" *and* impeachable.

Ostensibly, is it clearly racist to show up our historic first black president with these results less than a year into Trump's first term? Is it *prima facie* evidence that Trump is a "white supremacist"? No other reason has yet been cited for the impeachment call to arms by these titans of "liberal logic."

Moreover the very *last* thing Democrats want is another Ronald Reagan (or worse) economic boom to wish away into the cornfield of "The Twilight Zone" history. They haven't successfully gotten rid of the original R^2 legacy of economic success yet.

By all accounts, the primary grievance of the black community with America is "police brutality" and the disproportionate incarceration rate of black males. That is behind the NFL national anthem protests. At this point it is appropriate to review some statistics.

In the United States, there are 14.82 murders per 100K by blacks versus 2.17 per 100K for whites.[3] This means that per capita there are 7x more murders committed by blacks than whites. (For liberals, divide 14.82 by 2.17.)

[3] FBI statistics 2016

These numbers are not a "racist" *opinion*; they are *facts*. The corpses were not taken "out of context"; they did not distort anything to make a political point. They are just dead.

On the positive side, NFL pregame protests during the playing of our national anthem are a major improvement over cop shootings in Dallas and Baton Rouge. The NFL demonstrations against our anthem and our flag are non-violent. It is up to the League to decide whether or not these protests should be allowed to continue. It is *not* up to the League to decide whether or not I ever watch another NFL game.

The number one priority of anyone with OCD is to turn their problem into your problem. It is a universal symptom of the OCDL. The best defense against this motive is recognition, and *not* play *their* game which completely abandons rules of civil discourse and is devoid of all logic. ***It is not possible to have a reasonable discussion with an unreasonable person.***

The pregame national anthem was selected deliberately as a forum to *force* liberalism upon the general public because of liberals' obsession with "relevance" and attention. The purpose of the demonstration is to turn *their* problem into *your* problem. Their problem is that they are in a perpetual state of anxiety because of their mental disorder. They were born that way. They imagine there is relief, some sort of satisfaction in antagonizing you. Of course, they are wrong about that too. Liberals are consistent that way.

The pregame national anthem ceremony has always been intended to be a moment of national unity. It is an ice-cold deluge on the community organizer's arson spree. This makes it a perfect target for liberal malcontents.

The national anthem protest is also an open declaration by the individuals protesting that "I am a victim!" The companion follow up statement is "Pay me money now!!" Liberalism has taught protesters/ rioters that they are *owed* a big payoff for their victimhood status. It is called "reparations."

The anthem protests are a form of liberal bullying, which always involves encroaching on their victim's space, turning *their* problem into *your* problem. NFL fans who paid top dollar to enjoy a sports event are instead first exposed to a distasteful anti-American demonstration by Alinsky-ite "useful idiots" who do not understand they are being used to foment civil unrest. Watching the repulsive display of disrespect for our anthem, our flag, and our nation is not optional. It is front and center on the playing field at the point of maximum audience attention just before the opening kickoff for all to see. They do not protest during the off season, they are silent as a 1920s movie. But come game time in September, you *will* be inseminated with their ideology, a bonus that accompanies the price of admission. Think of it as liberalism's contribution to national harmony.

But could it be that the American people don't want to pay $300 a ticket to be force-fed a repulsive demonstration on social justice by BLM malcontents? Could it be they just wanted to spend a Sunday afternoon enjoying a sporting event free and clear of the non-stop ubiquitous daily political happy horsecrap?

The national anthem protest is a big middle finger salute to America by a mob of millionaire (the average NFL player salary is approximately $2M per year) thugs who have never had a real job in their lives.

It is received with much empathy by the laid-off coal miner in West Virginia; by the out-of-work welder in Des Moines who could be working on the Keystone XL pipeline; by the laid-off waiter in Seattle who was priced out of a job by the minimum wage increase there; and by the U.S. Marine private from Amarillo stationed in Afghanistan.

I use the term "useful idiots" in the classic Alinsky sense. The same operator saboteurs who gave us Occupy Wall Street (OWS), Black Lives Matter (BLM), Trump rally protests of the 2016 campaign, the pink-hatted women's march on Washington DC and Antifa have hijacked the NFL. Their purpose remains unchanged from their predecessors:

1. To provide the illusion of a countermovement to the grassroots TEA Party which formed early during Obama's first term. The left has never gotten over the TEA Party movement. And

2. To create civil unrest in America with the ultimate goal of anarchy.

#BlackLivesMatter (#BLM) is the follow-up racial conflict-based leftist anarchist group to #Occupy-WallStreet (#OWS), which was the failed leftist anarchist class-warfare model. The race based anarchist group #BLM is not to be confused with the declarative sentence "Black lives matter." The sentence is perfectly accurate because it is a subset of another accurate declarative sentence "All lives matter." In fact, there is no real need to break "Black lives matter" out of the larger, more inclusive declarative sentence "All lives matter." Presumably, liberals broadcast themselves as enthusiastically inclusive, except in this instance? At any rate, the declarative sentence "Black lives matter" and the anarchist group "#Black Lives Matter" are non-equivalent synonyms which are designed by liberals to be ambiguous.

Liberals love to wordsmith to manufacture confusion. Any criticism of the anarchist group "#BlackLivesMatter" can and usually will be intentionally conflated into repudiation of the declarative sentence "Black lives matter," serving as instant and irrefutable proof of white supremacist racism. To condemn the anarchist group "#BlackLivesMatter" does not mean you condemn the declarative sentence "Black lives matter," and it does not make anyone a "Racist!"

This is like the (liberal) night club owner who put up "Free drinks tonite!" on the club marquee, then didn't understand why his customers rioted when he explained to them "Free Drinks Tonight" was the name of the band, and drinks were full price. "They are obviously stupid, Your Honor," he later told the judge in the false advertising lawsuit that followed.

Liberals are cleverly accomplished at semantic shape-shifting. Americans should never confuse "clever" with "smart." The criminal who pulls off the armored car heist may well be "clever," but doing 20 years in stir for armed robbery is not "smart."

The left's initial response to the TEA Party was OWS which formed up in September 2011. Its goal was anarchy based on *class warfare*. It fizzled out in the winter of 2011, due primarily due to cold weather. Apparently "occupying Wall Street" is a real drag in the freezing cold of lower Manhattan. Who saw that one coming?

BLM came along in 2013 in the wake of the Trayvon Martin death in Florida, then gained momentum in 2014 after the death of the Michael Brown "Hands up, don't shoot!" episode in Missouri. Its goal was anarchy based on *race warfare*. It lasted longer because unlike OWS, it did not require occupying anything in the freezing cold. Also, it is easier to cultivate racial tension in America than class envy because of the strong American middle class, which socialists seek to sabotage.

Successful class warfare is dependent upon destroying the middle class, which eliminates the bridge between the very rich and the very poor. The American left has not yet vanquished the middle class.

However, the BLM momentum is clearly waning because America sees it for what it is: leftist-manufactured civil unrest.

An NFL player who would sabotage his own livelihood to the point of ruination for someone else's obsession must qualify for the very top end of the "useful idiot" scale. For the majority of players participating in the let's-take-a-knee 15 minutes of fame jackpot, the NFL is their only real shot at long-term financial security. They are being played by the far left but are too blinded by their desperation for victim status to realize it.

To deliberately antagonize their fan base has already done damage to the NFL. The questions are (1) how much damage is yet to be done; and (2) will it be permanent? My guesses are (1) substantial, and (2) yes because the players have learned nothing from the already-declining ticket sales and television ratings. Maybe they think it has no impact on them personally because they have contracts. The contracts will mean nothing when the revenue dries up. The operative word is "bankruptcy."

More questions about the NFL/BLM insurrection: what happens when the next new stadium comes before the *public* for approval and local taxpayer-funding subsidy? There are 32 NFL teams. For the sake of simplicity, let us say the average stadium useful life is 32 years, which is probably not too far off. Then higher math (I earned an "A" in *Differential Equations and Laplace Transforms*) leads me to the idea that a one-stadium-per-year replacement schedule is required to maintain the current state of the NFL stadium fleet. Without this replacement schedule, it will not take many years before game site venues become unacceptable to fans. It might be best for the NFL not to antagonize its public fan-base if they ever expect to *publically* finance a new stadium anywhere.

What about the current federal income tax exemption for the NFL's phony "nonprofit" status? The future is a mine field for the NFL given their current belligerent anti-American course.

Not all 32 NFL franchises are going to make it, given the current trajectory of fan withdrawal. I see the NFL crisis reaching critical mass before the end of the current season, as game ticket prices hit single digits for many franchises.

NFL players obviously think that America needs them more than they need America. ***"And falling feels like flying until you hit the ground." – Chris Stapleton song lyric.*** This misconception is the product of a failed education system where self-esteem is our most important product and *YOU* are the center of the universe. For the NFL, the "Great Awakening" is close at hand.

All of the financial carnage is for the cause of protesting alleged or imagined "police brutality." If we examine black murder victims in the United States**, we find:

Blacks killed by police = 1%

Blacks killed by whites = 2%

Blacks killed by blacks = 97%

The 600+ murders year to date in Chicago, which are part of the 97% statistic, are of no concern to liberals. Yet "Hands up, don't shoot!" which *never* happened, but has turned into an annual riot in Ferguson, MO, is *New York Times* (NYT) page 1 above the fold. Go figure.

The Chicago murder rate story does *not* fit the liberal victimhood narrative of racial oppression of blacks by whites. The narrative that Chicago *does* fit is that of a decaying northern city run by corrupt liberal Democrats turned into a combat zone. There is *no* room for the truth in the liberal victimhood narrative.

Conversely, the Ferguson storyline *does* fit the liberal victimhood narrative. It is the narrative that "Racism not only exists in the United States; it is metastasizing exponentially!" It is the liberal MSM's ticket back to the 1960s where they can join in this valiant fight against the ultimate evil of (white supremacist) America! The liberals who advance the liberal agenda of division in America, whether it is racial, class, gender, or sexual orientation have astonishingly ordained themselves as the saviors of the victims they have created. This is the power of the MSM for as long as anyone continues to believe what they are peddling. So now we understand.

This is how we have come to learn the name of Michael Brown in Ferguson, but we cannot name *any* of the shooting victims in Chicago?

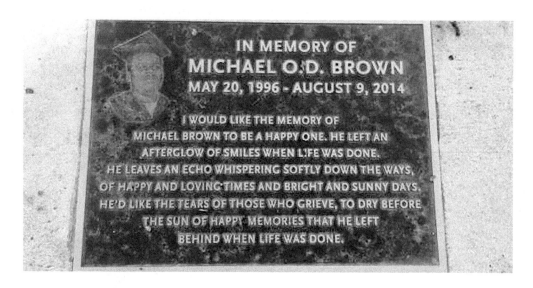

Could we conclude that liberals actually believe in the Joseph Stalin quote: ***"A single death is a tragedy; a million deaths is a statistic"***?

No, that is not what is in play here. What is in play is racial division which allows liberals to peddle victimhood and civil unrest to a minority. Could we sarcastically conclude from this that liberals believe only *certain* black lives matter? Only the ones who provide momentum to their errant liberal agenda? An emphatic "Yes!"

Obviously not every NFL player is participating in the pregame ceremony protest. Of the ones who are, it would be interesting to know what percentage of them grew up in fatherless homes. It would be equally interesting to know how many of the "disproportionately" incarcerated grew up in fatherless homes. Likewise with those convicted of murder. If we had access to that data, I suspect we would get a confirmation of what the *real* problem is.

"Though this nation has proudly thought of itself as an ethnic melting pot, in things racial we have always been and continue to be, in too many ways, essentially a nation of cowards." – **Eric Holder (02.18.09)**. *This* is the conversation on race relations in America that Eric Holder is too cowardly to have.

Mr. Holder is a Democrat. The Democrats are responsible for the current state of welfare which has long since destroyed the black family in America. Even more sinister, this was no accident. It was a conscious welfare-for-votes scheme invented during the Lyndon B. Johnson (LBJ) presidential era and continued by Democrats through today. It was a scheme to displace black fathers from their families with government checks.

Very simply, no father in the family means no discipline, no mentor, and no respect for authority. This is particularly crucial for young black males who will have to learn these things one way or the other. The father is the easy way. The penal system is the hard way.

How does America right the ship from this Democrat-inflicted epic catastrophe? Mr. Holder would have America believe the answer is to legalize the crimes and handcuff the police. Certainly, legalizing crime would have made his job as Attorney General easier. It could allow him to spend his workday pursuing "social justice," defying Congress to the point of contempt citation and harassing local police departments at taxpayer expense, and *reparations*.

Deeply embedded within the subject of American slavery based victimhood is the idea of "reparations". "Reparation" is defined as anything paid or done to make up for a wrongdoing, or the act of making up for a wrongdoing. An example would be money paid for breaking an item in a store. A wrongful death judgement (*e.g.*, O.J. Simpson vs. Goldman) would also be a reparation.

Within the context of the American socio-economic landscape, reparations means a tax on white people for the transgression of being white. The premise of this tax is that white people remain guilty for the crime of slavery which ended in 1865 at the conclusion of the American Civil War. For mathematically challenged liberals, that is over 150 years ago.

From a legal perspective, the asinine scam is a complete non-starter. It has no basis in constitutional law and is, in fact, in perfect diametric opposition to the Civil Rights Act of 1964, which prohibits discrimination on the basis of "*race, color, religion, sex or national origin.*" Proponents of reparations would argue that it is implied (somewhere) that the Civil Rights Act of 1964 does not apply to discrimination against *white* people. ***Irony is always lost on the stupid.***

The only plausible legal pathway for a reparations ploy by the left would be through a left coast federal judge like James Robart in Washington state (Chapter 7); then on the Ninth Circus Clown Car of Appeals in San Francisco; then on to death before the SCOTUS.

But the stakes are high. There is an entire industry of race-baiting malcontents (no need to name names) who are looking to parlay this ultimate jackpot on to their ticket to fortune and the Social Justice Hall of Fame….perhaps even having a national holiday declared in their honor. We can envision an entire platoon…no, make that a division of cash thirsty trial lawyers eager to make a career out of this crusade in the fashion of asbestosis or big tobacco. Then there are hordes of liberal politicians who will seize upon any calls to redistribute wealth, which is an open invitation to the all-you-can-eat buffet of graft and perpetual re-election. And too we have white guilt riddled liberals would then be able to pay for their psychological disorder with someone else's money. Finally, we must not overlook the minorities who will be cashing in on reparations with multiple EBT cards. The reparations bunco hoax has something-for-nothing possibilities that make the Nigerian prince email scam look like penny ante poker. Charles Ponzi would be proud of the reparations parasite mafia.

Do not look for this one to ever go away. Even with no legal future, reparations is a segue to liberal's two favorite divisive topics, slavery and victimhood. Stormy Daniels will die of old age long before the usual suspects listed above let go of their chance at the reparations meal ticket.

But just for grins and giggles, let's imagine that a reparations mandate survives the legal challenge process. Who should be liable for this "social justice" debt? Applying logic, we ask ourselves "Where did slavery start?"

We travel back in time to the 18th and 19th centuries. African *Muslims* rounded up and enslaved fellow Africans in chains to sell for *profit*. This was the crucial first step in the slavery process. The practice continues to this day with African Muslim groups like Boko Haram of #BringBackOurGirls notoriety.

I personally do not know many Americans descended from African Muslims. Only one comes to mind.

Based on their position of prominence in initiating the slavery migration, I think it is highly appropriate that African Muslim descended Americans, particularly those with *zero* slavery heritage, be the *first* to pay the reparations toll. Also, I think a 100% toll rate is appropriate. I would anticipate the lifelong "social justice" warrior Obama would plead *nolo contendere* to this judgement.

Let us approach the reparations "issue" from an entirely different perspective, that of open borders. The prosperity of the American socio-economic system has left many white liberals with the psychological phenomenon of "white guilt". They believe that America's ill-gotten prosperity results from exploitation of non-American non-white victims worldwide, not by anything I elucidated in Chapter 6. They are literally embarrassed by the success of America and their own standard of living. Their attitude is perhaps best summed up in a passage from Obama's book "Dreams from My Father": *"White folks greed runs a world in need."*

This is the "Blame America first (for everything)" cluster of perennial malcontents who would gladly give away American welfare, healthcare, education, cash, and even America itself to anyone who can crawl, stumble, run, swim, drive, fly or leap across our southern border. They flatly reject America's greatness (Chapter 6) as resulting from anything other than America's greed. Their magnanimous giveaway of America's wealth is a down payment on America's "global reparation" debt, which is long overdue.

We must note here that liberals do not seek to give away *their* wealth, which they are free to do at any time but never do. Instead they seek to give away America's wealth (translation: *your* wealth). This is a recurring theme with liberals: obnoxiously encroaching upon the space of others as therapy for their own massive psychological deficit...bullying.

Handcuffing police worked out very well in Baltimore, MD. Six police officers were charged with various crimes ranging from second degree murder to illegal arrest after black prisoner Freddie Gray sustained fatal injuries during transportation to jail in Baltimore (April 12, 2015).

The six Baltimore police officers were prosecuted by Baltimore State's Attorney Marilyn Mosby, who is black and whose resume includes an appearance as a contestant on the television show "Judge Judy." *"I heard your call for no justice, no peace,"* Mosby announced at a press conference early on after the Freddie Gray death. *"Your peace is needed while I try to deliver justice for this young man."* There was no mention of justice for the six police officers charged, half of whom were black.

Violence, rioting, and looting occurred in Baltimore during the time surrounding Freddie Gray's funeral in late April 2015. (Black) Baltimore Mayor Stephanie Rawlings-Blake ordered police to stand down during the riots.

There were separate trials for the six officers charged. The first officer's trial ended in a mistrial. The next three were acquitted on all counts. Cases against the remaining two were dropped in July 2016. Currently five of the six police officers charged by Ms. Mosby are suing her for malicious prosecution, defamation, and invasion of privacy. Eventually, there will be justice for *all*, even the police officers.

Ms. Mosby is a typical liberal who overpromised and under-delivered. This made for excellent cable TV theater while the spotlight was on Baltimore. The facts and evidence never supported her ludicrous overcharging spree. I personally take this opportunity to nominate her for the Mike Nifong* Award for Prosecutorial Excellence.

*Mike Nifong was the disgraced prosecutor in the Duke lacrosse rape case.

But who knows, Ms. Mosby may yet ascend to national prominence. This is exactly the resume enhancement the Democrat Party is looking for: Skin color? Check! Gender? Check! "Compassion?" Check! "Truth to Power?" Check! Crusader for "social justice?" Check! Results? Never mind.

Where does the Freddie Gray episode leave Baltimore? Ms. Mosby's performance was initially lauded by the black community in Baltimore, but outraged the Baltimore police who began a slowdown. The arrest rate plunged, and the murder rate doubled within a month. By the end of 2015, the murder rate in Baltimore spiked to the highest level this century and a 63% increase over the preceding year. In the light of clearly demonstrated non-support from city officials, the Baltimore police can hardly be blamed for a more passive job performance.

So here we are again with another Black Lives Matter success story: outrage followed by rioting at a racial flashpoint, police in retreat, *more* dead black citizens in the streets of Baltimore and the liberal MSM has no interest in covering the aftermath because it does not support their narrative preference. Welcome to Chicago, Baltimore!

Also, the post Freddie Gray incident increase in Baltimore murder rate can be directly attributed to the Eric Holder liberal attitude that the police are the problem and they need to be constrained…just as surely as the death of U.S. Border Agent Brian Terry's death can be directly linked to the asinine Obama/Holder "Fast and Furious" gun running to the Mexican drug cartels.

We return to Mr. Holder's *"nation of cowards"* accusation of America. We can start by acknowledging what the *real* problem is. The elephant in the room *ain't* the University of Alabama team mascot. It is fatherless black families. The liberal epithet "toxic masculinity" is a dog whistle for fatherless young males. Even more fundamental than that are liberals like Mr. Holder who created the *incentive* for fatherless black families. It is my prediction that the words "toxic masculinity" will become inseparable within the liberal lexicon by the end of the decade, in the fashion of "unfettered capitalism" and "undocumented immigrant," and "tax-cuts-for-the-wealthy." But the truth is there is no such thing as "toxic masculinity" outside of fatherless homes created by "toxic liberals", Democrats in pursuit of the votes for welfare transfer payments *quid pro quo*.

We must acknowledge how it was done, who did it and why. It was done with welfare bribery. It was done as a conscious effort by Democrats 50 years ago to guarantee themselves the black vote with the "compassionate" head-fake of low expectations. Their goal was to set up a permanent Democrat plantation of enslaved voters at the taxpayers' expense.

Now a half century+ later, this scam is run by the political descendants of LBJ and its founding Democrat fathers. That would be *you*, Mr. Holder. Why would they discontinue it? It has worked so well for so long. Using public funds to buy votes for themselves while basking in the sunlight of their own self-praise as "compassionate"…it hardly gets any better than that! Any dissenters are "heartless" and will be attacked not only by the scam *meisters*, but also their liberal enablers in the MSM. To protest the Democrat plantation scam is political suicide for any opponent.

Based on intermittent "bat signals" from Mr. Holder, we observe that he holds presidential aspirations for 2020. In that case he will need a running mate. The right tool for the job?

Anthony D. Weiner was able to plea multiple accusations of cybercrime down to a single count of transferring obscene material to a (15-year old) minor and is now doing a 21-month sentence in federal stir. He should be out no later than August 2019, in plenty of time for the 2020 campaign.

Everyone in this political kabuki dance is aware of their role. People are not stupid. What then is the way off the Democrat plantation?

Could it be that the way out is the same as the way in? I refer to the age-old common sensical axiom of economics: *"If you want less of an activity or behavior, you tax it. If you want more, you subsidize it."* This axiom can be applied to fatherless children subsidized with government welfare transfer payments.

Then welfare reform is the solution? Nobody said there were any easy answers. This situation has been over half a century in getting to where it is now. It will *not* be reversed overnight.

Let me the first to acknowledge that welfare reform would instantly receive a five "R" (for "RACIST!!!!!") rating from Democrats, liberals, and their MSM tools for two reasons: (1) it is the only thing that would reverse the 50+ years of failure they have dumped upon America; and (2) it would break the cycle of codependent bribery that keeps Democrats in political office. Liberals are repulsed to nausea by the very idea of welfare reform.

I am not so personally invested in my own ideas that I am not open to any better ideas. Before the chorus of "Racist!" begins from the left, I am also betting Dr. Sowell (photo below) would agree with me: ***"Few skills are so well rewarded as the ability to convince parasites that they are victims."***

Without question race tops the liberal totem pole of victimology. Liberals are superheros whose mission in life is to defend dark-skinned victims of white oppression. Muslims are at the top of the racial victims subcategory by virtue of their natural opposition to Judeo-Christians. Race towers over gender and sexual orientation on the podium of liberal victimology.

There is ample evidence to support this. We know that in the Middle East, homosexuals are hanged, stoned to death, and thrown blindfolded off the tops of buildings by Muslims as a "religious" practice. Liberals have no problem with this because somebody told them *"Islam is a religion of peace,"* and that it comports with what they *want* to believe. Muslims also publicly stone women to death for alleged civil offenses.

This also appears to be of little concern to American liberals because it cannot happen in America… at least until liberals are back in charge of immigration policy.

Iranian President Mahmoud Ahmadinejad gave a speech at Columbia University on 09.24.07. In response to a question about the recent execution of two gay men there after the speech, the exalted president remarked *"In Iran we don't have homosexuals like in your country."* Loud laughter broke out from the audience of near a thousand Ivy League prepsters. Ahmadinejad instantly silenced the laughter with his follow-up chilling comment: *"Perhaps you can tell me where they are."*

On June 12, 2016, Omar Mateen, a 29-year-old American-born Islamic terrorist of Afghan Pashtun parents, killed 49 people and wounded 58 others in an attack inside "The Pulse," a *gay* nightclub in Orlando, Florida. He was shot and killed by multiple Orlando Police Department (OPD) officers after a three-hour hostage standoff. In a 911 call during the shooting, Mateen identified himself as *"Mujahedeen,"* *"Islamic Soldier,"* and *"Soldier of God."*

Soon after, President Obama described the shooting as an *"act of hate"* and an *"act of terror,"* *not* an act of "Islamic terror." The MSM storyline was the predictable #1 narrative off the liberal journalism Rolodex: "The gun did it! We must ban all guns *now*!!!" with a touch of "lone wolf" seasoning to *"Kick it up a notch!"* — Emril Lagasse.

The fact that the shooter was a self-described Islamic terrorist who admitted hating gays was of no interest to the MSM "journalists." This aspect of the story was ignored because of Muslims toprung position on the liberal victimhood ladder, well above gays. It received little mention outside of Republican candidate Donald Trump, who condemned it for what it actually was: a _radical Islamic terrorist_ attack.

The message from liberals to LBGTQIAs* is quite clear: get to the back of the bus. When massacred by a psychotic radical Islamic terrorist, they were of no more use to liberals than black murder victims in Chicago.

*Liberals who cannot tell right from wrong are able to detect 80+ gender types. I must plead ignorance on the latest additions to the liberal alphabet soup of sexual orientation/identity. I had to look the "QIA" up on the internet.

I predict this alphabet soup will grow because of the liberal obsession to peddle victimhood to an ever-expanding market. Adding more letters to the soup expands the liberal base. It reinforces the liberal obsession with "diversity" and "inclusion." It serves to illustrate the Democrat-sloganeered "big tent party" label. "Pro-lifers, pro 1st and 2nd Amendment Americans, pro border security Americans, police, military, etc. need not apply" in the fine print below the "Big Tent" label.

To be clear, I do not disparage anyone's sexual or gender orientation. I condemn liberals who are desperate to manufacture an "issue" from a non-issue in an attempt to claim their imagined "moral superiority" while America's real problems are ignored.

If history is any indication, we might get a couple of new letters a year. I see "P" for pedophile, "N" for necrophile, and perhaps a couple of more "B"s for bigamist and bestiality as potential sexual-deviant behavioral nominees to join the current *"Star Wars"* bar scene line up. ***"Some men see things as they are, and ask why. I dream of things that never were, and ask why not."* – Robert F. Kennedy.** Right on, Mr. Attorney General!

As an addendum to this discussion, we see that Canada has a big lead on the United States in the alphabet soup gender sweepstakes. They are up to LG²BDT³IQ²A²P ² (count 'em, 15!), and are now requiring teachers to take inclusiveness training courses to accommodate these gender identities. Canada is the *pathfinder* ("Racist!" language again!) for the United States. This should be no surprise. Their Prime Minister qualifies for at least half of the letters. When I hear him correct his fellow Canadian country folk with "peoplekind" (which is *not* a word in any thesaurus I have found) instead of "mankind", my visceral reaction is "Nobody is that anal." Upon further review, I was obviously wrong about that.

Let me be clear about one thing: I pass no judgement on anyone for their gender identity, sexual orientation, or practice (as long as it is legal). What they do in privacy is of no concern to me, <u>as long as they do not pester me with it</u>. But anyone who thinks they are *not* going to pester you with it does not understand what liberalism is.

Liberals wake up in the morning irritated by their mental disorder. It goes downhill from there. Their number one priority is to turn *their* mental problem into *your* problem by any means at hand. They imagine that there is psychological relief from their mental disorder in annoying America with distracting and irrelevant causes such as public LBGTQIAWTF "acceptance." It is their right and responsibility to annoy you *ad nauseum* with their virtue signaled social justice big heartedness. It is a form of bullying, no different than the NFL pregame national anthem exhibition.

America faces dozens of problems more exigent than LBGT "acceptance." The problem I have is when it is unnecessarily force-fed to America.

The most notable recent example of my "force-fed" allegation that comes to mind was the ESPN coverage of the 2014 NFL draft featuring newly self-identified gay University of Missouri defensive end Michael Sam. I do not remember who the first player chosen in the 2014 draft was, but I will always remember Mr. Sam was drafted in the 7th (last) round by the St. Louis Rams thanks to the non-stop ESPN coverage. That was the last time I watched any of the annual ESPN NFL draft coverage. Since then, I have given up watching the NFL altogether due to other liberal "social justice" activism. When the sports news becomes how many players knelt during the national anthem and not the game scores, it is time to move on.

In a related matter, ESPN recently announced yet another 150 employee layoff. They have no clue why they are losing paying subscribers and revenue.

In full disclosure, even as a small kid I have always thought that *"America, the Beautiful"* was a much more aesthetically pleasing song than the *"Star-spangled Banner."* Sadly, in a moment of colossal oversight, I was not consulted when the *"Star-spangled Banner"* was adopted as the national anthem in 1931.

Star Spangled Banner

Another squandered opportunity by Washington D.C.

Now America is bombarded with an avalanche of sexual misconduct accusations, mostly years if not decades old. The defendants are predominately white liberal males; the plaintiffs are predominately white females. The reason the defendants are predominantly liberal is because liberals do not acknowledge the individual or individual responsibility. This leaves them with no moral compass. It is also why they are openly contemptuous of the law.

Is this the latest leftist iteration at civil unrest via gender warfare? If so, many liberal males are being hoisted on their own liberal petard in sacrifice for "the cause." Is the ultimate target Donald Trump? You can bet on two things: (1) the left is not doing this randomly, there is a target; and (2) the target is not Al Franken or Matt Lauer; they are merely collateral damage swept away by the neo-Puritanical "all-males-are-rapists" tsunami.

It has always been a little strange to me that liberals give women "minority" status since they comprise 50.8% of the U.S. population (2010 census data). But within the context of liberal victimology, where everyone except straight white males are victims, women are classified as an oppressed minority. The liberal goal here is *not* reality but to harvest the minority voter blocks, you understand. In that sense, the women's vote is the liberals' mother lode (double *entendre*), so to speak.

Despite the massive numbers, women rank at the bottom of the liberal victimology ladder. Perhaps this is because they have been voting in national elections for almost a century. (The 19th Amendment to the United States Constitution giving women the right to vote was passed in 1920.) Perhaps it is because women (and particularly single women) are more dependent on the government safety net than men. Most likely it is the Democrats' liberal position on abortion that irreversibly attracts women voters.

Women voter support is reversible if the Democrat Party continues to slide over the left edge of the flat political spectrum. As with other damage to the party brand during the last eight years, Democrats can thank Barack Obama to the abrupt leftward surge toward political irrelevance.

The evidence that race trumps gender in the liberal hierarchy was never more evident than in the 2008 presidential campaign. After eight years of George W. Bush and his highly unpopular Iraq War, 2008 was clearly the Democrats' year to retake the White House. Hillary Clinton had rescued the Bill Clinton presidency from the catastrophic Monica Lewinsky scandal in his second term with guerilla warfare on Bubba's female victims. After the Clintons left the White House, Ms. Clinton suffered through a menial Senate job for a resume enhancement while awaiting her turn in the Oval Office. The presidency was *owed* her in 2008.

But Democrat primary voters had other ideas. They dropped her in the primaries like the proverbial soiled prophylactic for the shiny new black kid with the teleprompter, Barack Obama. As Joe Biden so eloquently put it in a January 2007 interview with a New York Observer journalist, *"I mean, you got the first mainstream African-American who is articulate and bright and clean and a nice-looking guy."* As we found out later in the 2008 primary season, apparently Democrat primary voters agreed with Joe.

In an attempt to secure Ted Kennedy's endorsement of Hillary Clinton over Barack Obama for the 2008 Democrat nomination, Bill Clinton told Kennedy *"A few years ago, this guy would have been getting us coffee."* File that one under *"Nostalgia ain't what it used to be."* – Yogi Berra.

Early during the primary season (03.11.08), former 1984 Democrat vice-presidential nominee Geraldine Ferraro spoke out about the race for the Democrat nomination: *"If Obama was a white man, he would not be in this position."* Her observation was truthful, accurate, and relevant. Very simply put, her point was that if a white male had entered the race with the same resume and qualifications as Obama, how far would he get? Obviously, Ms. Ferraro has never heard of the Democrat concept turned reality called "affirmative action."

It was *not* what Democrats wanted to hear. **The truth to a liberal is like a cross to a vampire.** For her wanton display of truth and common sense, Ms. Ferraro was viciously attacked like a school of piranha on a wiener dog out for its Sunday swim.

As a political force within the Democrat Party, Ms. Ferraro was instantly excommunicated.

The point of this extended excursion into the sleazy past of Democrat primary history is to illustrate that on the podium of victimology, race is golden, gender is bronze.

Nevertheless, the Democrat Party advocates for women as far back as Teddy Kennedy at Chappaquiddick in the late 60s; Bill Clinton's *"You had better put some ice on that lip"* quote to Juanita Broaddrick a decade later; and James Carville's mid-90s quote *"Drag a hundred-dollar bill through a trailer park, you never know what you'll find,"* about another early Bubba victim, Gennifer Flowers. Evidently Mr. Carville did not approve of his boss' "taste" in his victims. Yet Again we learn that what Democrats *say* matters; what they do does *not*.

The Kate Steinle murder trial case in the "sanctuary city" of San Francisco is also excruciatingly vivid testimony to the lack of women's standing on the liberal victim ladder. Ms. Steinle (a white female U.S. citizen) was murdered on July 1, 2015 by a Mexican national illegal alien Jose Inez Garcia Zarate on the San Francisco Embarcadero (waterfront).

Zarate had 7 felony convictions and had been deported 5 times previously.

Zarate claimed he found the gun (which had been reported stolen from a federal government agency vehicle), then it accidently went off in his hand killing Ms. Steinle. It was an accident, happens all the time, no big deal. Coincidentally, Zarate was virtually incoherent on *"some sleeping pills he found in a trash dumpster."* That's where I store mine, too.

Zarate's initial account of the incident was that he was shooting at sea lions in San Francisco Bay. This changed when his legal team advised him *that* story would likely get him a lethal injection sentence. San Francisco liberals love their sea lions even more than killer whales and great white sharks do, and a heap sight more than Kate Steinle.

A jury of his "peers" acquitted Zarate of the murder and manslaughter charges, but convicted him of illegal possession of a firearm. The jury sent multiple messages to America with this verdict:

- To the race-obsessed left, brown people have been trampled upon by white people for centuries. It is about time the tables were turned. The 1995 O.J. Simpson verdict was just a down payment on this congenital American injustice. Consider the Kate Steinle verdict another reparations installment payment.

- The verdict is a classic liberal repudiation of individual responsibility because liberals reject the concept of the individual. This basic construct was set forth in *"The Communist Manifesto"* back in the 19th century.

- The gun did it. Guns are *evil*. It is OK to kill someone, just don't do it with a gun. We will *not* convict you of killing Ms. Steinle, but we *will* put you in prison for the gun!

- San Francisco is a sanctuary city! A few dead Kate Steinles are a miniscule price to pay for this exalted moral high-ground status. In truth this is a self-delusional psychological disorder disguising itself in the liberal psyche as "moral superiority." In child psychology, this is known as Oppositional Defiant Disorder (ODD), which is "a pattern of angry/irritable mood, vindictiveness, and argumentative/defiant behavior toward authority." In this case the petulant child meme is directed at the authority of President Trump, who would end the "sanctuary city" malevolent practice in America.

- The Kate Steinle verdict is classic liberal bullying of the majority by the OCD liberal minority. It is an overt demonstration that the twelve liberal jurors can impose their "San Francisco values" upon the rest of American society. *They* are in *control*, which is *the* prime obsession of OCD liberals. It is no different than forcing the "anybody-in-any-bathroom-any-time" rule upon the 99.7% of non-transgender Americans against our will in the name of transgender advocacy. In truth, it is merely *bullying* to satisfy the OCD primal urge.

- As Zarate's defense attorney Matt Gonzalez noted post-trial, it should have been Donald Trump on trial there for his campaign rhetoric. Typical liberal logic: Kate Steinle's death was *not* a crime, but Trump talking about Ms. Steinle's death during the campaign *was* a crime.

What happened next? A liberal San Francisco judge gives Zarate credit for time served on the illegal firearm charge and Zarate walks out into yet another deportation (*if* the local *gendarmes* bother to notify ICE of the release). The over/under on the next time he shows up stoned on the Embarcadero with another gun? Thirty days.

Synopsis: the entire liberal agenda is dependent upon peddling victimhood to various minority groups. The more, the better. This is euphemistically deemed "diversity and inclusion." In truth, it is a strategy of cultivating division, anger, jealousy, and hate. The minority groups do not represent individuals with dreams and aspirations because liberals do not acknowledge the concept of the individual. The victim groups represent monolithic voting *blocks* which will be manipulated with propaganda to keep Democrats in power. *It is bad enough that liberals see group identity <u>first</u>. The real problem is that is the <u>only</u> thing they see.*

9. CANDIDATE HILLARY: "MONICA BENGHAZI – 2016!!!"

"The superior man blames himself. The inferior man blames others." – **Don Shula.**

I will digress briefly from the beaten path to share my thoughts about the Hillary Clinton 2016 presidential candidacy. She described me during the campaign as *"deplorable."* I still consider that attempted insult as the ultimate validation of character.

As for her, I am torn among "evil," "corrupt," and "incompetent." In a moment of compromise, I will settle on "all of the above." Donald Trump has labeled her "Crooked Hillary." In point of fact, Hillary Clinton is as crooked as Gloria Allred's nose.

Any discussion of "Candidate Hillary" must include the 2016 Democrat primary, which was just as corrupt as she is. The Democrat primary was about "Super delegates." Approximately 15% (712 of 4763 total) of the delegates to the Democrat convention were designated "Super delegates." They are long-time party establishment hacks who will support the long time party establishment hack candidate, in this case Hillary Clinton. Their purpose is to take the candidate selection out of the hands of the people who vote in the primaries. In this capacity, they are about as "super" as the *"Great Depression"* was "great." At the 2016 Democrat National Convention (DNC) in Philadelphia, 85% of them voted for Ms. Clinton regardless of how voters in their states voted in the primaries. Do the math: a 70% (85% -15%) advantage in "Super delegates" who comprise 15% of the Democrat electorate gave Hillary Clinton a ~10% electoral advantage before a single primary vote was cast. Who couldn't win with that kind of head start?

That was not enough for Hillary. On top of this markedly unfair structural advantage, the Hillary campaign could just not refrain from further primary d!p$h!ttery.

Before a March 2016 town hall meeting in Flint, Michigan, Ms. Clinton was given questions by DNC official and CNN commentator Donna Brazile so she could rehearse her focus-group-tested responses regarding questions about the quality of water* there. The information about Ms. Brazile's question-leak to the Clinton campaign was made public via Wikileaks, an international non-profit organization that publishes secret information, news leaks, and classified media provided by anonymous sources. Ms. Brazile denied the accusation initially, then later confessed and was fired by CNN.

*Flint's water quality crisis happened because state officials made a temporary switch in the city water supply and did not properly treat the water **with an anti-corrosive agent. The untreated water corroded the pipes as it traveled to homes. Lead pipes leeched lead into the water, poisoning hundreds.**

In the heat of the ongoing primary battle with Sen. Bernie Sanders, Democrat National Committee (DNC) chairwoman Debbie Wasserman Schultz was forced to resign her position. WikiLeaks released a collection of hacked emails indicating that Ms. Wasserman Schultz and other members of the DNC staff showed bias against the presidential campaign of Sen. Sanders in favor of Hillary Clinton's campaign.

In July 2017, Debbie Wasserman Schultz' top information-technology employee, Pakistani-born Imran Awan (who was under investigation by the FBI for theft, fraud, and cybersecurity-tied abuses but was *still* employed by Ms. Wasserman Shultz) was arrested at Dulles International Airport as he tried to flee the country. Ms. Wasserman continued to defend Awan after his arrest. Can you spell "B-L-A-C-K-M-A-I-L"? Look for that plot to thicken as Ms. Wasserman Shultz descends the slippery slope into the roux. Anthony D. Weiner will enjoy her company there.

And then there was the bigoted anti-Semitic emails of Ms. Clinton's campaign manager, John Podesta, also exposed by Wikileaks. Podesta distracted the complicit MSM's attention away from the content of the emails to imaginary "Russian hackers" who were attempting to influence the election in favor of Trump. And so we learn the hazard of using "*p-a-s-s-w-o-r-d*" for your password. "Russian hackers"? A fifth grader with an i-phone on recess could have hacked Podesta's email.

At the end of the Democrat primary season, Ms. Clinton emerges victorious over Sen. Sanders and a couple of other anonymous dropouts. Evidently for the party that booed God at their last national convention (2012), "evil," "corrupt," and "incompetent" are certainly not a problem; they are resume enhancements.

Of course, we now understand that the Democrat primary was the undercard for the main event of "*deplorable*" political treachery, the 2016 general election. In their desperation to lock in Obama's "legacy" via a second Clinton invasion of the White House, America is treated to the "Trump dirty dossier"/ FBI/ FISA fiasco (Chapter 7).

I consider Hillary Clinton to be the worst presidential candidate nominee of a major political party in American history. Here are a dozen reasons I personally found Ms. Clinton unacceptable as President of the United States, in no particular order:

1) She has the accomplishment resume of a crash test dummy, only worse.

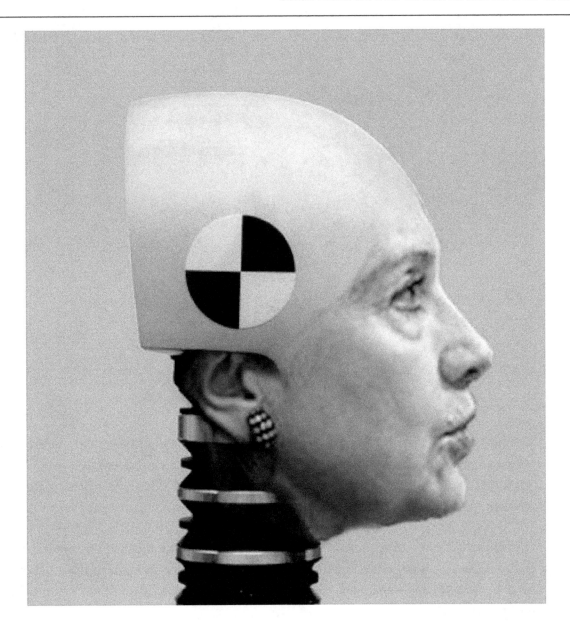

The 70s-80s Whitewater scam, the failed 90s Hillarycare debacle, self-appointed manager of White House *"bimbo eruptions"* (her words, not mine) control, her Senate vote for the second Iraq war which she later repudiated, the ludicrous *"Russian reset,"* the Benghazi massacre, numerous Middle East foreign blunders, and avoiding prosecution for multitudinous email crimes, plus the Clinton Family Foundation RICO (Racketeer Influenced and Corrupt Organization) Act felonies do not qualify her for anything but a nickel-dimer in Leavenworth.

The easiest way to end any pre-election debate was to ask the Hillary supporter to name a Hillary accomplishment, then watch them drown in their own psychobabble as a prelude to the counter accusation of *"Misogynist!"* To update her list of "accomplishments": it remains at zero.

2) She has the arrogant entitlement mentality of the pigs in George Orwell's novel *"Animal Farm."*

The broken record of *"Wouldn't you someday like to see a woman president?"* was bleated out at every campaign opportunity. I have no problem with a female president; Margret Thatcher was one of the top five leaders of the 20th century. I have a HUGE problem with Hillary Clinton, who couldn't lead a 2 year old to the latrine, as president.

One more "historic" affirmative-action presidency would have finished off the Constitution and America as it was founded via more bogus SCOTUS appointments in the mold of Ginsberg, Sotomayor, and Kagan, open borders, deficit spending, neglect of the military, Middle East bungling, etc.

3) She has the credibility of Baghdad Bob whether the tale be dodging sniper fire on an airport runway in Bosnia; or explaining she was named after Sir Edmund Hillary, who reached the summit of Mount Everest five years *after* she was born; or her defiantly belligerent *"What difference at this point does it make?!?!?"* testimony before the Senate investigation committee about the September 2012 Benghazi massacre.

Ambassador Stephens remains unavailable for comment.

Ms. Clinton's supporters claim she is the smartest woman on the planet. Which planet? Uranus? But mysteriously (schizophrenically?) she became Sgt. Shultz when testifying under oath. She can barely remember her own name. I foresee ample opportunities for her to improve her "I know nothing...NOTHING!" delivery in the near future, *vis a vis* the Uranium One/Clinton Family Foundation and "Trump Dirty Dossier" investigations yet to come.

The one thing we can remain assured about any Hillary Clinton testimony, past, present or future: if the testimony is *not* under oath and threat of penalty for perjury, she is lying. If she *is* under oath, then her memory will again "fail" her.

4) She has the charisma of *The Thing from Another World* (1951 Sci-fi movie), which is why she couldn't draw flies to an outhouse, let alone a crowd to a campaign rally.

Turnout was so embarrassing, she quit having them. If you were in the witness-protection program, a Hillary campaign rally was the safest place in America to be.

5) Her speech delivery has the aesthetic value of Freddie Krueger dragging his claw hand across a chalk board, another reason for staying off the campaign rally trail.

6) She has the spontaneity of the Bernie cadaver in *Weekend at Bernie's* (1989 movie).

Interviews have to be carefully scripted and her responses carefully rehearsed as with the staged Flint, MI, town hall question preview. This is why her public speaking comes across like a 5th grader at a spelling bee.

Obviously, Hillary was *not* interviewed by Bill O'Reilly, Sean Hannity, or Rush Limbaugh, who would have asked her unscripted unrehearsed real questions like *"Who gave the stand- down order for the Benghazi rescue mission?"*

7) She is as trustworthy a Gila monster in your boxer shorts. What would have been the consequences if Trump had approved the sale of 20% of America's uranium supply to Russia in exchange for $150 million in "donations" to *his* hypothetical family foundation plus a $500K cash "speaker's fee" payoff to his spouse at the close of the deal? *This* was the real Russian collusion. With Hillary in the Oval Office, the entire nation would have been up for sale in exchange for a "contributions" to the Clinton Family Foundation. But America was spared by the 2016 election result from the corruptocrat Clinton uber-jackpot.

Six billion dollars disappeared from the State Department budget while Ms. Clinton was Secretary of State. Meanwhile, the Clinton Family Foundation was awash in "contributions."

8) She has the loyalty of Kim Jong-un, who has murdered several of his family members to maintain power. Kim is also paranoid, but does *not* claim to be the victim of a "vast right-wing conspiracy."

She is the kind of person who would metaphorically put a knife in your back, then have you arrested for carrying a concealed weapon. Murdered DNC employee Seth Rich, who was accused of leaking DNC emails to WikiLeaks, was unavailable for comment.

For example, she declared Trump a menace to democracy itself for refusing to unconditionally accept the election outcome in response to a pre-election debate question. This meme was the MSM headliner for almost a week. Then immediately after she lost the election, she refused to accept the election outcome (*#RESIST*). A public procession of nonsensical denials of reality hypothesizing why she lost the election was led first with "Russian meddling." The full current delusionary parade is documented in her new book *What Happened*, which will no doubt be an instant best seller to people wanting another Monica Lewinsky chapter.

My reaction to the "Russian meddling" allegation is that it was not possible. I know this because Obama informed America at an annual end-of-year news conference (Dec. 16, 2016) that he had told Putin directly earlier in China to *"cut it out or there were going to be serious consequences"*. *"…And the dish ran away with the spoon."*

I voted against Hillary in the general election for many reasons, but Russian hackers, Macedonian content farmers, sexism, misogyny, the imaginary "vast right wing conspiracy" from the 90s, James Comey's schizophrenic buffoonery, "fake news" about her multifarious email felonies, the bankrupt DNC and Democrat Party, Twitter-bots, fake polling, talk radio, the imaginary "Alt Right media," etc., etc., etc. did not show up anywhere on my radar.

To hear her tell it, anyone who voted against her was *Islamophobic, homophobic, misogynistic, racist, deplorable*, etc. She left out *Clintonphobic*, which is *my* case. *Clintonphobia* is the result of watching the Clinton's 3+ decade crime spree across America go unprosecuted.

She did *not* blame herself for being the worst candidate in American political history. And she did *not* credit the American voter, who voted against the worst candidate in American political history.

As time marches on, America will be treated to fresh excuses designed to keep her in the public view and the cash flowing. And O.J. will pick up his search for Nicole's killer right where he left off as soon as he leaves prison. And the cow jumped over the moon.

Ms. Clinton is the ultimate victim. That is her not-so-new program. She is an opportunist. The sun is setting on her opportunity to grab power. *What Happened* is her final opportunity to cash in on what is left of her celebrity. She will spend the rest of her life publicly lamenting what coulda-shoulda-woulda been for as long as anyone will listen. I think legislation which requires her to shut up and go away would have bipartisan support.

9) She has the strength and stamina of an overcooked linguine noodle. We remember her collapse into the back of a Secret Service SUV on September 11, 2016, which was coincidentally the 4th anniversary of the Benghazi massacre…karma strikes again? After the collapse she was taken to her daughter's Manhattan apartment rather than a hospital to keep the cocktail of meds she was taking to (almost) keep her on her feet hidden from the public.

She has serious heart and circulation problems according to sources within her campaign. She has kept this hidden from the public. Although she claimed to be constantly "preparing for the next debate" during the campaign, her health problems kept her from the rigors of the campaign trail. I think it is unlikely that she would have been physically able to perform the duties of the POTUS based on the *prima facie* evidence available to the public: coughing uncontrollably, fainting, falling, lack of public appearances, etc.

10) She has the integrity and character of Anthony D. Weiner, more widely known on the internet and closest friends as "Carlos Danger."

Who looks the mother of a Benghazi victim in the eye over her son's coffin and tells her that her son's death was caused by a "crappy" YouTube video? Who gloats about getting a child rapist acquitted? Who intentionally commingles State Department business with private Clinton Family Foundation business for personal profit on an illegal "home brew" email server, then destroys the evidence (computers, cell phones, email servers) *after* it has been subpoenaed? Who approves a deal to sell 20% of America's precious uranium supply to the Russians in exchange for a $150 million *quid pro quo* contribution to her RICO foundation?

11) She has the empathy of Nurse Ratched (*One Flew Over the Cuckoo's Nest* - 1975 movie.)

Who shows up on the campaign trail to give a speech on "income inequality" wearing a $12,496 Armani "jacket"? She obviously feels your pain.

Fashion sense is not her long suit either. The "jacket" looked more like a sack from Ms. Potato Head's wardrobe closet, well within Chairman Mao's lofty dress code standards.

12) She has the authenticity of the laughable red plastic "Russian reset button" she dreamed up to launch her patented 2009 *"smart diplomacy,"* presumably juxtaposed to the "stupid diplomacy" of George W. Bush which preceded it. ***If you have to call yourself smart, chances are you are not.***

And thus the "Russian reset" button became the symbol of the eight year stretch of "Stupid is the new smart." which characterized the Obama era.

Her smile is as genuine as a Guy Fawkes mask with a matching cackle that belongs on a Halloween haunted house soundtrack.

"Ah don't feel no waz tarred. Ah come too far from whur I started from. Nobuddy told me that the road wud b easy. Ah don't believe he brot me this far to leev me." (Hillary Clinton at a March 4, 2007, patronizing speech at the black First Baptist Church in Selma, AL., utilizing Negro dialect). Highly authentic indeed. ***All liberals are frustrated actors.*** Just as her Senate testimony on the Benghazi massacre (*"What difference, at this point, does it make?!?!?"*), Ms. Clinton's Selma performance was at a minimum Oscar-worthy (the synthetic tube steak, not the Hollywood statuette).

She repudiated her Senate vote *for* the second Iraq war by joining the anti-war herd *after* the war became unpopular. Ms. Clinton obviously felt strongly both ways. When the war was a popular idea, she was an enthusiastic supporter. Later when it became unpopular, she condemned the war and never mentioned her initial vote again, treating it as some sort of "out of body experience."

She lauded KKK member Robert C. Byrd as her personal mentor in the Senate. *"From my first day in the Senate, I sought out his guidance, and he was always generous with his time and his wisdom,"*

Clinton wrote. Byrd set the record for longest filibuster on the floor of the U.S. Senate with a 14-hour filibuster against the 1964 Civil Rights Act. Byrd was a "Grand Kleagle" in the KKK and reportedly recruited 150 members to the group. Mentor indeed!

Her role in the Benghazi cover-up was even more *deplorable* than the massacre. The massacre could *possibly* be attributed to feckless incompetence. But the truth is the cover-up was premeditated. There was no "crappy" YouTube video. The whole deceitful yarn was spun to buy enough time through the corrupt media to get Obama re-elected less than two months later.

She was saved from her email corruption only by mitigating FBI corruption. FBI Director James Comey announced the FBI's prosecution recommendation to the Department of Justice during his July 5, 2016, press conference: he acknowledged that Hillary Clinton and her State Department colleagues had been *"extremely careless in their handling of very sensitive, highly- classified information."* But he then concluded that *"although there is evidence of potential violations of the statutes regarding the handling of classified information, our judgment is that no reasonable prosecutor would bring such a case. There are obvious considerations, like the strength of the evidence, especially regarding <u>intent</u>."* As we later learned, Comey wrote Hillary's exoneration memo in April 2016 before interviewing key witnesses, including Clinton herself. Now I know what the "F" in FBI stands for.

The Comey dismissal effectively temporarily pardoned Ms. Clinton for her email transgressions, at least through Election Day. What could possibly have led federal top cop Comey to (1) perform the legislator's job of retroactively rewriting the criminal code to include the requirement of *"intent"* which did not exist within *any* applicable statute; (2) perform the prosecutor's job of laying out a compelling case against Ms. Clinton; (3) then perform the jury's job of finding her not guilty; then (4) performing the judge's job of dismissing the case? Comey expanded to fill the vacuum of Attorney General Loretta Lynch when she declared that she would accept the recommendation of the F.B.I. and career prosecutors in the Hillary Clinton email *"matter."* Ms. Lynch's July 1, 2016, announcement followed a storm of criticism about an impromptu private meeting between herself and former President Bill Clinton on an airport tarmac in Phoenix.

To summarize, Mr. Comey did not understand that his job was to *enforce* the law. In a moment of supreme self-delusion, he thought he *was* the law.

I will translate the presser announcement utilizing Ockham's razor: (1) Comey thought Hillary was going to win the election so he gave her a pass. (2) Assuming Hillary did win, Comey knew no one would ever charge *him* with wrongdoing. There was one problem with the execution of Comey's plan: he believed the MSM-controlled fake pre-election polling. He rolled the dice and lost.

Hillary Clinton's participation as an enabler in her husband's philandering was equally *deplorable*. The Clintons were a tag team: the victims of Bill Clinton's sexual advances were attacked a second time by Hillary Clinton's smear machine in a counteroffensive *she* designated *"Bimbo Eruptions."* Classy, as usual.

What is truly scary is that through all of these sordid and shameful chapters (and more), *she doesn't think she did anything wrong*. This is the definition of a *sociopath*, the very *last* thing America needs for a Commander-in- Chief.

Of course I realize many of these criticisms are subjective. I was speaking with a half dozen or so former coworkers at a retirees' healthcare insurance seminar shortly before the 2016 election. It was impossible to avoid the conversation topic of the upcoming election.

One female former coworker took the lead and launched into a lengthy condemnation of Trump. Her monologue was accompanied by nonstop gesticulations: subconsciously shaking her head no, shuddering, wringing of hands, gnashing of teeth, etc. It was quite the performance. She was obviously sincere, but she was so "focused" on Trump's personal demeanor that policy issues never entered her field of vision. She was the typical "form-over-substance" voter who elected Obama twice because he made her feel good by reciting what she wanted to hear from his teleprompter.

When she finally gave her diatribe a rest, I asked her a rhetorical question: *"So you feel the same way about him (Trump) that I do about her (Hillary)?"* Drop the mic, exit.

I get it. *"One man's trash is another man's treasure."* – Anonymous. But there was far too much at stake to leave the 2016 presidential election to yet another "form-over-substance" whim that took America so dramatically backwards for the last eight years.

Another four years of a president who prioritized transgender bathrooms over the national debt, who prioritized golf over a Louisiana flooding catastrophe, the "global warming" hoax over ISIS beheadings in the Middle East, closing Guantanamo Bay over border security, destroying the coal industry over job growth and energy independence, bankrolling Iranian nukes over Israeli security, drawing imaginary "red lines" in the Syrian sand over meaningful reform of our broken VA healthcare system, nominating another Elena Kagan to replace Antonin Scalia on the SCOTUS, etc., would have terminated America as the beacon of hope for the rest of the world. ***When you are incompetent, you 'focus' on the irrelevant.***

Instead, America would have been transformed into a "Let's Make a Deal" cleptocracy operated by the Clintons. Do the math. If the Clinton Family Foundation grossed $150 billion selling 20% of America's uranium supply to Russia, how much could they make selling the other 80%? With my command of higher math, that would have them knocking on the Billionaire Club door.

The substantive difference between the two 2016 presidential candidates was vast, with repercussions which would impact America's future to the end of this century, possibly beyond:

Trump will drain the swamp.	Hillary IS the swamp.
Trump has never held public office.	Hillary represents decades of Washington DC corruption.
Trump cannot be bought	Hillary has already been bought through "contributions" to the Clinton Family Foundation by Wall St. and by Middle Eastern oligarchies who practice Sharia Law, murder homosexuals, and oppress women.
Trump is already a self-made billionaire.	Hillary wants the job to become a billionaire.
Trump wants the job of President to improve the lives of everyday Americans.	Hillary wants the job to become a billionaire.
Trump sacrificed his personal wealth for our country.	Hillary sacrificed her country for her personal wealth.
Trump supports the police.	Hillary supports Black Lives Matter (BLM), a George Soros-funded anarchist group who advocate murdering the police (*"Pigs in a blanket, fry 'em like bacon!"; "What do we want? DEAD COPS! When do we want 'em? NOW!"*)
Trump promises to undo the damage the Obama has done (e.g., Obamacare, coal industry, open borders, anti-military, racial unrest, etc.).	Hillary promises to double down on the damage.
Trump will enforce the law.	Hillary is a serial felon.
Trump represents taxpayers who work for a living.	Hillary represents parasites who vote for a living.
Trump will lower taxes which will grow the economy.	Hillary will raise taxes which will grow her personal power and control while devastating the economy.
Trump is an American patriot.	Hillary is an Alinsky-ite saboteur.
Trump is a capitalist.	Hillary is a communist.
Trump authored *The Art of the Deal*.	Hillary authored *It Takes a Village*.
Trump's spouse is a "peach."	Hillary's spouse was impeached.

Trump will attack radical Islamic terrorists and destroy them.	Like Obama, Hillary cannot utter the words "radical Islamic terrorist."
Trump is a member of the NRA.	Hillary seeks to destroy the 2nd Amendment while arming the Muslim brotherhood in Egypt with F-16s and tanks.
There are NO skeletons in Trump's closet.	Hillary's closet runneth over with skeletons....LITERALLY!!!
Trump raised $6M for vets at a fundraiser.	Hillary "lost" $6B from the State Dept. budget.
Trump called Rosie O'Donnell a "fat pig," then compounded the offense by failing to apologize...to the pigs.	Hillary told the families of the Benghazi dead heroes their deaths were caused by a YouTube video over the victim's caskets.
Trump owns dozens of hotels, buildings, and bars.	The Clintons have been disbarred.
Trump operates a multi-billion dollar corporate conglomerate which is audited by the IRS every year.	Hillary operates the Clinton Family Foundation for Bribery, Embezzlement, Money Laundering, Income Tax Evasion, and Fraud. It has NEVER been audited by the IRS because it could never withstand the cold light of day.
Trump has created thousands of jobs.	Hillary has never had a real job.
As a lifelong employer, Trump signs his paychecks on the front.	As a lifelong government dependent, Hillary signs her paychecks on the back.
Trump does not use email and tweets openly to millions of followers.	Hillary criminally deleted thousands of her emails to cover up other crimes from her illegal personal server...then lied about it...and then lied about lying about it.
Trump has zero foreign policy experience.	Hillary's foreign policy experience is light years WORSE THAN NOTHING (e.g., Benghazi).
Trump would appoint Supreme Court justices in the mold of Antonin G. Scalia, who would uphold and strictly interpret the Constitution as written.	Hillary would appoint Supreme Court justices in the mold of Ruth Ginsberg, who publicly denounces the Constitution.
Trump would stop immigration from Muslim terrorist nations.	Hillary will accelerate immigration from Muslim terrorist nations, turning America into the Western European type disaster. The immigrants would become Democrat voters.
Trump is pro-life.	Hillary is pro-abortion...tragically, HER mother was pro-life.

Now comes election night 2016. The first polls begin to close. The pundit class is abuzz with Hillary's pending victory celebration and the gigantic fireworks display on the Hudson River.

In the Eastern Time zone, Florida and North Carolina fall to the "deplorables," accompanied with pundit speak: "Trump has a very narrow path to victory," they reinforce themselves.

Time marches quickly on and the Central Time Zone results are at hand. Iowa falls to the hayseeds and pig farmers. More pundit speak: "It's now up to Hillary's northern firewall," with smug reassurance.

But it was not to be. First Ohio and Wisconsin fall to the sodbusters and coal mine grunts, then the Trump Neanderthal horde overruns Michigan. Hillary's northern firewall collapses in a heap of ashes, which Trump Hoovered up with a Dust Buster. "Does anybody realize he could actually win this thing?" gasps Chris Wallace, the dean of Fox News Channel (FNC) pointy-headed pundits. The group-think now takes an ugly turn to "Hillary has a very narrow path to victory."

It is effectively over by midnight, but for good measure Pennsylvania and its 20 electoral votes is called for the Obama-deemed "bitter-clingers" shortly after 2AM.

The Keystone state was the wooden stake in the heart of the vampire. It left the "Never Trump" posse at FNC: Chris Stirewalt (the political savant from Possum Gulch, WV), Trump slayer *emeritus* Megyn Kelly, Karl Rove (the "Whiteboard Wizard from Waco"), *et. al.* gaping at one another speechless with a collective "Whiskey! Tango!! Foxtrot?!?!?" look on their faces. Yes, the election outcome was the mother of all buzzkills in New York and Washington.

In flyover America, the mood was quite different. American patriots like myself witnessed the second historic defeat of collectivism within our lifetime. The first occurred at the Berlin wall approximately three decades ago. And now the oxymoronic "democratic socialism" in the form of "Obamunism" was defeated in America.

It was amid this atmosphere of drunken despair and desperation that the nonsensical "Russian hacker" script was conceived. Yes, "Russia" heinously meddled (as yet undefined) in America's 2016 election… more or less like Obama interfered in the 2015 Israeli election, you mean? This is a threat to American democracy itself! (Israeli democracy doesn't matter because they are no longer our ally, you understand.)

"Russia" is the perfect strawman for the job: they have no forum to defend themselves even if they cared. And even if they did attempt to defend themselves, who would believe them? Nobody likes Putin anyway.

Now well over a year of MSM-manufactured hype and hysteria based on 0.000 evidence whatsoever, it appears the "Russian hacker" meme has reached exhaustion. That is, unless Special Prosecutor Robert Mueller and his cadre of Hillary-donor lawyers can pull a rabbit out of a hat or elsewhere, the "Russian hacker" farce is *kaput*.

Mueller will be looking for red meat to barbeque at the conclusion of his inquisition to justify his expense reports. Someone has to go down for this crime, which has not yet been identified, to justify the last year+ of MSM/Democrat histrionics. The usual suspects (Hillary Clinton, Debbie Wasserman-Shultz, John Podesta, Mrs. Carlos Danger, Cheryl Mills, etc.) are off limits because they have the wrong party affiliation. If I were Scooter Libby's attorney, I would consider advising him to take an extended vacation in a country that has no extradition agreement with the United States.

Mrs. Clinton now seems to be making the case to America that she is the rightful winner of the 2016 election. She thinks presidential election outcomes should be determined by the popular vote rather than the Electoral College as prescribed by the Constitution. Obviously she thinks this change should be retroactive to include the 2016 election.

This is like changing the winner of the Super Bowl to the team that gains the most yardage instead of the team that scores the most points *after* the game is played. It is a masterpiece of oxymoronic "liberal logic."

To recap the election outcome, Ms. Clinton won the popular vote nationwide by 2.9M votes (65.9M to 63.0M). She won the state of California by 3.4M votes (7.4M to 3.9M). Over 50% of driver's licenses in California are issued to illegal aliens. Her popular vote "victory" is no mystery.

The vote that actually counted was the Electoral College. The final Electoral vote count was Trump 304, Hillary 227. Trump carried 30 of the 50 United States. Apparently 8 states dropped out since Obama ran for president in 2008. ***"…it is just wonderful to be back in Oregon, and over the last 15 months we've traveled to every corner of the United States. I've now been in fifty-seven states. I think one left to go…"*** **– Barack Obama (05.09.08).** The 8 dropout states must have seen what was coming.

The impassioned liberal plea to eliminate the Electoral College is not new, and is a companion to their open borders strategy. Ms. Clinton wants to do it for her own selfish reasons, just like everything else she has ever done.

There is often much banter about the Electoral College after an election, much more so after the 2016 election. But why do we have an Electoral College in the first place? Does it actually have any redeeming qualities that make it worth keeping?

None of what I have heard answers *my* questions about the purpose of the Electoral College and whether we should discontinue it for a straight popular vote. Even the analysis I have heard from trusted conservative sources on the subject has been muddled.

So here is my take on the issue. The short answer is that we have an Electoral College system for the same reason we have a Senate within our legislative branch.

When America's founders initially defined our government in the Constitution, they gave us a legislative branch with 2 houses: (1) a House of Representatives based on *population* within the states; and (2) a Senate based on *statehood* itself, giving 2 senators to each state. The Senate provides a means for *all* states, no matter how small, to have some voice and participation in legislation through the Senate. The proposed Senate component of the legislature was also an enticement for smaller colonies to join the newly forming United States. Without the Senate, Wyoming or New Hampshire would have virtually no participation in the legislative process, while California and New York would dominate the vast majority of legislation. That thought is sickening.

The House has 435 members; the Senate has 100 members. The Electoral College is an extension of this logic. It is a mathematical blend of the House and the Senate, giving one presidential electoral vote for each member of *Congress* (House plus Senate) for a total of 535. In this manner, every state, no matter how small, has some input to the determination of the executive branch owing to its 2 Senators. Due to the far larger total of House representatives to senators (435 to 100), the math blend is properly heavily weighted toward more-populated states BUT does not ignore less-populated states. So even South Dakota's 3 electoral votes (2 Senators plus 1 Representative) are important, and candidates are incentivized to campaign during the general election in South Dakota. The Electoral College system is a simple yet elegant mathematical solution to how to fairly determine presidential elections and represent every state, just like in the Senate. As usual, our 18th-century founders got it right.

Of course, liberals object to the Electoral College method for a number of reasons:

- It was defined in the Constitution, which they seek to destroy because it gives Americans freedom from government tyranny. The American Constitution to a liberal is like a cross to Dracula...it is an obstruction to the totalitarian *control* of the people that they obsess over. Liberals view getting rid of the Electoral College as a stepping-stone in the path to getting rid of the entire Constitution. The only thing that prevented Obama from becoming the totalitarian Marxist dictator he dreamed of was the Constitution. This is also a major reason why they seek to invalidate the 2nd Amendment. In addition to disarming future government dissenters (*"deplorables"?*), it is an attack on the entire Constitution by extension.

- Through the Electoral College, liberals have yet again been victimized by the racist, slave-owning founding fathers. The Electoral College was used to steal the election from Hillary

Clinton. Note that Trump strategically targeted electoral votes during his campaign. If Trump had instead mis-targeted the irrelevant overall popular vote, he likely would have won that too. Hillary only targeted campaign donors.

- Their supporters, who are largely dependent on government welfare, are concentrated in large population centers in the most populous states. To allow smaller states a base-participation starting stake (i.e., Senate based electors) dilutes the power of their straight popular vote.

The question you must ask yourself is "Do I want my president to be determined by the process defined by America's founding fathers in the Constitution? Or do I want to scrap that for the straight popular vote as advocated by anti-Constitutionalist liberals?"

Alternatively stated, "Do I want my president determined by a rural taxpaying Midwestern farmer? Or an illegal alien on welfare in Los Angeles? Or New York City? Or Chicago?" If we scrap the Electoral College method for a popular vote method, the 2016 election map (dark equals Democrat) would have looked like the one below. It is juxtaposed with a map of violent crime rate in America, for reference. The two maps are virtually identical. This is not a coincidence. Seriously, is this how we want to elect our president? Liberals enthusiastically answer this rhetorical question in the affirmative!

2016 Election Map.

Crime Rate.

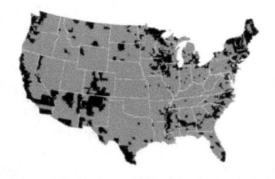

The juxtaposition of these two maps exposes another nugget of imaginary "liberal logic": clearly violent crime in America is committed by people who vote Democrat. Therefore, everyone should give up their 2nd Amendment right. Yes, the cattle rancher in Texas should give up his firearms to reduce the murder rate and save lives in Chicago. Makes perfect sense to a liberal.

What does the future hold for the temporarily grounded Hillary? Anybody's guess, but she *will* make another mega grab for money and power if circumstances even remotely permit. From her perspective, the 2016 campaign never ended. The *What Happened* political fictional non-thriller gives her the platform for campaign-like potshots at everyone but herself.

She faces multiple hazards in yet another comeback grab for the U.S. Treasury brass ring:

1) Failing health. Hillary barely made it through the 2016 campaign upright. We remember the 09.11.16 collapse into the back of the getaway SUV leaving a 9/11 memorial ceremony in New York. Karmatically, it was four years to the day after the Benghazi massacre. The uncontrolled coughing spasms and lack of critical campaign appearances in her self-described "firewall" states were telling. From here, she only gets older. I don't know what the "over-under" on Hillary's remaining years is now, but I'll take the "under."

2) Hillary attracts scandals like a black hole attracts light and matter. In her case, "scandal" is a euphemism for "felony." There is a reason for that: Hillary is a sociopath who genuinely does not believe rules or laws apply to her. Do not bother to challenge this assertion; the examples are more plentiful than seagull droppings on Buffett Beach. Ms. Clinton graduated from *capo* to mob boss after she left the White House in January 2001. The current rap sheet of malodorous misdeeds now includes trafficking in classified government documents, obstructing justice, treason, and multiple RICO felonies via the Clinton Family Foundation. This list is dynamic with much opportunity for growth via future investigations. Forget the nickel-dimer peccadillos (e.g. "Whitewater," the cattle-futures scam, "Bimbo eruptions" management director, etc.) of yester-century. Quite the resume! Seth Rich is still unavailable for comment. Forget the "smart diplomacy" as Secretary of State during Obama's first term. The ludicrous red plastic Russian reset button, the Arab Spring, Benghazi, and making $6 Billion disappear from the State Department budget were a few of the lowlights. As for the four dead Americans at Benghazi, she opined in a congressional hearing *"What difference, at this point, does it make?!?!?"* Equal parts feckless incompetence and soulless evil. Forget the 2016 campaign d!p$h!ttery (e.g., rigged primaries and debates, staged riots at Trump campaign rallies and most recently the revelation of financing the salacious and fallacious Trump "dirty dossier"). We should make this crucial distinction regarding campaign tactics: when a Republican is seen in the same photo frame with anyone who had Russian dressing on their salad this century (or last), it is deemed "collusion," which is a capital offense. When a Democrat finances a

Russian-sourced fictitious document such as the Trump "dirty dossier" with a 12-million dollar payoff, then uses the document to justify illegal government surveillance of a political opponent, it is called "opposition research." It is also a demonstration for the neophyte politician Donald Trump on how Washington *really* works.

3) The illegal James Comey acquittal for email wrongdoing was only going to hold up if Hillary had been elected president. Election victory was always her ace in the hole, her "get out of jail free" card...*literally*. Losing the election may well have won Hillary an all-expense paid extended vacation in Leavenworth. The truth about her role in the Uranium One sale of American uranium to Russia in exchange for "contributions" to the Clinton Family Foundation could and should reopen all the email felonies FBI Director Comey so magnanimously and erroneously flushed down the toilet. Ms. Clinton could barely get up the escalator with the mountain of baggage she carried into the election last time. She made it only on the back of the MSM. The baggage load has doubled *(minimum)* since then.

4) Clinton fatigue. This was a problem *before* the 2016 election loss. For anyone over 40, the last ugly Clinton tour in the White House is an all-too- vivid memory. Hillary's *What Happened* tour is a real-time replay of the worst moment in liberal history, rivaling the collapse of the old Soviet Union in the early 1990s. It does nothing but exacerbate Clinton fatigue. Eventually, I predict even liberals grow wary of the epic Hillary victimhood storyline and will forsake this latest pathetic Clinton grab for cash.

Aside from the felonious hijinks by the outgoing neurotic Obama administration, the politically-hijacked FBI, and the outlaw Clinton campaign, my biggest takeaway from the Trump "dirty dossier" hijinks is that the presidential election winner should take office *immediately* after the election. Leaving an outgoing defeated lame duck Marxist community organizer in the White House in charge of the government intelligence apparatus for over two months after an election is a recipe for malicious mischief of unprecedented magnitude.

The 2016 campaign was the Democrats' fresh coat of paint (as if anything about Hillary Clinton could ever be described as "fresh") on a worn-out sales pitch: identity politics. It was sheer genius. "It worked with the black guy; it'll work again with the woman...followed by eight more years of Bolshevik rule, out-of-control spending, no southern border, and finally American bankruptcy. America will collapse and our long- awaited communist egalitarian utopia will emerge." The liberal dream for America was at long last within reach.

It is particularly grating for liberals to lose the 2016 election to an old white guy, a loud boisterous billionaire who has nothing but contempt for the asinine liberal "political correctness" they feed America daily. Virtually the entire DC political class (both D and R brands) is also livid that an outsider with zero political experience could ride the escalator down at Trump Tower straight into the White House with naïve ideas like "Drain the Swamp!" and "Make America Great Again!" You may be able to sell that to the hayseed hicks in flyover land, but that's not how *this* Vaudeville show works.

Much of the resistance to the Trump agenda is nothing more than a giant *"WELCOME TO THE SWAMP. MEMBERS ONLY!!!"* sign for Trump and the American people who elected him. The message is all too clear: *"Trained professional swamp creatures. Do NOT attempt!"*

Professionals at what? They are professionals at enriching themselves at the public trough. While just 1% of the American public are millionaires, 66% of senators and 41% of house representatives are millionaires. These statistics also give us insight as to why representatives want to become senators: better graft opportunities.

They are experts at voting themselves a pay raise for a two-day work week and a subsidy exemption from the Obamacare fiasco they inflicted on America. They are experts at obstructing the will of the American voter while clearing the path for the wealthy K Street lobbyists, as we have witnessed on the crucial issues of Obamacare, immigration, deficit spending, energy independence, job growth, etc. Instead the Swamp creatures are all over imaginary Russian "collusion," imaginary "global warming," gun control, transgender bathrooms, and outlawing our nation's energy own resources like a mob of starving Venezuelans on a stray flamingo.

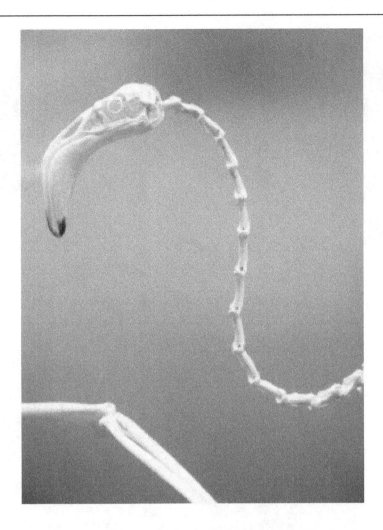

I hear threats of a federal government shutdown every few months. The battle usually develops over profligate spending. It is always an empty threat because both sides do not want their ride on the American cash gravy train to stop or even slow. Their re-election is dependent on the faux prosperity of borrowing from *future* generations and bringing home the bacon to their homeland voters *now*. Each baby born in America today signs on to $39,500 of debt. Add college on top of that.

The Washington DC kabuki theater budget battle marches toward the next mystical drop-dead government shutdown hour with cable news coverage warning America to hold its collective breath; the end is near...until miraculously just before the stroke of midnight, a spokes-joker for each party appears grinning before the cable news cameras to announce that an agreement has been reached by Congress to continue spending America into oblivion at the same rate as before the deadline.

Most critically, Congress will continue to be paid on time!

The same wash/rinse/spin cycle repeats itself at least semi-annually. The over-spenders always win. *"No man's life, liberty, or property is safe while the legislature is in session"* — **Mark Twain.** If you ran your personal finances the way Congress runs America's budget, your new mailing address would be the cell next to Bernie Madoff at the Federal Correctional Complex, Butner NC.

The only reason America's current $20 Trillion national debt is a dormant issue is because the interest rate owed on the debt is near zero. When the interest rate hypothetically reaches 5%, the interest payment becomes $1 Trillion per year (for liberals, .05 * $20T = $1T). This equals 27.4% of the current $3.65 Trillion federal budget. Pretty scary, huh? Only if you want to avoid national economic collapse. I am certain Cloward, Piven and Obama would have no problem with it.

Will Hillary Clinton become a candidate again? *Greed* is second on the standard list of the seven deadly sins. The religious connotation of greed is an artificial, rapacious desire and pursuit of material possessions. As defined outside Christian writings, greed is an inordinate desire to acquire or possess more than one needs, *vis a vis* material wealth. Hillary is driven by sociopathic greed for money and power.

Lust is third on the standard list of the seven deadly sins. Lust is a psychological force producing intense desire for an object or emotion. Bill Clinton is driven by lust for sex much more so than greed.

From her perspective, Hillary realizes that the American people made a big mistake in 2008 and a colossal mistake in 2016. She is certain that she is just one more plastic reset button away from a successful charge at her presidential windmill in 2020. Or maybe a better "Russian dossier" and more helpful participation by the FBI/DoJ next time around.

The allure of the public treasury to the Clintons, and particularly Hillary, is like the music of the Sirens of Greek mythology. Without question, Ms. Clinton has *much* to overcome to earn another grab at the U.S. Treasury, er, presidency. Her health, potential felony convictions, self-delusion and other psychological disorders, and the "Clinton fatigue" suffered by the American people are all *major* obstacles she must overcome to make another credible run at the presidency. Her misfortunate *What Happened* tour wherein she takes her 2016 campaign into imaginary extra innings has compounded the fatigue factor to the breaking point.

Any one of these obstacles is enough to sink a future Hillary run. Collectively, they are surely insurmountable, at least for the national office of president. I think it much more likely that their own party will discard them as a liability the way Bill discarded Monica. However, a run for a local office in a dysfunctional liberal enclave might work. Mayor of New York City comes to mind. Bill ("Big Tird") De Blasio would not be a tough act to follow.

I personally do not think we have yet seen the fat lady sing on the epic Clinton American farce. From an opposition standpoint, I would very much prefer to see her make another White House run. She is the gift to conservatives that keeps on giving, like Nancy Pelosi, Maxine Waters, Sheila Jackson Lee and more recently, Frederica Wilson. If you attempted to create a liberal parody to mock, you could not approach the absurdly comical entertainment value of these Democrat masterminds. This is also why I oppose the "Dump Pelosi" movement that bubbles to the surface at least a couple of times a year. Since she was elected House Speaker in 2007, Democrats have gone from a +31 member majority to a -47 minority in the 435 member House. I propose to fellow conservatives that we not do anything to interfere with that trajectory.

So far we have seen liberal stage a pink-hatted women's march in Washington D.C. in protest of the Nov. 8, 2016, Trump election victory. The Ashley Judd onstage "Nasty Woman" performance there was Oscar- worthy. We saw the impassioned television plea for an Electoral College *coup d'état* by a sanctimonious herd of Hollywood "B" listers who *actually* thought that would work. And then we were treated to another promotion that reeks of sheer liberal genius: people were urged to gather on the Boston Common on Nov. 8, 2017, to *"scream helplessly at the sky"* on the anniversary of the 2016 election. The Boston event has since spawned imitators across the country, including Philadelphia; Austin, Texas; and even one at Trump Tower in Chicago. Yes, *these* are the intellectual elite who think *they* should be in charge of America's (and your) future. *"No society can survive this level of stupidity."* – Mark Steyn.

Although this lunacy rave sounds like the plot of a three-panel Dilbert cartoon episode, it may sweep the nation and eventually surpass the August 17, 2017, solar eclipse turnout. I can envision the Nov. 8 date becoming a global leftist event like May Day (May 1), Earth Day (April 22) or Kwanzaa (Dec. 26). *"You can sum it up in one word: 'YaNeverKnow.'"* – Joaquín Andújar.

As for myself, I help out whenever I can. In support of another Hillary White House run, I have designed bumper stickers for the occasion. An example which commemorates two of her many high profile "accomplishments" below:

I have more available upon request.

SYNOPSIS: Hillary Clinton is the ultimate loser. She was cheated on by her philandering serial-sex-offending husband while in the White House. She failed miserably in two presidential bids: in 2008, she lost the Democrat nomination race to a neophyte with a blank resume. She lost the 2016 presidential election to a businessman who had never run for elected office before. This despite a corrupt, rigged primary process, nonstop biased corrupt MSM propaganda, and the entire corrupt federal bureaucracy running interference for her.

Post-election America is insulted daily by this bitter crass individual who seeks to absolve herself of all personal responsibility for her election defeat. She continues to peddle victimhood to herself. Nobody else is buying. There is no better validation that America got the 2016 election right than her classless post-election behavior.

10. OBAMUNISM:
KRYPTONITE FOR AMERICA'S GREATNESS

"The danger to America is not Barack Obama but a citizenry capable of entrusting a man like him with the Presidency. It will be far easier to limit and undo the follies of an Obama presidency than restore the necessary common sense and good judgment to a depraved electorate willing to have such a man for their president.

The problem is much deeper and far more serious than Mr. Obama, who is a mere symptom of what ails America. Blaming the prince of fools should not blind anyone to the vast confederacy of fools that made him their prince.

The Republic can survive a Barack Obama, who is, after all, merely a fool. It is less likely to survive a multitude of fools such as those who made him president." **– Czech Republic newspaper** *Prager Zeitung* **op. ed. (04.28.10).**

Where do you even start? First, by acknowledging there is nothing negative that can be said about Barack Obama that will not be considered *"Racist!"* I understand that. I would never deny a liberal the joy of screaming "Racist!" It is the sole remaining pleasure they get in life.

Likewise, the act of voting for someone other than Obama in an election will be considered *"Racist!"* (Liberals are accomplished at reading your mind and your motives; however, you will *never* be smart enough to read theirs.) This phobic phenomena got him elected twice.

Although Obama was billed as "America's historic first black president," correcting a long-standing misconception by Nobel Lauriat (black) novelist Toni Morrison who deemed Bill Clinton *"our first black president"* in 1998, he is in fact biracial. By all indications, the ideas from his white half are every bit as bad as his black half. I admit this is highly subjective. His supporters may very well believe the opposite is true; it is indeed debatable.

It does not matter at this point where Obama was born. His personal history is irrelevant. The damage to America has already been done. But America should have seen this coming. In Obama's own words from pages 100-101 of *Dreams from My Father: A Story of Race and Inheritance*: *"To avoid being mistaken for a sellout, I chose my friends carefully. The more politically active black students. The foreign students. The Chicanos. The Marxist Professors and the structural feminists and punk-rock performance poets. We smoked cigarettes and wore leather jackets. At night, in the dorms, we discussed neocolonialism, Franz Fanon, Eurocentrism, and patriarchy. When we ground out our cigarettes in the hallway carpet or set our stereos so loud that the walls began to shake, we were resisting bourgeois society's stifling constraints. We weren't indifferent or careless or insecure. We were alienated."*

He never outgrew this sophomoric malevolent malcontented mindset. Pre-president Obama had ties to sordid miscreants, gloating terrorists, rabble rousers, anarchists, Islamic racists and convicted felons. If he had ever been exposed to a sane thought about America in his life, I am at a total loss to identify the source: his communist childhood mentor, Frank Marshall Davis? His Marxist father? His communist mother? Michelle Obama? Reverend Wright? Bill Ayers? Tony Rezko? Father Pfleger? Louis Farrakhan?

Here are a few chosen *sane* thoughts about Obama from a few of America's greatest minds:

"People who oppose Obama are said to be racist...so I guess I'm a racist." – Herman Cain.

"I think this man (Obama) really thinks he can change the world, and people like that are infinitely more dangerous than mere politicians." —Dr. Thomas Sowell.

"He's beyond learning. He has another agenda and, firstly, I don't think Obama is his own man." —Dr. Walter E. Williams.

"...the underlying problem is a false narrative that continues to be pushed, not only by the prosecutor but by Hillary Clinton and Barack Obama and the protesters and all of the rest who are pretending that we have an epidemic of black men dying at the hands of police. That is not an epidemic. That is exceptional. That is rare. What is normal is young black men dying at the hands of other black men, and they do not want to talk about that." – Jason Riley.

"He built this racial divide. It was a wound that had been healing for a number of years, a number of decades... and he reopened it with his divisive politics. Who would have thought that after the election of the first black president in the history of the United States, we would need a period of reconstruction to try to put this country back together?" — Milwaukee County Sheriff David Clarke.

"I will not sacrifice my country for some faux historic moment. This is not about the color of his skin, it's about the content of his character. President Barack Obama constantly shows himself to be to be a disgrace to America and a clear and present danger to our republic." – Col. Allen West.

"I have never believed for a moment that Barack Obama has the best interests of the United States at heart." —Dr. Thomas Sowell.

And my favorite *stereophonic* American philosophers, Diamond and Silk on the neo-reality of the post-Obama era: *"It sounds like Barack Obama is living on a planet in La La Land. He's the one who's running around still acting as though he's the president - he's not."*

"Let's say somebody were in the White House wanted to destroy this nation. I would create division among the people, create a culture of ridicule of basic morality and the principles that made and sustained the country, undermine the financial stability of the nation, and weaken and destroy the military. It appears coincidentally that these are the very things that are happening right now." – Dr. Ben Carson.

What do all of these Americans have in common? Two things: (1) I agree 100% with *all* of them. (2) Unlike Obama, they are *all* 100% black.

All of these Americans would be labeled *"Racist!"* by the left were it not for their skin color. Make no mistake about it, they are all "defective" in the eyes of the left. They *will* be attacked and discredited because they are conservative, but the mindless *"Racist!"* hysterical *ad hominem* attack will not work for an all too obvious reason.

Let's contemplate the last comment from Dr. Carson. If I wanted to sabotage the United States of America with access to the resources of the presidency, what would my strategy be?

- I would saddle future generations with debt, effectively enslaving them to work for someone else paying it back. *"The problem is, is that the way Bush has done it over the last eight years is to take out a credit card from the Bank of China in the name of our children, driving up our national debt from $5 trillion dollars for the first 42 presidents — number 43 added $4 trillion dollars by his lonesome, so that we now have over $9 trillion dollars of debt that we are going to have to pay back — $30,000 for every man, woman and child,"* Obama said on July 3, 2008, at a campaign event in Fargo, ND.

  "That's irresponsible. It's unpatriotic," said candidate Obama. For the only time in Obama's life, he was on the right track. George W. Bush's over-spending habit was unhealthy for America.

- I would confuse, confound, and demoralize my military by leading from behind, vacating America's victory in Iraq, performing inane social experiments, underfunding, announcing America's withdrawal timetable to the enemy, releasing Islamic jihadists from Gitmo to return to the battlefield, treat Army deserter Bowe Bergdahl like a returning war hero, withhold government benefits from Ft. Hood victims by deeming the Islamic terrorist massacre there *"workplace violence,"* etc.

- I would refuse to enforce immigration law and our nation's borders, allowing millions of uneducated, unskilled illegal aliens across our southern border to swamp our education, healthcare, welfare, and election systems. Uneducated imported voters have the added attribute of being susceptible to liberal propaganda, making them easier to manipulate. Eventually these invaders would become my voting base, displacing the white working middle class. *This* would be my *"fundamental transformation of the United States of America."*

- I would socialize the healthcare system to grow government and satisfy my obsession with *control*. I would call it *"The Affordable Care Act."* I would undercut economic growth by hijacking America's healthcare system and replace it with the new "Obamacare." I would manufacture uncertainty for small businesses by constantly reinterpreting the ambiguously-written 2,700 page law. I would force Americans to buy insurance they don't want or need, or pay an ever-increasing fine. I would strangle the economic system with costly and unnecessary regulation composed by unelected bureaucrats. I would smother the financial system with Dodd-Frank legislation and call it the *"Wall Street Reform and Consumer Protection Act."*

- I would oppose any and all pathways to energy independence: fracking, off-shore drilling, ANWR drilling, the Keystone XL Pipeline to bring American crude oil to American refineries. I would start a "War on Coal" to eliminate it as an economical source of energy. I would sell 20% of America's uranium supply to the Russians. I would unilaterally commit America to the *"Paris Climate Accord,"* a massive global redistribution of wealth scam which targets American "greenhouse gas" emissions, while postponing source emissions from other nations. ***There can be no graft without redistribution of wealth.*** The *non-binding* international agreement would give me the premise to further regulate America's energy industry out of business, like coal. The "accord" was approved by the same "usual suspects" that condemned America's recognition of Jerusalem as the capitol of Israel.

- I would instigate a national "War on Cops" with remarks like *"The Cambridge police acted stupidly"* and *"If I had a son, he'd look like Trayvon."* Then I would send the DoJ to handcuff the police in every community with a police shooting fatality of a minority, regardless of circumstances.

- I would arm America's enemies, e.g., the Mexican drug cartels, with assault weapons. I would arm the Muslim Brotherhood with American F-16 jet fighters and M1A1 tanks.

- I would pave the way for Iranian nukes with a cargo plane-load of untraceable cash and an un-verifiable non-proliferation agreement.

- While negotiating with the Iranians, I would *refuse* to negotiate with the opposition Republican party, instead ruling with a *"pen and phone"* by fiat. Who needs a constitution?

- I would unilaterally pull out of Iraq, allowing the formation of a Middle Eastern caliphate called ISIS. Then I would distract, confuse, and confound America from my military and strategic foreign policy failures with red herrings like "climate change" and transgender bathrooms. After all, *"ISIS is the JV team."*

- I would trigger a Middle Eastern refugee crisis with a feckless "red line" threat in Syria, then begin a program of unvetted Middle Eastern mass invasion to America to recreate the ongoing Western European crisis. The goal is twofold: (1) make whites a minority in their own country; (2) import a new Democrat voting base.

- I would nominate leftist activist affirmative action type judges to the SCOTUS like Sonia Sotomayor and Elena Kagan, who will obliterate the line between the law and my "social justice" crusade.

- Perhaps most importantly of all, I would weaponize the federal bureaucracy (IRS, DoJ, EPA, BLM, FBI, etc.) into a thugocracy for my own political use, undercutting America's faith in its own government, and its own election process in particular. I would demoralize America with the realization that it now has a two-tiered justice system: one for the politically connected and another one for the rest of us.

Any of this sound familiar? It should unless you've been in a coma for the last ten years.

And with this cargo of non-sensical, counter intuitive sabotage and hatred, America set sail on an eight year voyage into the future with our historic first gaslighter* in chief at the helm. The predictable result was a reenactment of "The Poseidon Adventure" (1972 movie).

*Gaslighting is a form of psychological manipulation that seeks to confuse and confound a targeted individual or group, making them question their own memory, perception, and sanity. Its origin is the plot of the 1944 movie "Gaslight".

Hillary Clinton's pre-presidential candidate resume was substantially worse than nothing. In contrast, Barack Obama's pre-presidential candidate resume was substantially blank. It consisted of some *still*

sealed academic records, a rouge's gallery of prior acquaintances, a non-descript term in the Illinois State Senate, a cup of coffee in the U.S. Senate, and a flashy teleprompter read at the 2004 Democrat National Convention: *"We are one people, all of us pledging allegiance to the stars and stripes, all of us defending the United States of America."* Yes, Barack Hussein Obama was very accomplished at reading what people wanted to hear off his teleprompter. I will always think of him as "the Manchurian Telepromter."

For traditional form-over-substance shallow-minded liberals, the DNC *performance* was all it took. He told them what they wanted to hear; he made them feel good. Fast forward 13 years to November 8, 2017: these are the same deep thinkers who thought screaming at the sky on the first anniversary of Hillary Clinton's 2016 election defeat was the bromide for what ails America.

Of course the psychosocial disordered "white guilty" took the bait. The Civil War of the 1860s and the Civil Rights movement of the 1960s were clearly not enough to expunge the original American felony of slavery from our nation's sordid history. Perhaps electing the first "black" president would finally remove the stubborn nasty stain of slavery from America's otherwise pristine blue dress.

It goes without saying that blacks bought into Obama's socialist foolishness. They envisioned the mother of all government reparation giveaways immediately post-election. We recall the interview with the Florida woman who said after an Obama speech in the run-up to the 2008 election: *"I won't have to worry about puttin' gas in my car; I won't have to worry about payin' my mortgage."* Then there were the women in line in Detroit to apply for an Obama "stimulus" giveaway post 2008 election who thought that free money came from Obama's *"stash."* And who could forget Ms. Free Obamaphone's *"Romney sucks!"* rant in Cleveland, OH, in the run-up to the 2012 election?

Inexperienced voters below 35 also eagerly jumped onto the Obama bandwagon to oblivion. ***"If you are not a liberal at 25, you have no heart. If you are not a conservative at 35, you have no brain."*** – Various.

They could hardly be blamed. They are the product of a failed education system that has been drifting ever leftward for decades. Witnessing the destruction their misguided votes caused was going to be the first real shot at education most of them would have.

We add in Women, Hispanics, Native Americans, LGBTQIAs and a few other less-populous victim groups, and we have Obama's 2008 *Coalition of the Gullible*. It was easily enough to swamp the bewildered aging relic John McCain.

The Republicans were in no shape to defend the presidency in 2008. Eight years of George W. Bush and his highly unpopular and misguided Iraq War were enough. During the entire eight years, Bush was under relentless attack by the MSM and he refused to fight back. This resulted in a mid-30s public approval rating. He dragged the Republican brand down with him.

The Obama campaign was a tsunami of media hype designed to disguise no resume, no qualifications, and some really perniciously destructive ideas. But to the *Coalition of the Gullible*, none of that mattered. It was all eclipsed by Obama's skin color. No one ever asked *"Where's the beef?"*

"I have a dream that my four little children will one day live in a nation where they will not be judged by the color of their skin, but by the content of their character." – Dr. Martin Luther King, Jr. (08.28.63). Sorry, Dr. King. That was so 20th century. *This* is the 21st century.

The 2008 presidential campaign was *de facto* the grand finale of *"American Idol,"* and Obama was the man for the job. As Democrat gaffe *meister emeritus* Joe Biden reminded us, *"I mean, you got the first mainstream African-American who is articulate and bright and clean and a nice-looking guy."* Doesn't happen often. Is that your point, Joe? Nothing racist about that "observation"…no siree.

Obama's primary battle with Hillary Clinton was quite contentious and acrimonious. But from the get-go, Democrats were perfectly willing to drop the aging high mileage, baggage overloaded, cadavers-in-the-closet Hillary for the shiny new black kid on the scene. Apparently the historic "first black president" of the United States had more appeal to identity-obsessed liberals than the historic "first female president." Remember the race *vis a vis* gender positions on the liberal victim ladder (Chapter 8. Victimology).

Throughout the campaign Obama continued to read populist-scripted drivel at the American people off his teleprompter. For a while I wondered why his head kept turning from side to side like he was at a Wimbledon Center Court final match. He never looked directly ahead at the camera on him. Then I realized his head was bobbing back and forth between his twin stereo teleprompters.

The campaign trail teleprompter reads were quite often interrupted by fainting damsels in the front row. These fainting events were apparently caused by the confluence of warm weather, crowded venues, and the sheer aura of *The Messiah*. Or more likely they were gullibles taking a dive for the cause. Regardless, Obama's response was consistently a marvel of adaptation and leadership: he took command as the first responder in chief issuing directives like "Give her some air"; "Somebody get her some water, please"; and "Can we get some paramedics down front?" Truly, this man was ready for the "3 AM phone call," just not from the Benghazi area code.

The 2008 Democrat season got off to a sour start immediately after the Iowa caucuses in early January. Obama won the state. The day after the caucuses, Bill Clinton telephoned Sen. Ted Kennedy and pressed the veteran of the vast right-wing Chappaquiddick conspiracy for his endorsement of Hillary. Recounting the conversation later to a friend, Teddy fumed that the ex-president had told him *"A few years ago, this guy would have been fetching us coffee."* Obviously, Teddy had a sound working knowledge of the liberal victimhood hierarchy and immediately endorsed Obama. Mary Jo* was unavailable for comment.

*Mary Jo Kopechne died in a car accident at Chappaquiddick Island on July 18, 1969, while she was a passenger in a car being driven by U.S. Senator Ted Kennedy.

Much of the friction in the Democrat primary season resulted from Hillary's come-from-behind antics in the spring of 2008, which was the genesis of the so-called *birther* movement. The Hillary campaign challenged Obama's *"lack of American roots."* Later, the Clinton campaign had to fight off accusations that they had circulated a photo of Obama in Somali apparel, stating in classic non-denial denial form that they *"did not find the photo offensive in any way. It's not a divisive photo."*

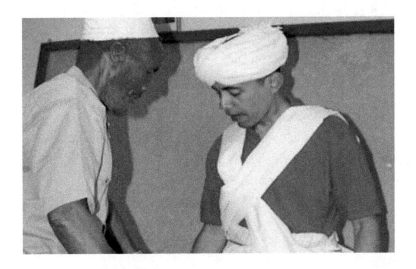

In full disclosure, I do not find the photo divisive, either.

In March of 2008 there was the CBS "60 Minutes" interview with Steve Kroft where Hillary stated that *"Obama was a Christian, <u>so far as I know</u>."* Nothing *veiled* about that unambiguous testimonial. At this point I probably should note that Ms. Clinton is not and never has been a member of the KKK, <u>*so far as I know*</u>. Her warm embrace and declaration that KKK Grand Kleagle/Senator Robert C. Byrd was her *"personal mentor in the Senate"* were taken out of context, yet another vicious personal attack by the *"vast right wing conspiracy"*.

As the Hillary campaign became more desperate, anonymous' emails surfaced:

"Barack Obama's mother was living in Kenya with his Arab-African father late in her pregnancy. She was not allowed to travel by plane back then, so Barack Obama was born there and his mother then took him to Hawaii to register his birth," asserted one chain email that surfaced in April 2008.

Eight years later (09.26.16) during a 2016 campaign debate at Hofstra University, Ms. Clinton stated, *"He (Trump) has really started his political activity based on this racist lie that our first black president was not an American citizen."* It was one of the most incredible exhibitions of political shape shifting I have ever witnessed. Moreover, Ms. Clinton can still remember dodging sniper fire in 1996 on the Bosnian tarmac with reporter-on-the-scene Brian Williams in tow covering the harrowing carnage.

The truth is that the birther conspiracy was conceived during the 2008 election campaign by Hillary operatives if not Hillary herself. Donald Trump had *nothing* to do with the 2008 election campaign.

The Democrat primary season mercifully comes to a close in early June with Barack Obama the winner based on "super delegate" pledges. "Super delegates" are unelected party hacks empowered with delegate voting rights to make sure the party nomination does not fall into the "wrong" hands. In this case, the young black guy gets the nod over the old white female based on the liberal victimology hierarchy (LVH). The polling reaction to Hillary's primary chicanery was a succession of "dead cat bounces". Her treachery was a futile attempt to upend the long standing LVH, which will *never* happen. In 2016, old white guy Bernie Sanders would get the short end of the Democrat LVH stick.

To place the cherry on top of his sundae, Obama delivered a primary victory speech (06.03.08) in St. Paul, MN: *"…This was the moment when the rise of the oceans began to slow and our planet began to heal…"* in his best Southern Baptist minister delivery, head darting left and right in between teleprompters. *Nothing is impossible for the man who doesn't have to do it himself.*

Of course, long before that point I had come to the conclusion that unless Obama was under oath and threat of perjury, there was no point in listening to him because he was lying. It turns out in hindsight I was 100.000% accurate.

It was scary enough that the *Coalition of the Gullible* went for the chum. Scarier by far was this moment when Obama convinced Himself that He was *The Messiah*! ***"We are the ones we've been waiting for."*** Translation for mortal consumption: *"I am the one you've been waiting for."* Egomania run amok!

The primary show is now over, and the circus makes its way to Denver, CO., for the Democrat National Convention (DNC) in late August. For Obama's climatic acceptance teleprompter read, the stage at Invesco Field at Mile High Stadium is converted into "Obamapolis." It was a clinical exhibition of pathological narcissism by Himself to exalt Himself.

The phony Styrofoam Greek columns instantly became a metaphor in my mind for the entire Obama "Nightmare on Pennsylvania Avenue" experience that was about to befall America. The columns were as false as a 2004 Dan Rather update on George W. Bush's Texas Air National Guard record.

Then along comes the 2008 debt crisis October surprise. Seeded by Democrat presidents Jimmy Carter and Bill Clinton decades ago, and cultivated by contemporary socialist Nano-wits Maxine Waters, Barney Frank, and the usual suspects, the game of financial musical chairs ended on George W. Bush's watch. That's all the information the MSM needed to convey to the American public: that Bush and his greedy Wall Street accomplices had sunk America financially.

To make bad circumstances even worse, the 2008 Republican nominee was handpicked by the MSM largely because John McCain stuck both middle fingers in the eyes of the Republican base every opportunity he had. The only enthusiasm shown for the Republican ticket on the campaign trail was for vice-presidential nominee Sarah Palin. Her popularity with the base was not enough to carry the moribund McCain across the finish line. Barack Hussein Obama was elected the 44th President of the United States.

The Obama era thuggery was in full pro even as the votes were being cast. In Philadelphia two members of the New Black Panther (NBP) party stood in front of the entrance to the polling station in paramilitary attire. One carried a night stick, and pointed it at voters while both "gentlemen" allegedly shouted racial slurs: *"white devil"* and *"you're about to be ruled by the black man, cracker,"* *et. al.* Perhaps this was the *"civilian national security force"* Obama alluded to in his July campaign speech in Colorado Springs.

Civil rights voter intimidation charges against the NBP thugs King Samir Shabazz and Jerry Jackson were dropped in May, 2010, by the Eric Holder-directed Department of "Justice." Before the election votes are even counted, America is force-fed an affirmative-action anal extrudate sandwich.

Holder later, during a March 2011 House Appropriations subcommittee hearing, rationalized *"When you compare what people endured in the South in the 60s to try to get the right to vote for African Americans, and to compare what people were subjected to there to what happened in Philadelphia...does a great disservice to people who put their lives on the line, who risked all, for my people."* Yes, Mr. Holder, I understand that justifying unacceptable behavior by citing other bad behavior is Liberal Debate Tactic #6. It misdirects the narrative in this case back to the 1960s, a place where all liberals wish to return.

With this declaration Holder was serving notice that there would be two standards of "justice": one for _his_ people and another for everyone else.

A few days before Obama's *emaculation* (borrowing Rush Limbaugh nomenclature) on January 20, 2009, radio talk show *meister emeritus* Rush Limbaugh was asked to submit a 400 word essay on his hope for the new president by an American print publication. Limbaugh responded with "...I don't need 400 words, I need four: 'I hope he fails.'" Of course the liberal MSM went tapioca over Rush's terse statement.

Limbaugh advertises that he has been certified right 99.8% of the time by independent audit. Turns out this was *not* one of the 0.2% minority again. Rush understood early on that Obama's interests and the American people's interests were diametrically opposed. That should have been obvious to any American paying a modicum of attention to the pre-election clues: the self- avowed Marxist, the notorious associations, the pathological narcissism, the sealed academic records, the unanimous MSM endorsement, the generic campaign sloganeering and the blank accomplishment resume *all* should have been red flags. **"Barack Obama is the least qualified person in any room that he enters." – Rush Limbaugh.**

Obama was an empty suit, a blank canvas that anyone could fill out anyway they saw fit. *"Hope and Change"*— to what??? *"Yes We Can"* — what??? Clint Eastwood nailed it four years later during the 2012 Republican National Convention with his empty chair Obama mock interview.

Yes, Obama had the perfect resume for the task of mismanagement of America into global mediocrity…and beyond.

For me personally, Obama's ambiguous promise (threat?) to the American people on October 30, 2008, was chilling: *"We are five days away from fundamentally transforming the United States of America."* Do not expect the *Coalition of the Gullible* to ask *"To what?"* Nor should we expect actual investigative journalism from the MSM, which was mesmerized by the historic nature of the Obama candidacy, the "crease in his slacks", and the orgasmic "thrill up my leg". Yes, the MSM was truly on the "right" side of history once more with their inextinguishable commitment to the "last Kennedy brother*". Nor should *you* dare publically ask *"Transformation to what?"* That would have been *"Racist!"*

* So designated by oddball MSNBC "Hardball" host Chris "Thrill Up My Leg" Matthews in a half drunken shower of spittle (08.26.09).

To be sure, Obama's *"fundamental transformation"* was *nothing* good, which is precisely what you would expect from a (self-described) Marxist "community organizer" from Chicago who had never had a real job in his life. In fact, it turned out to be far worse than anyone imagined.

Now it is time for the "Master of Disaster" to preside over the United States of America. The overview from 30,000 feet revealed only two real problem areas with his administration: (1) domestic policy; and (2) foreign policy. Other than these two petty peccadillos, Obama's White House tour of duty was flawless.

He did an *exceptional* job of pardoning the turkey every Thanksgiving. He welcomed the NBA champion Golden State Warriors to the White House with the class and suave style of a Harvey Weinstein female lead-screen casting call. His annual NCAA brackets were prescient and visionary (picking all four number 1 seeds to make the Final Four had Las Vegas odds makers in "shock and awe"), so much so that ESPN devoted an hour-long show to the Obama NCAA bracket exposé. His interview with GloZell set a new standard of excellence (called "rock bottom") in journalism for decades to come. His "slow jam" simulated newscast with Jimmy Fallon during the 2012 campaign season had all major network news divisions rethinking their program formats. Obama had the legendary White House parties with Beyoncé and Jay-z; the Manhattan, Hollywood, and San Francisco fundraisers; the golf outings; and the all- taxpayer-expense-paid (separate planes for POTUS and FLOTUS) vacations in Martha's Vineyard (summer) and Hawaii (winter) covered like fire ants on a Georgia picnic.

In matters involving policy, not so much. Let us review some of the lowlights of the American "Nightmare on Pennsylvania Avenue."

Obama began his emaculation celebration early with a self-aggrandizing January 17 train ride from Philadelphia to Washington D.C., the intention of which was to mimic the Abraham Lincoln train ride of a century and a half before. The emaculation ceremony itself was epic in the tonnage of garbage dumped on the Washington Mall by Obama supporters.

The 2008 election was over, and it was time for Obama to preside over the United States government. My thought at the time was that he did not know how; he only knew how to campaign. Obama was a one-trick pony. It turns out I was right.

The missteps of the newly-emaculated Obama began immediately. In an openly-insulting gesture to America's oldest and most trusted ally, Obama removed the bust of Sir Winston Churchill from the White House and returned it to England. Apparently Obama's rude jab was retaliation for 19th century British colonialism, which did not have Obama's approval. And thus we gain insight into Obama's masterful foreign policy skills. Ostensibly no one informed Obama that Churchill didn't do colonialism; instead he focused on defeating the Nazis.

Then with much pomp and circumstance, Obama signed an executive closing the Guantanamo Bay detention camp in Cuba which was to be *completed no later than one year post signing.* During the ceremony, he asked his legal counsel how the Gitmo detainees would be *disposed of.* The response was that *a process* would be set up for that. Now, almost nine years later, Gitmo is still open. However, Obama did manage to offload most of the Gitmo detainees, many of whom are back on the battlefield of *jihad* attacking American sons and daughters in the military.

The presidential campaign then became a springboard for the campaign for his next elected office: President of the World. Farfetched? How difficult would it be if Obama was able to successfully cede the governing authority of the United States to the United Nations? Then it becomes a manageable leap from President of the United States to Secretary General of the U.N. The only thing standing in his way is the United States Constitution, which he despises.

This is the backdrop for his beyond cringe-worthy World Apology Tour (WAT) in April 2009. Obama crisscrossed the globe pretending that the United States, by far the greatest nation in the history of this planet, was in fact a cesspool of racism and hatred. Because *his* election proved that? *"I believe in American exceptionalism, just as I suspect that the Brits believe in British exceptionalism and the Greeks believe in Greek exceptionalism."* – Barack Obama at a NATO summit (04.03.09). Obama could not wait to announce to the world how overrated America was. And this was the kickoff of his eight year voyage to full fill his WAT prophesy.

Obama was firmly convinced that the world is governed by dazzling rhetoric distributed liberally from his twin teleprompters as his head darted back and forth between them. His delivery and substance have not been seen since *The Wizard of Oz* (1939 movie).

The WAT was the right tool for this job. The WAT was his formal introduction to the world outside the United States. The balance of mankind ("peoplekind" for Canadians) would be awestruck by his teleprompter reads just like Americans before the 2008 election. Tell them what they wanna hear: America is no good, and now the rest of the planet has a friend in the White House who will straighten out 2+ centuries of malodorous American misdeeds.

"There are times when America has shown arrogance, been dismissive, even derisive." Obama told an audience in Strasburg, France, in an apparent attempt to apologize for saving them twice in the last century from German invaders. He addressed an audience in Ankara, Turkey: *"The United States is still trying to work through some of our own darker periods in our history."* As it turns out, certainly *none* darker than *his* presidency (double *entendre*). *"We have at times been disengaged, and been at times thought to dictate our terms."* *"We have to acknowledge potentially we've made some mistakes; that's how we learn."* *"Unfortunately faced with an uncertain threat, our government made a series of hasty decisions. In other words, we went off course."* Etc., etc., etc. His rambling asinine confessionals to no one in particular were bad enough, but I personally found his use of the words *"we"* and *"our"* particularly offensive. There ain't no *"we,"* amigo.

The Japanese cities of Hiroshima and Nagasaki were planned as WAT stops. A secret communique dated Sept. 3, 2009, was released by WikiLeaks. Sent to then Secretary of State Clinton, it reported Japan's Vice- Foreign Minister Mitoji Yabunaka telling U.S. Ambassador John Roos that *"the idea of President Obama visiting Hiroshima to apologize for the atomic bombing during World War II is a 'nonstarter.'"* A tip of the cap to the adults in the room, the Japanese!

Obama's World Apology Tour (WAT) was not a particularly big hit in the United States. That was not a problem for Him because the next presidential election was four years away. His self-perceived global popularity had outrun His newly elected position yet again and He was now running for the mythical President of the World.

Obama's next stop on the world stage: Cairo (06.04.09). At the University of Cairo, the Chosen One delivered a one hour rambling omega male retreat: *"…I consider it part of my responsibility as President of the United States to fight against negative stereotypes of Islam wherever they appear…."* He apologized for the 9/11 attack: *"…9/11 was an enormous trauma to our country. The fear and anger that it provoked was understandable, but in some cases, it led us to act contrary to our ideals."* And Obama praised Islam for their many contributions to civilization during the millennium before last: *"It was innovation in Muslim communities that developed the order of Algebra; our magnetic compass and tools of navigation; our mastery of pens and printing; our understanding of how disease spreads and how it can be healed. Islamic culture has given us majestic arches and soaring spires; timeless poetry and cherished music; elegant calligraphy and places of peaceful contemplation."* Pretty much everything but low sodium Spam.

And then in a willing suspension of all reality *"throughout history, Islam has demonstrated through words and deeds the possibilities of religious tolerance and racial equality."* The three thousand victims of the Muslim 9-11 attack were unavailable for comment.

How different would the 2008 election result been if Obama had made his World Apology Tour *before* the election? Under the circumstances of eight years of George W. Bush and his Iraq War, the uninspiring 2008 Republican nominee, the subprime mortgage collapse, the zombie-like mental capacity of the *Coalition of the Gullible*, liberals' awestruck fixation on Obama's skin color, probably no difference. But at least Americans would have been exposed to exactly who they were voting into the White House.

Throughout his first term as president, Obama was sustained by the oft-repeated phrase "Let's give him the benefit of the doubt." Across America liberals were temporarily elated that affirmative action had found its way into the White House.

The American Recovery and Reinvestment Act was signed into law by President Obama on February 17, 2009. Advertised at a price tag of $787 Billion "to rebuild America's crumbling infrastructure," it did precious little of that. Instead, the money was pilfered to fund public-sector unions jobs (and raises), payoff ACORN, the SEIU, and Obama's campaign donors and bundlers. At the signing ceremony, Obama assigned Vice-President Joe Biden, who thinks "jobs" is a three letter word and long division is "higher math," the task of overseeing the so-called "Porkulus" expenditures. That virtually assured none of the money would ever be spent on anything worthwhile.

The "Porkulus" instantly added approximately a trillion dollars to the national debt with virtually no perceived public benefit other than the retirement of Obama's campaign IOUs. It set the tone for the next eight years of liberal "fiscal responsibility." Some have commented the Obama regime spent money like a drunken sailor. This is highly inaccurate, and an insult to drunken sailors everywhere. Drunken sailors stop spending when they run out of money. Obama printed and borrowed more. Running out of money does not even slow down hardcore liberals.

Next up on the Obama regime social justice checklist was *"The Homeowners Affordability and Stability Plan,"* a proposal to retire homeowner debt resulting from the Democrat-created housing bubble collapse. The plan was proposed on February 18, 2009, and offered $75 Billion in new government "Porkulus" funds to avoid home foreclosures. It was classic socialist tampering with the free market to (1) create a problem; then (2) throw boatloads of taxpayer money at the resulting blowout.

From the wake of the good ship "Porkulus" emerged "the TEA Party," a metaphorical anchor. With conservative/libertarian grassroots, loosely organized, and almost entirely conceptual, the TEA Party instantly became the strawman, nemesis, and the piñata of the psychologically-disordered left. We must acknowledge that OCD liberals have an acute psychological need of a focal point for their overflowing hatred. The phantasmal spirited TEA Party was made to order, like *"Slimer"* in the 1984 movie *"Ghostbusters."*

I personally consider myself a member of the TEA Party, even though I have attended only one rally on April 15, 2009. I very much concur with the idea of "Stop spending money we don't have," which is nothing short of unpatriotic 'Racist!' hate-filled rhetoric and fiscal insanity to liberals.

For the rest of Obama's tenure, the non-existent TEA Party lived rent-free in the left's head (with plenty of room left over). The MSM was on the case, misreporting and prejudging virtually every negative public incident as caused by a "TEA Partier" (e.g., the Aurora, CO., movie theater massacre).

To this day the left is still trying to mimic the formation of the TEA Party with George Soros-funded anarchist knock offs: first Occupy Wall Street (OWS), followed later by Black Lives Matter (BLM), then later the fascist "Antifa." Each iteration was more defiant, more belligerent, and more thuggish than the one before. The "Antifa" practice of preemptively violently attacking anyone suspected of conservative thought became so Nazi-esque that eventually even Democrats had to acknowledge the truth. That doesn't happen often. I refer to these organized anarchist attempts to hijack and counter the 2009 TEA Party grassroots movement collectively as "Code Stink." ***Imitation is the sincerest form of flattery." – Charles Caleb Colton.***

As the 2012 presidential election drew nigh, Obama's weaponized Internal Revenue Service (IRS) selectively targeted conservative TEA Party-like organizations for denial of tax exempt status. In May 2013, it was learned that from April 2010 to April 2012 (pre-election), the IRS had placed a hold on the processing of applications for tax-exempt status that it had received from hundreds of organizations with such presumably conservative indicators as *"Tea Party,"* *"Patriots,"* or *"9/12"* in their names. During that period, the IRS approved only four applications from conservative groups while green-lighting applications from several dozen organizations whose names included the likely left-leaning terms *"Progressive,"* *"Progress,"* *"Liberal,"* or *"Equality."* During a 2014 pre-Super Bowl interview with FNC anchor Bill O'Reilly, Obama offered, *"Not even mass corruption — not even a smidgen of corruption"* within the IRS. Perhaps the misunderstanding is in *your* definition of *"smidgen."* Or as Bill Clinton once noted *"It depends on what the meaning of the word 'is' is."*

Then in October 2017, *after* Obama left office, the truth finally emerged (purely coincidental, you understand): the bureaucratic IRS admitted in federal court that it wrongfully targeted Tea Party and conservative groups during the Obama administration because of their political viewpoints and issued an apology to our clients for doing so. In addition, the IRS consented to a court order that would prohibit it from ever engaging in this form of unconstitutional discrimination in the future. Little good it did five years after the fact except to reinforce what we already knew about the character of Obama and the "Deep State" thugocracy. Obama was re-elected to do four more years of heinous damage to America. Of course, the IRS corruption during the 2012 election cycle was a Brownie Scout cookie sale compared to the FBI d!p$h!ttery that occurred on Obama's watch in the 2016 election cycle.

By mid-2009 Obama's approval numbers had taken a major tumble as the giddy liberal euphoria of the election victory wore off, and he was upside down in the polls.

Presidential Approval Index

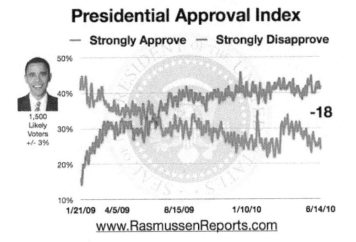

This did not slow his community organizer self. He still had his skin color and the MSM to hide behind. The polls were wrong and the people just didn't understand. So much social injustice, so little time.

Which brings us chronologically to the July 21, 2009, arrest of Harvard professor Henry Louis "Skip" Gates at his Cambridge, MA, home. Professor Gates was returning from a trip and found his front door jammed, and he tried to force it open. Meanwhile a neighbor called in to 9-1-1 a possible burglary in progress at the Gates home. When Cambridge police sergeant James Crowley responded to the call, a real life plot of "Amos and Andrew" (1993 movie) broke out. The B&E charge against Gates was dropped, but he was charged with disorderly conduct. Add high-profile social justice warrior Barack Obama into the mix and a local one-liner buried in the weekly "Crime Report" section of the paper becomes a national front page above the fold story for a week, bigger even than the uber classy Melania's shoe selection for her 2017 Hurricane Harvey visit.

"I don't know, not having been there and not seeing all the facts, what role race had to play. But I think it is fair to say, number one, any of us would be pretty angry; number two, that the Cambridge police acted stupidly in arresting somebody when there was already proof that they were in their own home; and number three, what I think we know separate and apart from this incident is that there's a long history in this country of African Americans and Latinos being stopped by law enforcement disproportionately."

So Obama admits that he doesn't know, but that did not stop him from condemning the Cambridge police officer for *"acting stupidly."* It hardly gets any more stupid than that. Professor Gates wasn't arrested for being in his own home; he was arrested for *disorderly conduct.* Perhaps we can imagine Gates shouting *"stupid"* and a few other choice belligerent expletives at Sgt. Crowley, who only showed up to do his job in response to a 9-1-1 call?

The remedy for this unfortunate situation is clear enough: the Cambridge police should no longer respond to 9-1-1 calls at Professor Gates' residence. That would preempt any future instances of mistaken identity and disorderly conduct on the part of Professor Gates.

Later, Obama said that he regretted his comments and hoped that this would become a *"teachable moment."* For whom? Me??? I am not a racial interloper. I was minding my own business. I actually found it somewhat bewildering that a mistaken 9-1-1 call and a misdemeanor could dominate the American MSM news cycle for a week.

Obama invited Professor Gates and Sgt. Crowley to the White House for a "beer summit" a few days later, ostensibly to provide Sgt. Crowley a forum to confess his racist transgressions. It was a welcome relief that a food fight did not break out, allowing America to finally move on. At the time, I interpreted Obama's *"teachable moment"* to be: "You can take the organizer out of the community, but you can't take the community out of the organizer." In reality what we witnessed were the seeds of the far left's "War on Cops" sewn in Cambridge, MA, by Obama.

The long hot summer of 2009 is finally over. The city of Chicago had been working on its bid for the 2016 Summer Olympic Games for over two years. From an original field of seven cities, Chicago made the final four along with Madrid, Tokyo, and Rio de Janeiro. Enter the heavyweight celebrity "Dream Team" to make the final pitch for America's Windy City: Barack and Michelle Obama, Oprah Winfrey, Michael Jordan and even Hillary Clinton.

Obama's "American Idol" stock took a nose dive when Chicago was the first eliminated from the final four. Perhaps the International Olympic Committee (IOC) was looking for more *diversity* in the presentation team? Or perhaps they have never heard of American affirmative action?

But Obama rebounded quickly. A week after the IOC disappointment, Obama was awarded the Nobel Peace Prize. The official basis for his award remains uncertain. Perhaps the Nobel committee was impressed by his swift and decisive action in closing down Gitmo (which is still open today). Perhaps the committee foresaw his "red line" decree in Syria, which triggered the mass Muslim Invasion of Western Europe. Perhaps they too thought it was a good idea to arm the Mexican drug cartels with assault weapons via "Fast and Furious." Most likely the Nobel Peace prize was a reward for his skin color, just like the office of American president.

Regardless, it was awesome. Yet again, America is overwhelmed by its prodigal *wunderkind*. I know my opinion of the prize took a major step-change with this award to the Community Organizer in Chief. Obama joined other notable Nobel Peace laureates such as Mikael Gorbachev (1990) for ending the Cold War despite the heckling and harassment of nincompoopian cowboy Ronald Reagan; Yasser Arafat (1994) for achieving lasting peace in the Middle East; Jimmy Carter (2002) for handing Iran over to the Ayatollahs; and Al Gore (2007) for his invention now known as *"the Internet."*

Nobel asininity is not limited to its Peace Prize. *E.g.*, leftist economist Paul Krugman was awarded the Nobel Prize for Economic Sciences in 2008. Immediately after the 2016 presidential election (November 9, 2016), Sir Paul wrote in a New York Times op ed *"So we are very probably looking at a global recession, with no end in sight. I suppose we could get lucky somehow. But on economics, as on everything else, a terrible thing has just happened."* We all know what happened to the American and global economy next. This leads me to wonder if the silly some beach can make change for a dollar.

In a related story, Adolph Hitler was Time Magazine's prestigious "Man of the Year" in 1938.

On November 5, 2009, a mass shooting took place at Fort Hood, Texas. Maj. Nidal Hasan, a U.S. Army psychiatrist, fatally shot 13 people and injured more than 30 others. It was the deadliest mass shooting on a military base in American history. Maj. Hasan was a practicing Muslim who was heard screaming *"Allahu Akbar!"* while firing his weapon at unarmed U.S. soldiers in the Ft. Hood Soldier Readiness Processing Center.

Yet again, the Obama regime refused to acknowledge the massacre as a radical Islamic terrorist attack, opting instead for the kinder, gentler *"workplace violence"* misnomer. By refusing to identify the cause of the attack, Obama was successfully able to block the victims from Purple Heart awards and benefits. This was the only instance in his eight years in office that he showed any concern whatsoever for the budget deficit. Military morale is a small price to pay for a balanced budget, you understand.

In the wake of Obama's callous attitude toward the Ft. Hood victims, Congress passed legislation changing the criteria to cover instances where an attacker was in contact with foreign terrorists before an attack and was inspired by the foreign group. This then paved the way in 2015 for a decision to award Purple Hearts and the associated benefits to the victims. It was not until Dec. 6, 2015, a full six years later that Obama referred to the Ft. Hood massacre *indirectly* as a terrorist attack without using the words "radical," "Islamic," or "Muslim." Another tip of the cap from our military to the *Coalition of the Gullible* who elected Obama.

To close the chapter on Ft. Hood, Maj. Hasan was tried and convicted of multiple counts of murder and attempted murder. He awaits execution on death row at Ft. Leavenworth. "Workplace violence" is indeed a serious crime.

When Obama took office in January 2009, he immediately "focused like a laser" on annexing America's healthcare and 15% of the American economy to government *control*. Government healthcare was never about healthcare. It is about government. Socialized healthcare has been a liberal utopian fantasy since Karl Marx authored *"The Communist Manifesto"* in the mid-19th century.

The Affordable Care Act (ACA), more commonly known as Obamacare, was signed into law on March 23, 2010. It was, is, and always will be completely dysfunctional. It was never designed to work. It was only to be the bridge between the traditional free market-driven pre-Obamacare health insurance system and the government-operated single payer post-Obamacare system. Single payer means VA quality healthcare for everyone at Park Ave. penthouse prices after all private healthcare insurers are eliminated from the market. The single payer system would give the corrupt Obama regime complete *control* over their political opponents' health care. After seeing what they did with the IRS, the EPA, the DoJ, and the FBI, it doesn't get much scarier than that.

A key assumption by the authors of Obamacare was a permanent Democrat majority in Congress and *control* of the White House for the foreseeable future. This assumption was only logical because long-term Democrat *control* would be the natural result of the eternal gratitude of the American voter for the magnificent gift of Obamacare from the Democrat Party. Lawmakers cleverly excluded themselves, their families, and their staff from this magnificent "gift."

But reality is a buzzkill. Obamacare was a major issue in the 2010 mid-term elections. The American people immediately made the Democrats the minority party in the House in the 2010 elections, firing Nancy Pelosi as Speaker of the House in the process. The Senate could not be turned over as quickly because of six-year terms, and Democrats held on there until 2014.

Obamacare was the brainchild of liberal mastermind architects Dr. Ezekiel *"Death Panel"* Emanuel and MIT economist Dr. Jonathan Gruber. Anyone who has ever listened to either one of these narcissistic egotistical pinheads rattle on for more than one sentence will understand why their *opus magnum* failed. These two could not organize a two-player bingo game at the annual family picnic.

"Dr. Death Panel" is the brother of Chicago mayor Rahm Emanuel. He has done for America's healthcare system what his brother did for the murder rate in the Windy City. He exudes the personality of a ghoulish *"Carlos Danger"* with terminal hemorrhoids. If I had to give a three word description of Dr. D, it would be "banal and anal".

A self-described *"bioethicist,"* Dr. D has written extensively on who should get healthcare, who should be denied, whose life is worth saving, and who should decide all of this. In September 2014, he wrote an article which appeared in *The Atlantic* magazine titled *"Why I Hope to Die at 75."* Allow me to translate: You will die from heath care rationing; he will be the one on the death panel denying you a reprieve. This is the "central planning" concept of *"The Communist Manifesto"* run completely amok. As I approach my golden years, Dr. D is the last man on earth I want designing my health care system. Nor do I want people who have no problem with partial-birth abortion in charge of *anybody's* health care.

Dr. D has devised some sort of convoluted mathematical points system called the *"Complete Lives System"* to decide who gets health care and who is denied. I reject the premise of *any* mathematical formula dreamed up by an oxymoronic "liberal genius." To liberals, math is the application of qualitative terms like "some," "more," "less," "a lot," "few," "much," etc., *not* actual numbers.

We can imagine this tool in the hands of Barack Obama: liberals get healthcare. Conservatives, libertarians, and independents do not. This is the same criterion the Obama IRS used when deciding which political action groups get tax-exempt status. Why would anyone expect their driving principles to change? Obamacare death panels would turn what used to be an IRS financial penalty for Obama's political opposition into a death sentence. Obama has the conscience of the cold-blooded communist dictators he admires so greatly; he would have no problem with it.

The liberal economist Jonathan Gruber was every bit as repulsive as Dr. D. He is Rodney Dangerfield with the comedic talent of Luca Brasi ("The Godfather" character).

His chief function in the assembly of the Obamacare Frankenstein monster was to deceive the American people into supporting it by lying about its economic impact.

"Lack of transparency is a huge political advantage," Gruber said in an October 2013 panel discussion at the University of Pennsylvania. *"And basically, call it the <u>stupidity</u> of the American voter or whatever, but basically that was really, really critical for the thing to pass."* I'm guessing *"basically"* is one of Gruber's favorite words…*basically* speaking. Gruber made the comment while discussing how the law was *"written in a tortured way"* to avoid a bad score from the Congressional Budget Office (CBO), which couldn't score a touchdown against tall grass.

Gruber was later called to testify before members of a House investigation committee. He gave testimony on December 9, 2014, in which he apologized for his remarks, calling them *"glib, thoughtless, and sometimes downright insulting."* In truth, he was apologizing for getting caught on tape, not for his offensive remarks. A skunk cannot change his stripe. Gruber is *de facto* the Mother of All Clucks. Now, in any discussion of my personal resume, I emphasize that I do *not* have any degrees from MIT in economics.

We should acknowledge that Dr. Gruber has secured immortality for himself in the "Urban Dictionary" with his Obamacare performance. Gruber-speech is defined there as *"Telling someone a lie because you think they are too stupid to know the truth. It's usually used when you want to cheat the person out of something and you lie to them to pull off the scam, relying on the gullible nature of people. The name comes from Jonathan Gruber's many comments about how the Obama Administration exploited the stupidity of the American voter to pass Obamacare. Newt Gingrich coined the phrase in Nov. 2014."* This prestigious honor easily eclipses Obama's 2009 Nobel Peace Prize.

This brings me to my definition of a pathological liar: someone who if given an equal probability of outcome will chose to tell a lie rather than the truth. I attribute this behavior to a derived childish self-satisfaction in the cleverness of deceit. To liberals, *Grubering* is its own reward, which is why it universally pervaded during the Obama administration.

Some Obamacare Senate bribery deals were so egregious they had their own titles (*e.g., "the Cornhusker Kickback," "the Louisiana Purchase"*). House Speaker Pelosi delivered a primer on how the legislative process works to the American people: *"We won the election; we write the bill,"* in justification of rejecting any and all Republican input on the healthcare bill. Later (03.09.10) as the legislative process neared completion *"We have to pass this bill to find out what's in it, blah, blah, blah."* Pelosi actually makes Spicoli ("Fast Times at Ridgemont High" male bimbo) look smart.

The new 2,700 page bill did not include the 10,000+ pages of regulations that were to follow.

The United States Constitution (including 27 amendments) takes up approximately 15 pages of print. All legislation signed into law should be limited to Constitution-size maximum to preempt the kind of scam the Democrats pulled on the American people with Obamacare.

As Dr. Gruber informed us later, the law was intentionally written in such a way that it was ambiguous at best, but more often than not just incoherent. The only coherent part of the law was the oft utilized phrase *"...or as deemed by the Secretary,"* which essentially meant the Obama regime could make it up as they went along...which they did.

Hard deadlines written into the base law were ignored. Financial penalties to favored political supporter groups were waived or postponed. The goal of the evasive tactics was always the same: get Democrats through the next election before the eventual damage to voters was unleashed. The strategy failed more often than not as Obamacare notable Democrats Mary Landrieu ("Louisiana Purchase" negotiator), Ben Nelson ("Cornhusker Kickback" negotiator), and Michigan congressman Bart Stupak (abortion funding opponent) went down to election defeat. Many more Democrats followed, an expression of America's gratitude for the Democrats' colossal socialist stunt. I think the Democrat party will not be finished paying for the Obamacare pariah for many election cycles yet to come.

Although now law, Obamacare still had to survive a SCOTUS challenge. Before the SCOTUS, administration lawyers argued that the purchase mandate was a fee allowed under the Commerce Clause of the Constitution, not a tax. The Commerce Clause grants the power *"to regulate commerce with foreign nations, and among the several states..."* to the Federal government. The Obamacare ruling by the SCOTUS in National Federation of Independent Business v. Sibelius (HHS Secretary) case was decided on June 28, 2012. The SCOTUS ruling was a 5-4 ruling to uphold Obamacare.

In the ruling, Chief Justice John Roberts completely rejected the Obama administration's unprecedented argument that the individual mandate was constitutional under Congress' power *"to regulate commerce...among the several states."* However, Justice Roberts went on to add after his announcement teaser, *"Such legislation is within Congress's power to tax."* In short, as the deciding vote, the Chief Justice completely rejected the administration's argument, then awarded them the victory. The whole convoluted absurd ruling sounds like something ex-FBI Director Comey would come up with. Or maybe there's just something wrong with the Washington DC water supply.

Along the way I did a financial impact assessment on myself if I were forced onto Obamacare. Pre-Medicare, my annual premiums would have been approximately $6,000+ per year ($500 per month) for the cheapest "Bronze Plan." Annual deductible was approximately $7,000+. In *none* of the past 10 years would I have met the deductible. My $6,000+ per year premiums would have served simply to enrich Washington DC. Of course I still had private coverage and was *not* forced onto Obamacare...

yet. But the Obama plan was all too clear: force all private healthcare insurers out of business, then fleece the American people with the "Affordable" Care Act *unaffordable* premiums and out-of-reach deductibles. Obamacare is a Bolshevik's wet dream: so much cash (less overhead) to redistribute, so little time!

Of course the Marxist-designed Obamacare was a colossal redistribution of wealth scheme in the form of healthcare, which is roughly 1/6th of the American economy. The macro idea was to (1) force everyone onto Obamacare; (2) charge exorbitant premiums with equally exorbitant deductibles; (3) then give subsidies to the Democrat base parasite class. The Marxist overseers would direct the flow of healthcare (including death panels) and collect their fat overhead salaries. The death panels would be a huge weaponry upgrade in Obama's arsenal of dirty tricks over such tools as the IRS harassment and FBI thuggery that is now being exposed.

So Obama was re-elected in 2012 and the hideous monstrosity of government overreach into healthcare rambles on like a loose cannon for another four years. *"The forest was shrinking, but the trees kept voting for the axe because its handle was made of wood, so they thought it was one of them."* – Anonymous. It might eventually have served its purpose as the nexus to single-payer well enough except for a major spanner in the works: Hillary Clinton lost the 2016 presidential election.

Late in the 2016 election cycle, Bill Clinton blasted the core principles of Obamacare as unworkable at a Flint, MI, campaign rally. In a rare moment of truth and clarity, Clinton told the crowd *"You've got this crazy system where all the sudden 25 million more people have healthcare and then the people who are out there busting it, sometimes 60 hours a week, wind up with their premiums doubled and their coverage cut in half...it's the craziest thing in the world."*

Meanwhile, Hillary promised to build on the Obamacare catastrophe. Mr. Clinton later realized he was telling truth and walked it back with the old "taken out of context" disclaimer, which is alibi *numero uno* in the liberal Rolodex.

What Obama wasn't counting on was ever leaving office. Or, in the event he was not able to annul the 22nd Amendment, which limits a president to two terms, he would be succeeded by a sock puppet like Joe Biden who would soldier on for the Bolshevik cause at Obama's micromanaging direction. The last thing Obama expected after eight years of his socialist/social justice agenda was to be followed in office by an American patriot, Donald Trump in particular.

As we have come to learn, the only thing that matters to Democrats *now* is Obama's "legacy." Since he was unwilling, unable, and unprepared to work with Republicans, very little of his agenda ever took the form of signed legislation. It rather took the form of executive orders and bureaucratic regulation. His true legacy will be somewhere in the microscopic to non-existent range.

The partisan Obamacare cannot survive as it was written. Republicans attempted to bail Democrats out of the Obamacare hole they had dug for themselves in 2017, but Democrats blocked the effort. Democrats have too much political capital at stake to abandon Obamacare now. They have too much invested in Obama to abandon his legacy now. Bailing out the Titanic on its way to the bottom would have been an easier task than escaping the political death sentence for this American horror story.

Now Democrats are stuck with it until it drags them to the bottom, which they are currently nearing. The Democrats' election strategy will be to blame the failure of Obamacare on Republicans, *none* of whom voted for it. Even with the help of their corrupt comrades in the MSM, this will *not* sell. The Democrats gave America Obamacare; the Republicans gave America tax cuts. Which will America choose in the 2018 Mid-term elections and beyond? Wendy's burger "A" or burger "B"?

The only other legislative accomplishment of the Democrat-controlled Congress before the House was returned to the Republicans in 2010 was the *Dodd–Frank Wall Street Reform and Consumer Protection Act* (commonly called Dodd-Frank) which was signed into law by President Obama on July 21, 2010. The stated intent of the law was to protect America from a repeat of the recent subprime mortgage crisis, which was caused by Democrats. The true purpose of the act was to punish American financial institutions for succumbing to Democrat pressure to make home loans to people who could not possibly ever pay the loans off.

The law was a mammoth (2,300 pages with 22,000 pages of accompanying regulations) incoherent partisan gumbo of more bureaucracy and regulation for America's financial institutions. It effectively replaced the Sarbanes–Oxley (Sox) Act, a 66-page law passed with bipartisan support in 2002 and signed into law by President Bush. Sox was directed at correcting the corporate financial malpractice at Enron, World Com, etc.

The subprime mortgage crisis and its aftermath was exactly what you would expect when you elect Marxists like Barney Frank and Maxine Waters and put them in charge of overseeing the housing market: (1) a housing price bubble; (2) a housing price collapse; (3) stifling punitive scapegoating legislation called Dodd-Frank to distract from the real culprits in Congress and target business, which socialists hate.

Although it is not possible to understand the Dodd-Frank impact from the 2,300 page text, it is possible to examine the overall performance of the economy.

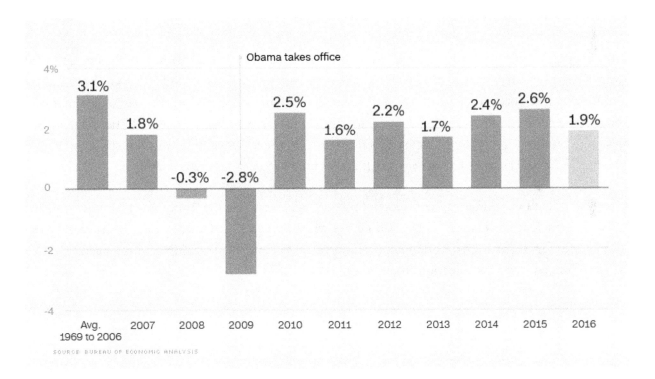

SOURCE: BUREAU OF ECONOMIC ANALYSIS

The average GDP growth during Obama's tenure in the Oval Office (excluding the -2.8% in 2009) was 2.1% compared with the long term (1969-2006) average of 3.1%. In no year in the Obamanomic era did America's GDP growth reach 3%, a record unequalled in America history. America has been treated to a new expression in the Obamaspeak jargon: "the new normal" in reference to economic mediocrity.

Dodd-Frank contributed substantially to America's economic anemia by drying up loan capital through over-regulation and micromanagement. This result is of no concern to Democrats who see business as a rival to government. Besides, any substandard economic result (or anything else) would be blamed on George W. Bush with a major assist from the MSM propaganda factory.

So aside from the unmitigated catastrophe Obamacare, what will Obama's legacy? The first "black" American president? That is not an accomplishment. Skin color belongs on a law enforcement BOLO ("Be On the Look Out"), not a resume.

We should not overlook Obama's skill as an administrator. Every competent manager should be asking himself "Are we doing the right things?" as opposed to "Are we doing things right?"

Then the July 2010 announcement by the administration that NASA had been retasked to *"reach out to the Muslim world"* should come as no surprise to America. What surprised me was that no other agencies (e.g., the EPA, the FBI, the IRS, the BLM, etc.) followed suit in tribute to the vast Muslim contribution to America (minus the 9-11-01 attack, of course).

How about "He got Osama Bin Laden"? The truth is OBL was located due to intelligence gathered from Khalid Sheikh Mohammed (KSM), who was the mastermind of the 9-11 World Trade Center and Pentagon terror attacks. KSM was water-boarded in Gitmo and gave up the name of OBL's personal courier. The courier then led the CIA to OBL's safe house in Abbottabad, Pakistan. Obama was *opposed* to water-boarding, which he outlawed. Obama was also *opposed* to Gitmo, which he attempted to close. Without the tools Obama *opposed*, there would have been no OBL raid.

OBL was killed in a courageous and successful Navy SEAL raid on the Abbottabad complex on May 2, 2011. President Obama was on the golf course when Secretary of Defense Leon Panetta gave the *"Go!"* order for the raid. Obama donned a windbreaker to cover his golf shirt and the Secret Service whisked him away for the Situation Room photo op.

None of these details prevented Obama from taking full credit for success of the raid in his same day *"I/me/my"* address to the American people. If the raid had been unsuccessful, he would have been back out on the golf course with a media blackout on the failed raid.

SYNOPSIS: For four years America struggled economically, racially, spiritually, and hopelessly under the dictums of the Marxist-driven Obama regime. The affirmative action prayer "Let's give him the benefit of the doubt" punctuated each absurd daily assault on America. The meaningless campaign slogan *"Hope and change"* **disappeared faster than the bank in an armed robbers' getaway car rear-view mirror.**

But wait! There's more!!! Read on, Pilgrim.

11. OBAMUNISM 2.0: AMERICA NO MAS!?!?!?

"True Revolutionaries do not flaunt their radicalism. They cut their hair, put on a suit, and infiltrate the system from within." – **Saul D. Alinsky.**

On March 26, 2012, Obama was caught on a hot mic in Seoul, South Korea, with Russian President Dmitry Medvedev: *"On all these issues, but particularly missile defense, this, this can be solved, but it's important for him to give me space…After my election I have more flexibility."* Medvedev's response: *"I understand. I will transmit this information to Vladimir, and I stand with you."*

Allow me to translate Obama's message to "Vladimir": "After I win this next election, I will no longer be accountable to the American people. You won't have to roll me for America's lunch money. I will just give it to you."

Contrary to how this may sound, this "Kodak moment" was not treason or even the "collusion" candidate Trump was guilty of based on evidence that is yet to be uncovered over a year and a half later. The difference was that Trump *never* actually spoke to *any* Russians. Trump was the victim of a salacious <u>*fictional*</u> Russian "dirty dossier" financed by the Hillary Clinton presidential campaign. *This* is the very definition of "collusion."

As for the "dirty dossier" itself, my guess is that the real subject was Bill Clinton. Then after being paid $12+M by the Hillary campaign, the "Global Fusion" authors did a cut of Bill Clinton's name from the dossier and paste of Donald Trump's name into the dossier…just a hunch.

We have learned since the 2012 meeting between Obama and Medvedev that the non-criminal charge of "collusion" is an impeachable offense, referring to things we wish were true, but actually never happened. We have also learned that firing a partisan hack incompetent loose cannon employee such as

FBI Director James Comey is now deemed obstruction of justice by no less than highly self-esteemed uber authority and brain amputation survivor Maxine Waters (D-CA), who doesn't know the word "fear"…or any other word. President Trump has deemed her *"low IQ"*…he is quite generous. You would think her accomplice role in creating the housing bubble of a decade ago would have been enough damage for one lifetime…wrong again!

Self-described socialist Rep. Waters, who maintains a residence in high end Hancock Park in the California 33 rd Congressional District, represents California's 43rd Congressional District miles away. It is apparent that she is much appreciated there for her efforts to bring Venezuelan style socialism to Los Angeles by the posters which pock mark her district.

The title of this book ascribes liberals in general as being from Uranus. Ms. Waters, who played the role of cheerleader for the rioters during the 1992 Watts riots, is a little further out than that…I'm thinking Pluto.

Political commentator savants Diamond and Silk have described Maxine Waters as a *"domestic terrorist"* for her violence-inciting rhetoric. Their description will be inaccurate if California succeeds from the United States. At that point, she becomes an international terrorist. WARNING! America should *not*

touch Congresswoman Waters' toxic socialist infested ideas or her self-destructive hatred of President Trump with a 10 foot condom tipped pole.

Perhaps Obama's legacy will be his "red line" in Syria? *"We have been very clear to the Assad regime, but also to other players on the ground, that a <u>red line</u> for us is we start seeing a whole bunch of chemical weapons moving around or being utilized. That would change my calculus. That would change my equation."* – Barack Obama, who doesn't know a second derivative from second base, a second mortgage, or the second hand on a clock, at a 08.20.12 press conference, pretending as if he knows what calculus is.

U.S. government intelligence sources soon after confirmed that Syrian President Bashar al-Assad *was* continuing to use chemical weapons on his opposition in Syria. Obama did nothing to back up his red line. This was deemed *"strategic patience"* in Obamaspeak, the contemporary equivalent of *"Newspeak"* in George Orwell's novel *1984*. Bury *"strategic patience"* in the time capsule along with *"workplace violence,"* *"man-caused disasters,"* *"teachable moment,"* *"shovel-ready jobs,"* and *"period,"* as in *"If you like your health care plan, you'll be able to keep your health care plan. <u>Period!</u>"* Or as W.C. Fields once remarked as he handed over his IOU to a sucker *"Worth its weight in gold."*

Obama spent the rest of his presidency explaining he either did not make the *"red line"* comment, or that you just misunderstood what he meant. Evidently he is a subscriber to the Jonathan Gruber theory on *"the <u>stupidity</u> of the American voter."* *"First of all, I didn't set a red line; the world set a red line,"* Obama responded at another press conference on Sept. 04, 2012. The entire *"red line"* episode was Exhibit "A" for the case that Obama was *never* up to the task of Commander-in-Chief.

Perhaps Obama's legacy will be Benghazi? On the night of Sept. 11, 2012, the American consulate in Benghazi, Libya, was attacked by the radical Islamic terrorist group Ansar al-Sharia. U.S. Ambassador to Libya Christopher Stevens and three other Americans were killed in the attack. The attack was clearly premeditated, utilizing mortars and rocket-propelled grenades (RPGs).

Since this attack occurred less than two months before the 2012 presidential election, the Muslim-descended Obama remained hyper-sensitive to negative Muslim publicity. The Obama regime needed a scapegoat, a villain, a focus of hatred for the Benghazi massacre. Something that would distract Americans away from crucial relevant questions like:

1. Where were Obama and Hillary during the attack?

2. Who gave the stand-down order for rescue forces that would likely have saved the Benghazi victims?

3. Why were Ambassador Stevens' earlier pleas for security upgrade in Libya ignored?

4. What was the ambassador doing in Benghazi in the first place?

Why not an obscure YouTube video to distract America?

To be clear, the truth about the nature of the Benghazi was known immediately by U.S. intelligence and virtually concurrently by the Obama regime. The YouTube cover-up story did not have to hold up for more than a couple of months until after the early November election. Obviously this would only be possible with a corrupt and complicit MSM.

Yes, Muslims were *not* at fault for the attack! America must have done something to provoke them!! A crappy anti-Muslim YouTube video allowed by the crappy 1ˢᵗ Amendment of the crappy U.S. Constitution is the culprit!!!

And so the saga begins, much the way the "Russian hacker" meme took on its life, i.e., out of thin air… dreamed up by people who have nothing better to do than manufacture mischief and mayhem. Nice work if you can get it.

The producer of the *YouTube* video *"The Innocence of Muslims"* was a Coptic Christian living in Southern California named Nakoula Basseley Nakoula. He was arrested and charged with eight counts of probation violation from earlier crimes not related to his video, jailed without bail, and deemed a *"danger to the community."* Today he lives in a homeless shelter in the Los Angeles area.

Obama's mission assignment to his inner circle of jerks was crystal clear: get Him through the 2012 election without damage from his Benghazi incompetence. U.N. Ambassador Susan Rice, who is also a pathological liar, was selected to *Gruber* the American public with the YouTube fantasy. Ms. Rice was a guest on several Sunday news talk shows on Sept. 16, 2012, five days after the Benghazi attack. The same Ms. Rice who later claimed that admitted Army deserter Sgt. Beau Bergdahl had served his country *"with honor and distinction."* America didn't buy that one, either.

Ms. Rice's Sunday broadcast message to America was unmistakable: the Benghazi attack was a *"spontaneous reaction to a hateful Internet video"* which our government condemns. The CIA reports on the Benghazi attack made *no* mention of a YouTube video. The reports did mention that there had been prior numerous threats against the American Embassy, and that Islamic terrorists were the perpetrators of the fatal 09-11-12 attack.

Obama's White House staff added the video cause to the ambassador's broadcast message, and deleted all reference to prior threats and "Islamic terrorists," which had long since been amputated from the Obamaspeak dictionary.

Barack Obama's remarks to David Letterman on his *"Late Show,"* less than a week after the Benghazi massacre (Sept. 18, 2012): *"Here's what happened. ... You had a video that was released by somebody who lives here, sort of a shadowy character who made an extremely offensive video directed at Mohammed and Islam... making fun of the Prophet Mohammed. And so, this caused great offense in much of the Muslim world. But what also happened, extremists and terrorists used this as an excuse to attack a variety of our embassies, including the one, the consulate in Libya."* Obama's account of the radical Islamic massacre at Benghazi was effectively a repeat of his Ft. Hood "workplace violence" whitewash.

Obama then addressed the U.N. a week later on Sept. 25, 2012: *"That is what we saw play out in the last two weeks, as a crude and disgusting video sparked outrage throughout the Muslim world...I have made it clear that the United States government had nothing to do with this video, and I believe its message must be rejected by all who respect our common humanity,"* said Obama. *"It is an insult not only to Muslims, but to America as well...We understand why people take offense to this video because millions of our citizens are among them. I know there are some who ask why we don't just ban such a video. The answer is enshrined in our laws: our Constitution protects the right to practice free speech."*

So in a single teleprompter recital, Obama knowingly lied about the cause of the Benghazi attack, then trashed the U.S. Constitution and the 1st Amendment in particular on the world stage. The pathetic pandering performance was well received in Paris, Pakistan, and Phnom Penh (please excuse the alliteration).

The bodies of the four American Benghazi Islamic terrorist attack victims were flown into Andrews Air Force Base on October 25, 2012. The victims were Ambassador Stevens, Foreign Service information management officer Sean Smith, and ex-Navy CIA contractors Tyrone Woods and Glen Doherty.

According to Patricia Smith, mother of slain Sean Smith, Secretary of State Hillary Clinton *"looked me squarely in the eye and told me a <u>video</u> was responsible"* on the Andrews AFB tarmac. Charles Woods, father of slain Tyrone Woods, reported that Secretary Clinton said to him at the Andrews AFB ceremony, *"We will make sure that the person who made the film is arrested and prosecuted."* As we know, Hillary later denied she said anything to anybody about a video (while she and Brian Williams ducked sniper fire on the Andrews AFB tarmac). ***One of the seven danger signals of a pathological liar is when they begin telling lies to undo the earlier lies they have told.***

Hillary later reflected her deep concern for the Benghazi incident in testimony before a Senate committee hearing on Jan. 13, 2013: *"…what difference does it make?"*

Obviously, precious little to her or anyone else in the Obama cabal. Ambassador Stevens remains unavailable for comment.

The Benghazi cover-up morphed into a cover-up of the cover-up as the 2012 election drew near. It was a bridge too far to expect the MSM to keep the truth about Benghazi from the American people. "Spontaneous protesters" don't spontaneously bring mortars to their protests. If no one in technically advanced America saw the *"hateful YouTube video,"* who actually believes a mob of Islamic thugs in Libya were triggered by a YouTube video no one ever heard of? Maybe the spontaneous protestors all got "crappy YouTube video" spontaneous alerts on their new iPhone 10s?

Now the Obama's *new* mission *re*assignment to his inner circle of jerks is changed into convincing America *nobody* ever said the Benghazi attack was caused by the YouTube video...lying about the lies... *Gruber* the American people yet again; they're stupid; they'll buy it...besides, to challenge America's historic black president on *anything* would be *"Racist!"*

I thought a more creative approach would have been to issue a statement lamenting the recent passing of Ben Ghazi (August 28, 1930 – February 3, 2012), who played the villain in "Road House". "Our thoughts and prayers are with the family."

That should have been good enough to *Gruber* most American voters.

This effort came to a climax during the second 2012 presidential debate at Hofstra University on Oct. 16, 2012. CNN correspondent Candy Crowley was an Obama sycophant disguised as the debate "moderator."

During the debate, Gov. Romney asserted that it took President Obama fourteen days to call the Benghazi attack an act of terror. Ms. Crowley quickly inserted herself into the line of fire by explaining to Gov. Romney that *"He (Obama) did in fact call it an act of terror...I want to move you on."* Of course she wanted to move on from this potential land-mine in Obama's path. At this point, Gov. Romney realized he was outnumbered on stage 2 to 1 and discontinued his discussion of Benghazi. *This* is the hazard of a CNN moderated debate: Romney was the meat in a liberal sandwich.

Later, well after the election was over, Ms. Crowley said that Obama *was* late in identifying the attacks in Benghazi as terrorism, quite contrary to what she said during the Presidential debate. Gov. Romney could not be caught up in what later would later be described by the MSM as a misogynistic attack on the defenseless damsel "moderator" Ms. Crowley. This is why you don't want a liberal female "moderator." It is also why you don't want a "moderator" from the egregiously biased CNN. Ms. Crowley's career as an impartial journalist went up in smoke on Oct. 16, 2012. I wonder if she thinks her 15 minutes of fame were worth it.

The Benghazi exchange during the Hofstra debate is symbolic of a much broader issue: general liberal media bias, intervention and activism. For the Media, this activism is a manifestation of their self-worth and moral superiority. They, too, want to bathe in the glory of wealth redistribution, giving other people's money away and "social justice." They want to earn the moral superhero status they envision for themselves by uplifting the poor, the downtrodden, and the oppressed people of color with taxpayer money. They want to go down on the right side of history in sacrifice for "The Messiah." What better way to showboat this self-delusion than putting your big fat corrupt thumb on the scale of a presidential debate on behalf of America's historic first black president?

So the Obama regime and the MSM has America chasing the cover-up red herring of the Benghazi cover-up while the substance of the Benghazi massacre escaped America's attention, by design.

Who was Ambassador Stevens doing at Benghazi in the first place? We know at the time there was a civil war in progress in Syria between the government forces of Bashar Al-Assad and government protestors now joined by ISIS. Assad had embarrassed Obama on the world stage by calling Obama's "red line" empty rhetoric. We know that Obama is a vindictive, petty, small man who focuses on the irrelevant. We know of Obama's impulsive obsession with arming America's enemies: the Mexican drug cartels with assault weapons (*"Fast and Furious"*); the Muslim Brotherhood in Egypt with F-16 fighter jets, and M1A1 tanks; Iran with nukes and cash for terrorism.

No plausible explanation for Ambassador Stevens' presence at Benghazi has ever been given. It doesn't take Team Scorpion (TV series) to figure this out.

Who gave the "stand down" order to rescue forces who could have saved the four American victims at Benghazi? This could be the best kept secret since the KFC recipe. Rather amazing how this was never pursued with any tenacity of purpose, wasn't it? I suspect that is because you don't want to know…or at the very least there is someone very near the *top* of the food chain of command who doesn't want you to know. But if Benghazi was in fact the Middle Eastern encore to *Fast & Furious*, one thing is certain: dead men tell no tales. No survivors meant no one would ever tell what the purpose of the Benghazi visit was.

The whereabouts of Obama and Hillary during the Benghazi crisis are anybody's guess. What do *you* do after a tough day at the office? No 3AM calls on their itinerary; Ambassador Stephens and Benghazi will have to take care of themselves.

Why were Ambassador Steven's pleas to the State Department for security upgrades ignored? Senator Ron Johnson (R-WI), who was on the receiving end of Hillary Clinton's infamous *"What difference, at this point, does it make?"* outburst in the Senate Investigating Committee hearing, later wrote an op-ed in the Milwaukee Journal Sentinel describing Ms. Clinton's job performance re: Benghazi as *"dereliction of duty."* Sen. Johnson's claim was that the State Department *"failed to honor repeated requests for additional security"* and *"actually reduced security in Libya."*

Hillary's State Department swatted this question away with correspondence evidence that comingled *"requests"* and *"concerns"* from Ambassador Stevens, then minimized the *"requests."* But the truth is that the State Department and Secretary Clinton simply ignored Ambassador Stevens' numerous requests. It is likely they did not want the publicity of having to increase security at an outpost in a Muslim country. Our historic first Muslim-descended president wanted to create the illusion that He was the carrier of peace to the Middle East. Arming up American diplomatic outposts there is hardly consistent with Obama's peacemaker vision of Himself, likewise uttering the words "Islamic terrorist." At any rate, ignoring the requests for security upgrades in Libya ultimately cost Ambassador Stevens and the other three American victims at Benghazi their lives.

Perhaps Obama's legacy will be abusing valued trusted allies Great Britain and Israel while embracing vile worthless contemptable enemies Iran and Cuba.

Israeli Prime Minister Netanyahu became the focal point of Obama's acrimony toward Israel. Netanyahu and Obama were like Batman and the Joker. During the 2015 Israeli election cycle, the Obama State Department gave $349,276 in U.S. taxpayer-funded grants to a political group in Israel to build a campaign operation, which subsequently was used to try to influence Israelis to vote against conservative Benjamin Netanyahu. Yes, *this* is how I want my tax dollars spent. "Netanyahu" is Yiddish for "I am not a yahoo." Conversely, "Obama" is Swahili for "Flaming yahoo." Now I understand.

Perhaps Obama's legacy will be his battlefield savvy. With no military training whatsoever, he stepped into the role of Commander in Chief and instantly snatched defeat from the jaws of victory in the Iraq War, which had already been won.

After a little more than a month in office, Obama announced that America's combat mission would end by Aug. 31, 2010, a year and a half later. To understand this stellar decision, you must understand the liberal mindset: they hate war more than you do. They must "virtue signal" their hatred by opposing everything military, including repudiating a victory that had already been won. So Obama pulled out of Iraq creating the crucial incubator for ISIS expansion. This triggered an exodus by America's allies from Iraq. The American withdrawal was completed by the end of 2012.

Liberal management of our military is our enemies' best friend and the surest path to America's defeat. The crippling "rules of engagement" fabricated by the anti-war left sabotaged the war effort in Vietnam.

The vacuum that formed in the wake of the American withdrawal led directly to the formation of ISIS. It leaves me to wonder what Obama thought was going to happen in oil-rich, government-unstable Iraq after the American beat cop left. Obama's campaign promise to get America out of Iraq was effectively accomplished by surrendering to America's radical Islamic enemies.

As sectarian violence in Iraq proliferated post American withdrawal, Obama needed a scapegoat for the daily increasing chaos. His story was that George Bush failed to negotiate a *status of forces agreement* (SoF) which would have allowed American forces to remain in Iraq *legally*. It is unclear to me why Bush didn't need the SoF agreement to invade Iraq in the first place. And of course Obama could not have obtained said agreement for undisclosed reasons. *This* is why you do <u>*not*</u> want a self-imagined lawyer in charge of your armed forces. It's too bad the Germans and Japanese didn't use the *status of forces* tactic to force the Allies to leave at the conclusion of World War II. Obviously, they needed better lawyers.

Obama's Iraq performance as Retreater-in-Chief was the segue to the ascendency of ISIS in the Middle East. This should be of little to no concern for Americans, as Obama assured us in a January 2014 interview for *New Yorker* magazine: *"The analogy we use around here sometimes, and I think is accurate, is if a jayvee team puts on Lakers uniforms that doesn't make them Kobe Bryant."* Yet again the Sportscaster-in-Chief bedazzles us with his knowledge of basketball utilizing a laser-focused metaphor. Foreign policy? Not so much. A career at the incredible shrinking ESPN beckons at the conclusion of his White House gig.

An emboldened ISIS wreaks murder and mayhem in the Middle East with brutality that is beyond barbaric and completely inhuman. Many of the ISIS victims are Christians. As Western civilization becomes numb to mundane beheading videos, ISIS becomes more psychotic in its lust for attention. Burning alive videos and drowning in cage videos are next as mere beheadings no longer entertain the cable news cycle.

"Now let's make two things clear: ISIL is not 'Islamic.' No religion condones the killing of innocents, and the vast majority of ISIL's victims have been Muslim. And ISIL is certainly not a state...it is a terrorist organization, pure and simple," – Barack Obama informs us (09.10.14).

So let me get this *straight* (offending LGBTIQZWTFers in the process). Obama encourages any person to declare him/her/itself any gender he/she/it so desires on any given day, and use whichever bathroom suits his/her/its whim. But Obama forbids ISIS from declaring themselves *"Islamic"* or a *"state."* Their self-described religious affiliation and political status have been vetoed by the Messiah, the self-appointed global thought policeman.

Meanwhile, President Obama focuses like a laser on his "social justice" merit badge. His top priority issues: global warming, transgender bathrooms, the Washington Redskins team name, alleged police brutality, importing the Ebola virus into America, closing Gitmo, military social gender experiments, importing Central American and Middle Eastern refugees into America, etc. Add in golf outings, White House parties with Jay-Z and Beyoncé, and taxpayer- financed Hawaiian and Martha's Vineyard vacations, and you have a full itinerary. ISIS will just have to wait for the next president. Fortunately for America, President Trump was elected and cleaned the Obama ISIS mess up *post haste.*

On Nov. 12, 2015, President Obama declared in an interview with ABC sycophant George Stephanopoulos that ISIS had been *"contained,"* asserting that *"the terror cell had been stalled in Iraq and Syria."*

Within 12 hours of Obama's timely update, ISIS executed a series of deadly attacks in Paris, France, on Nov. 13, 2015. The body count was 130 dead, over 400 wounded. George Stephanopoulos did not conduct a follow-up interview. Never mind…back to NCAA bracketology.

The era of "strategic patience" creaked to a halt on Jan. 20, 2017, when Donald Trump became Commander in Chief. Instead of admitting transgender enlistment and sex change operations, the American military focus shifted to defeating the heinous sub-human radical Islamic enemy called ISIS. No more micro-management, no more prohibitive rules of engagement. The results have been stark and devastating to the now near extinct ISIS.

The MSM has ignored the Trump success story with ISIS, along with America's miraculous 2017 economic rebound, the vast improvement on border security, the collapse of Obamacare, etc. The MSM has bigger fish to fry, focusing instead on Melania Trump's shoes, how many scoops of ice cream Donald Trump consumes, Trump trashing the White House bust of MLK, how Donald Trump fed koi (fish) in a pond with the Japanese Prime Minister, Trump's height and weight as reported on his annual routine physical exam, etc. ***"One picture is worth a thousand words."*** – Frederick R. Barnard.

This is Job One for the MSM. With each Trump success, the psychotic MSM redoubles its effort to manufacture the illusion of failure. They have long since sacrificed their own credibility to the Trump Derangement Syndrome (TDS) mental disorder. _Donald J. Trump demonstrates daily to the MSM why he is a billionaire and they are not. They don't understand that, either._

The fact that the MSM is unwilling to cover the annihilation of ISIS should be no surprise to anyone. Remember they too are typical liberals who cannot distinguish between _"radical Islam"_ and _"Islam."_ That is the same reason Obama refused to meaningfully pursue ISIS.

Perhaps Obama's legacy will be his unequalled skill as a negotiator on behalf of America. Case in point: the Beau Bergdahl hostage negotiation.

In June of 2009, Sgt. Beau Bergdahl walked off his post in Afghanistan and was captured by the Taliban. He was held captive for almost 5 years. Then in May 2014, after covert negotiations with the Taliban, the Obama regime agreed to a prisoner swap to free Bergdahl. The exchange involved five Taliban general-level Gitmo detainees for the American army sergeant, who later plead guilty to the charge of desertion.

Aside from the sheer magnitude of the giveaway, the Obama-approved deal had _major_ flaws:

1. The exchange required congressional approval based on the National Defense Authorization Act. Obama blew the NDAA requirement off. Yet his abuse of power went unchallenged due to the threat of the omnipresent _"Racist!"_ allegation.

2. The exchange set the dangerous precedent that America was now willing to negotiate with terrorists. That means there _will_ be more kidnapped Americans.

3. There were no real restrictions on the five Taliban _capos_ post-release, who were in the wind immediately after landing in the Persian Gulf nation of Qatar. Their return to the battlefield to kill American soldiers is highly probable.

Yet again we have an example of Obama willing to negotiate with our nation's enemies, but not with Republicans.

In celebration of his magnificent negotiation effort, Obama held a photo-op White House Rose Garden ceremony with Sgt. Bergdahl's parents on May 31, 2014. He congratulated Himself for a job well done, stating _"And he wasn't forgotten by his country, because the United States of America does not ever leave our men and women in uniform behind."_ Especially deserters. Ambassador Stephens was still unavailable for comment.

You can't make this stuff up. Aside from the fact that Bergdahl was a deserter, Obama had no interest whatsoever in his release. His only motivation was to empty Gitmo so he could fulfill his obsession of closing it down and ceding the base back to Cuba. The negative impact on troop morale of lauding a deserter as a returning hero was Obama's *pièce de résistance*.

At least six American soldiers were killed in the search for Bergdahl. Later at the conclusion of Bergdahl's court martial trial, Bergdahl received a dishonorable discharge and was credited with time served in Taliban captivity, no additional prison time. The judge was Army Colonel Jeffrey Nance, who was obviously auditioning for a seat on the 9th Circus Court of Appeals post-military career. Within hours of the Nov. 3, 2017, sentencing, President Trump tweeted, *"The decision on Sergeant Bergdahl is a complete and total disgrace to our country and to our military."* No kidding.

Just like the national debt, opioid addiction doubled during the Obama presidency years.

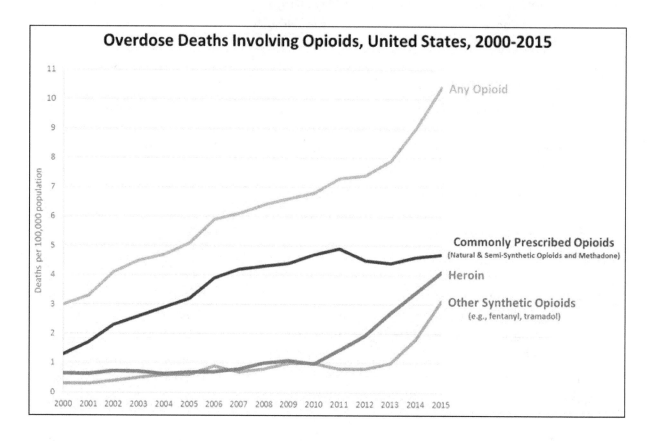

Over the same time period, the federal government almost doubled its issue of food stamps:

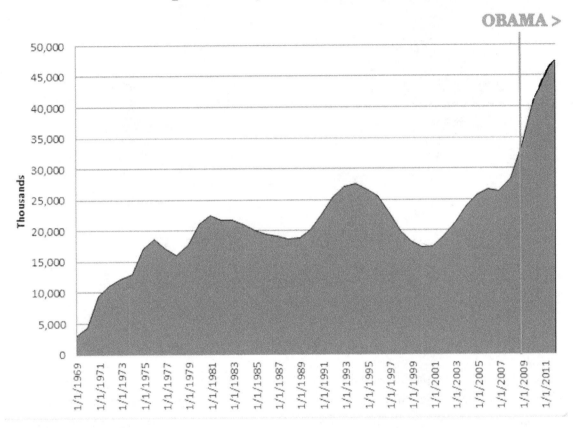

Average Participation - Food Stamps

OBAMA >

The similarities in the shapes of the opioid deaths and the food stamps graphs strongly suggests they are directly related. Why would that be? Would it make sense that opioid addiction would be driven by economic distress, just like food stamp utilization? An emphatic *"Yes."* This *is* the Obama opioid epidemic.

Let us visualize the opioid epidemic in terms of supply and demand. Demand is driven by eight years of public economic frustration, hardship, and failed socialist government overreaching economic policies. The stress of a comatose national economy is the key demand factor. Supply is maintained through an open southern border, plus over-prescription of pain killers by disengaged doctors.

The case study for this national tragedy is ubiquitous: first weed, then on to painkillers for more kick, then the habit concludes with Mexican-manufactured heroin which crosses the Obama open southern border. Those who are genetically susceptible succumb to addiction somewhere between PDQ and instantly.

Now let us examine the national opioid epidemic demographic.

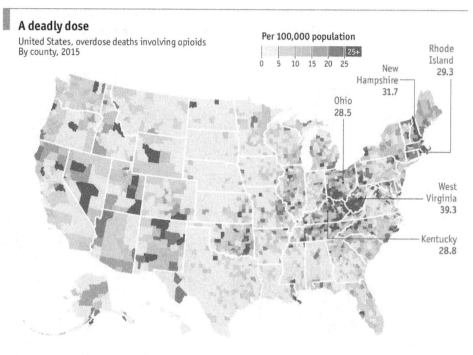

A deadly dose

United States, overdose deaths involving opioids
By county, 2015

Per 100,000 population

0 5 10 15 20 25 25+

Rhode
Island
29.3

New
Hampshire
31.7

Ohio
28.5

West
Virginia
39.3

Kentucky
28.8

Source: Centres for Disease Control and Prevention

Aside from a few sparsely populated western regions, America's opioid addiction problem is concentrated in Appalachian coal country and New England. In addition to the generally unsatisfactory eight year national performance of "Obamanomics," Obama's War on Coal was a second even more devastating gut-punch to the economy of Appalachia.

The cause of the New England problem is more elusive. Without specific data on the volume of painkillers prescribed, it is impossible to guess. A liberal education system which teaches young people self-esteem, social justice, and revisionist history in lieu of subject matter they can use to function successfully in American society is a usual suspect. Doctors who want to medicate every malady they see may be another.

As time ran out on the Obama presidency, his 14% approval rating among the American military pretty much established that there would be no Obama third term. In lieu of a third term, his legacy became his final presidential obsession. He needed an accomplishment to earn his foreign policy merit badge; the 2009 World Apology Tour and Nobel Peace prize did not qualify him.

In early 2015, the Obama regime opened back-channel discussions with Iran on a sanctions-relief-for-a-nuclear-development exchange. The Iranians correctly sized up Obama as an inexperienced and untalented negotiator who was desperate for a deal to populate his otherwise empty foreign policy resume. I doubt they were impressed with the unwritten rules of liberal American affirmative action, either.

Obama chose executive action because he knew he could never get the 2/3 majority for a ratified treaty in the Republican majority Senate for his "legacy" deal. This means his foreign policy legacy can be undone by the executive action of a successor. His failure to work with domestic political opposition again dooms him to the title of "historic first black president" and *nothing* more.

So in typical Obama amateur-hour fashion, bribery with the public treasury unlocks all doors. He loads up the front of the Iranian nuke deal with absurd American concessions: $150 B including plane-loads of cold foreign untraceable cash plus the lifting of trade and international banking sanctions against Iran. Iran's ante was a shell and pea game with their nuclear facilities: shutting down some facilities, limits on the operation of centrifuges that can produce nuclear fissionable material, limiting yellow cake production, etc. I trust the Iranian to live up to their end of the bargain like I trust a scorpion in my shoe.

But the Iranians got the cash *up front* plus the lifting of the international trade and banking sanctions, allowing them to make international business deals with Western allies. To abandon the deal post-Obama would be a major disruption within the international business community. This was Obama's insurance policy that his Iranian nuke "masterpiece" would never disappear into the wind.

Will the Iranian nuke deal live on? Anybody's guess, but mine is *"Highly doubtful."* In their lust for a nuclear weapon which they fully intend to use either on Israel, Western Europe, or the United States, they will violate the terms of the agreement...at which point President Trump will *not* be *"strategically patient."*

As a president, Obama went 0 for 8. That would have been bad enough in a baseball doubleheader. But 0 for 8 years as leader of the free world was a catastrophe. Obama's performance in the White House was far beyond merely feckless, inept, or incompetent. To completely whiff on eight years of opportunities takes ill intentions plus conscious and premeditated effort.

What could the motive for this behavior be? The standard every day vanilla OCD liberal hatred of America does not explain the behavioral pattern I witnessed. Is there something more?

On August 26, 2015, a double murder/suicide in Virginia occurred that captured the national news cycle. The murderer was a fired television station employee named Vester Flanagan. Flanagan shot and killed two employees of the Roanoke, VA, CBS-affiliate television station WDBJ. The victims were doing an onsite live telecast interview at a lakeside resort site 25 miles southeast of Roanoke. Interviewer Alison Parker and her cameraman Adam Ward were killed, while executive director of the local chamber of commerce interviewee Vicki Gardner was critically wounded.

Flanagan fled the on camera attack scene and was tracked via his cell phone. He committed suicide after a high speed chase.

The reaction to the shooting by Virginia Governor Terry McAuliffe was instantaneous, predictable, and irrelevant: yet again, the gun did it! He called for tighter gun control laws which have worked so well in Chicago.

Vester Flanagan was a 41-year-old black homosexual. He had disputes with the two murder victims, and many of his former co-workers in many other work locations. He had been fired before due to unacceptable on-the-job behavior. He had filed multiple lawsuits and complaints over alleged race and sexual orientation discrimination. In short, Flanagan was a malcontent and a troublemaker.

By all appearances Flanagan was antisocial, introverted, paranoid, and bipolar. He had ongoing confrontations with his two murder victims when he was fired by WDBJ in February 2013, two and a half years before the fatal shooting incident. He was escorted off site by police in a state of rage after being fired.

Vester Flanagan saw himself the *victim* of American bigotry and injustice. He was fully invested in the victimhood that the American left peddles continuously to foment civil unrest. He was a victim of bitter clingers who *"cling to guns or religion or antipathy to those who aren't like them...as a way to explain their frustrations."* Based on Flanagan's behavior and the suicide note he left behind, my guess is that the only thing he hated more than America was himself.

This just in: America was not responsible for Vester Flanagan's skin color, sexual orientation, *or* paranoia. America was *not* responsible for his victimhood-fueled anger...liberalism *is* responsible.

Flanagan was angry, but he was never in a position to arm America's enemies; or saddle America with another $10 T in debt; or pull out of Iraq leaving a void for ISIS to form; or set back American racial relations half a century by facilitating a war on law enforcement; or weaponize the entire federal bureaucracy against his political opposition; or sabotage America's energy future with bureaucratic obstructionism; etc. However, Flanagan *did* maximize the damage within his reach.

Obama did likewise. Whereas Hillary Clinton thought the American Treasury was her personal cash cow, Obama's motivation was simple hatred of America driven by his personal victimhood which he re-gifted to America, including Vester Flanagan.

What is the origin of Obama's animosity toward America...or more specifically white America? Perhaps there is a clue in his memoir "Dreams from My Father" (1995). In the book he describes an episode involving his white maternal grandmother, Madelyn Dunham: *"...a woman who once confessed her fear of black men who passed by her on the street, and who on more than one occasion has uttered racial or ethnic stereotypes that made me cringe."*

Evidently this revelation to the young Obama in Hawaii crushed his fragile psyche to the point he felt compelled to write about in his memoir. It likely created a node for a lifetime of Obama's distain for whites. It is equally likely the first documented incident of "snowflake" behavior.

As for Obama's gender and sexual identity, it is anybody's guess just like his academic records. We know in his book "Dreams from My Father" he describes an unnamed white girlfriend. He later admitted that "she" was a *"compression"* of multiple *alleged* girlfriends who never came forward to be identified.

There is the case history of one Genevieve Cook, who admits to being in a 1 ½ year "relationship" with Barry Obama in the early 80s. The Australian born Ms. Cook described Obama as being *"an imposter"*. Shocker.

Sometime later we have Michelle and their two daughters. Before then is virtually blank. It would have been simple enough to fabricate everything before Michelle. Genevieve could have been a blow up doll named Gerry for all I know.

Then too, we have Obama's deep involvement in the transgender bathroom issue during his *second* term. Why was this issue so important to him? Why did he wait until *after* his last election to expose his acute anxiety about the transgender bathroom *crisis*, which was inexplicably overlooked in America for nearly two and a half centuries?

Barack Hussein Obama (aka Barry Soetoro) has always been a shape-shifting opportunist. Perhaps he saw a traditional family as his ticket into mainstream politics.

You are free to do your own math. I come up "metro bisexual" with perhaps a couple of other letters from the LBGTQIAOMG alphabet soup added to "kick it up a notch".

The same Flanagan commentary is appropriate for Obama: America is not responsible for your skin color, sexual orientation, or mental disorders. Nor is America responsible for your victimhood-fueled anger…liberalism *is* again responsible. The truth is Obama would have hated any Western country he grew up in. It is America's misfortune that it was here.

Now let us revisit Obama's campaign-closing remark on Oct. 30, 2008: *"We are five days away from fundamentally transforming the United States of America."* It was campaign rhetoric, superficially devoid of real meaning. In the sense that it sounded good when read off a teleprompter by Himself, it was red meat for his *Coalition of the Gullible* base; it made them feel good. To be sure, it was intentionally ambiguous, fill in the blanks, choose your own adventure nonsensical word salad. My contention is that even though it meant whatever to his cheering *Coalition*, it meant something *very* specific to the race-obsessed Manchurian Teleprompter.

Being a minority in America is a substantial portion of Obama's deep-seeded hatred of America. What Obama envisioned was to *"fundamentally transform"* the United States into a majority *non*-white country.

Perhaps he took his cue from ex-New Orleans mayor Ray Nagin, who so artfully announced *"We as black people, it's time, it's time for us to come together. It's time for us to rebuild a New Orleans, the one that should be a chocolate New Orleans. And I don't care what people are saying Uptown or wherever they are. This city will be chocolate at the end of the day,"* during an MLK Day speech on Jan. 16, 2006, less than 5 months after the Hurricane Katrina catastrophe.

Nagin is in federal stir now, doing 10 years for a score of convictions including wire fraud, bribery, money laundering, income tax evasion, *et. al*...the typical lineup of Clinton-esque felonies.

Obama's failed red line bluff significantly exacerbated an already bad Middle Eastern refugee crisis. Obama's solution? In a classic "never let a good crisis go to waste" maneuver of uber pinheadery and political opportunism, Obama decides to double down on his red line blunder. He decides to import tens of thousands of unvetted Middle Eastern refugees to America. There is no reason that America should not share in the fun that Western Europe is having with the invading hordes of unvetted Middle Eastern refugees. It comports nicely with Obama's vision of a "chocolate" America.

This accomplishes multiple Obama objectives. (1) It creates a wave of future government dependents who will vote Democrat. Democrats are more than supportive of all things Islam. (2) It is a step-change in the American racial mix toward Obama. (3) It superficially mitigates Obama's earlier Syrian red line embarrassment.

The Middle Eastern refugee relocation effort is a complement to Obama's refusal to enforce our Southern border...and the trainloads of unvetted illegal immigrants coming to the United States from Central America. How many machete-wielding MS-13 gang bangers were on board? "Racist!" question.

It is more than a coincidence that all of this Obama- manufactured demographic shift designed to *"fundamentally transform the United States of America"* was staged in Obama's second term, when he was no longer accountable to the American voter. We recall again his chilling hot mic moment with Russian President Medvedev in March 2012: *"This is my last election ... After my election I have more flexibility."*

We return to Dr. Sowell's comment at the beginning of the chapter: *"I have never believed for a moment that Barack Obama has the best interests of the United States at heart."* As usual, the good Dr. Sowell was right.

Like Hillary Clinton, Barack Obama will be remembered for what he *is*, not for what he accomplished. Obama displaces Bill Clinton as America's first "black president," a reference to Toni Morrison's observation quoted earlier in the book. Obama won two presidential elections due primarily to his skin color and extraordinarily weak Republican opposition candidates.

Then in the midterms when his skin was not on the ballot but his policies were, he suffered the worst defeats of any sitting president in American history. In 2016 it was time to validate his eight-year body of presidential work; his personally-endorsed successor was handed one of the biggest upsets in American presidential election history.

Obama's only legislative accomplishments early in his first term are unmemorable. His trillion dollar "Porkulus" and all its "shovel ready" jobs evaporated in the wind before his signature ink had dried... just like the meaningless feel good *"Hope and Change"* bumper sticker slogan. Gov. Gary Johnson (R-NM) had perhaps the best review of the "Porkulus" during the 2012 Republican presidential debates: ***"My neighbor's dog has created more 'shovel ready' jobs than Obama's economic stimulus package."***

The governor nailed it!

In May 2009, Obama decided to save General Motors and Chrysler union jobs from its own poor management by confiscating corporate equity from the bond holders and giving it to the United Auto Workers (UAW). I too missed the Robin Hood Amendment of the United States Constitution. Fortunately for Obama, the SCOTUS overnight review of the case did not. Just as with their landmark Obamacare ruling yet to come, the SCOTUS ruled in favor of America's historic first black president. This put the taxpayer on the hook for the automaker's failing business. Through the public trough, Obama effectively repaid his campaign debt to the UAW. GM declared bankruptcy on June 1, 2009.

Obama's socialist legislative *opus magnum* Obamacare passed through Congress with 0.000 Republican support. As a result of Obama's failure to work within the legislative spirit of compromise, Obamacare will also disappear into the wind sooner rather than later.

Obama's decision to *"go it alone"* with his Jan. 14, 2014, announcement that *"I've got a pen and I've got a phone"* after he lost the House majority in 2010 shows how little the *alleged* "constitutional scholar" understands about the U.S. Constitution. There is nothing Obama can do with *"pen and phone"* that the next president cannot undo with the same executive order tactic. Even more significantly, his announcement shows his open defiance and complete contempt for the American voter who elected our Congress.

Continuing the Iranian nuke deal is totally at the discretion of his successor and will also likely be undone. The damage Obama did to American race relations and law enforcement is largely psychological and should heal with time. Black unemployment (now at a 21st century low) will help a great deal. Likewise the damage done with longstanding American allies Great Britain and Israel are healing already.

On Oct. 24, 2016, Obama appeared on "Jimmy Kimmel Live" for a cross demonstration of comedic talent and political forecasting skill. With two weeks left before the election, Obama read a tweet from then-Republican presidential candidate Donald Trump: *"President Obama will go down as perhaps the worst president in the history of the United States!"* Obama then cleverly countered, *"Well, @realdonaldtrump, at least I will go down as a president,"* Obama said, dropping his "mic" smartphone. The crowd went wild. My guess is that the same crowd also cheered when Obama announced *"ISIL is the JV team."* Stick to bracketology, Charlie Foxtrot.

In a moment of "self-reflection" (translation: pathological narcissism) after Trump's 2016 election, America's historical first Muslim descended president wonders whether his election had come "10 or 20 years too early." Now I understand what MY problem was.

The good news is there are other worlds for the Messiah to "fundamentally transform": Netflix will now be the beneficiary of His prescient omnipresence.

Netflix has announced that Barack Obama will have a monthly talk show on the network. Former U.N. Ambassador and fellow pathological liar Susan Rice will also be employed to work on the show. May I suggest the show name "Airhead America"? I know the perfect co-host.

Let's see how well they rebound from being drug backwards half a century. Sadly, I do not have a Netflix subscription to cancel. This pretty much assures I never will.

Obama's presidential tour of duty was beset with failure from Day 1 to Day 2,922. In military speak, it was FUBAR (all caps!). Race-obsessed liberals will look past his performance and pronounce his presidency as a success based solely on his skin color.

Liberals could have handled the transition from the liberal Obama thugocracy to the liberal Clinton cleptocracy *en route* to America's funeral smoothly. The key liberal requirement of identity qualification (first "black" president to first "woman" president) was all that mattered. But the transition from a president who smoothly reads lies they want to hear off a teleprompter to a coarse New York construction worker who *ad libs* the truth like the guy next to you on a bar stool is more than their miniscule psyches can handle. Liberal heads are now exploding like Martians listening to a CD of Slim Whitman's greatest hits in *Mars Attacks!* (1996 movie).

The glass is half full? Perhaps America is fortunate that the only lasting damage from the Obama era will be (1) his two substandard (I am in a generous mood) SCOTUS nominees, who would have been more properly placed on the farcical 9ᵗʰ Circus Court of Appeals in San Francisco. I foresee decades of absurd votes devoid of all common sense and reality from the Obama SCOTUS nominees; (2) the nearly $10T in new debt that Obama dumped on generations of Americans yet to come; (3) Obama's upfront financing of Iranian nukes and terrorism. These ignominious stains on America's future will *not* be going away.

We should also site the damage done to America's election system via the Obama controlled U. S. federal government interference. Without doubt, the Obama antics have deeply eroded America's confidence in our election system. He started small in 2008 with the New Black Panther polling interference. This escalated to the systemic IRS obstruction of conservative Political Action Committees in the 2012 election cycle. The grand finale was the 2016 FISAgate/FBI/DoJ conspiracy to frame Donald Trump for the crimes Hillary Clinton actually committed.

Although Hillary lost the election, she manufactured an evergreen excuse for any and all future Democrat election losses: "Russian collusion". The recipe for this ongoing low budget Saturday Night Live (SNL) skit is clear enough: ubiquitous "Deep State", MSM and DNC corruption plus a "special prosecutor" with a staff of discredited partisan shysters, an unlimited budget, no guiding directive, no oversight and no scruples. All of this is brought to you by an Attorney General who is MIA.

It remains to be seen if the election subversive mayhem caused by Obama and Hillary has done permanent damage to the American election process. However, we clearly owe yet another tip of the cap to "affirmative action" for this stain on our republic.

Also, the Obama war on law enforcement gained enough traction under the misguidance of his DoJ that it has carried forward into the post Obama era. Leftists see the retreat of law enforcement as an expedited pathway to anarchy. The end game of this leftist strategy is what we are now witnessing in the Rahm Emanuel declared "Trump free zone" of Chicago: an every soaring body count.

In truth, the Obama war on law enforcement is just a tangential franchise of the left's identity politics mainline sales business. The blue uniform replaces skin color and everyone in the uniform is a *"Racist!"* It is the standard Alinskyite identify, isolate, ridicule and condemn the target propaganda barrage that accompanies every other target of the left.

The cell phone is a key weapon: every individual becomes a CNN camera crew. Every incident involving a police officer no matter how small becomes a flash mob site with dozens of video cameras rolling. As the police retreat to passive law enforcement in the face of overwhelming "citizen witness" negative publicity, our liberal inner city is quickly super saturated with violent crime. What started out as a politically cute "Trump free zone" instantly devolves into a lawless third world combat zone or worse, Chicago. ***"If the rule you followed brought you to this, of what use was the rule?"*** – Anton Chigurh (*"No Country for Old Men"*)

Perhaps the lone bright spot from the Obama era is that America now understands that affirmative action does *not* work…a *very* expensive lesson. Nor does electing a "community organizer" *emeritus* to do a man's job. And perhaps America realized that eight years of the "omega president" *must* be followed by the "alpha president" in order to right this great ship.

Near the end of Trump's first year in office, Obama was speaking at a conference of mayors in Chicago (12.06.17) when he thanked himself for the post-Obama improving employment numbers the country is currently experiencing, crediting his climate change policies for the upswing.

"As we took these actions, we saw the U.S. economy grow consistently," Mr. Obama said. *"We saw the longest streak of job creation in American history by far, a streak that still continues by the way." "Thanks, Obama,"* he added.

This should not be confused with his June 2, 2016 town hall style meeting in Elkhart, IN with employees of Carrier who had announced that 1,400 jobs had been outsourced to Mexico. *"What we have to do is to make sure that folks are trained for the jobs that are coming in now because some of those jobs of the past are just not going to come back,"* Obama said bluntly during the event broadcast on PBS.

So let me get this straight: 7½ months *before* Obama left office, *"…those jobs of the past are just not going to come back."* Then 10½ *after* he left office, he was taking credit for economic growth. The liberal imagination and hubris is truly limitless!

The truth is that Obama is *not* responsible for the economic recovery, he is responsible for the economic mess preceding the Trump recovery. What Obama is responsible for is the thugocracy he spent eight years cultivating while in office, and must now be exterminated.

However, in one sense Obama was correct. After eight years of socialist nonsense, the American economy was primed for a spectacular recovery from a healthy dose of capitalism led by a savvy and successful American businessman. As the distance from the comatose Obama economic era of over taxation, over regulation and Obamacare mandate increases, the economy picks up speed. It is already in the best shape in over half a century. Consumer confidence and prospects for further economic improvement are off the charts as Maxine Waters (D-CA) continues to bleat out *"Impeach fawty five!"* (Ebonics to American English translation: *"Impeach Forty Five!"*)

Then later in an interview on *"60 minutes"* which aired Jan. 15, 2017, President Obama opined: *"I'm proud of the fact that, with two weeks to go, we're probably the first administration in modern history that hasn't had a major scandal in the White House."* Apparently there is no limit to liberal self-delusion. Ambassador Stephens and Agent Brian Terry* remain unavailable for comment.

* US Border Agent Brian Terry was murdered in Arizona on 12.14.10 while attempting to apprehend a group of armed subjects. The suspects had been preying on illegal immigrants with the intent to rob them. The assault weapon Agent Terry was murdered with was provided to the Mexican drug cartels by the Obama/Holder "Fast and Furious" "gunwalking" operation.

Then on July 17, 2018 Obama delivered a teleprompter read in Johannesburg, South Africa in which he praised South African President Cyril Ramaphosa for changing that country's constitution so farmlands could be seized from *white* landowners without compensation. The adulation Obama poured out upon Ramaphosa went far beyond normal diplomatic courtesy. In fact, Obama claimed the radical leftist Ramaphosa was "inspiring new *hope* in this great country." He left out *"change"* so as not to plagiarize Himself. *This* was the "fundamental transformation America" Obama envisioned in his impassioned Oct. 30, 2008 campaign teleprompter read at the University of Missouri - Columbia campus.

SYNOPSIS: Obama is now reduced to taking quixotic pot shots at his successor from liberal safe houses as President Trump repairs eight years of *uber* liberal damage. And so the chapter closes on America's "Nightmare on Pennsylvania Avenue."

12. "CLIMATE CHANGE": A HOAX BY ANY OTHER NAME...

In any discussion of *"global warming,"* it is imperative to understand motives that are driving the narrative. The advocates of *"global warming"* are without exception leftists who are obsessed with power and *control*. For them, *"global warming"* is a tool, a means to their own personal end.

Al Gore's Energy Transitions Commission (ETC) demanded $20 Trillion (with a <u>T</u>!) over the next two decades which they say will help the world meet the goals laid out in the Paris Climate Accord agreement. In effect, they want to create a supersized Solyndra, which received a guaranteed U. S. government loan of $535 M in mid-2009 based on Obama "Porkulus" funding, then declared Chapter 11 bankruptcy in August 2011. Why does the 1968 movie *Planet of the Apes* come to mind?

I suppose American taxpayers should feel relieved that the ETC demand was spread out over 20 years rather than cash up front, like Solyndra. I wonder who will be on the hook for the $20 Trillion. My guess is same people who are now on the hook for Solyndra *and* the dysfunctional United Nations: that would be the American taxpayer. Long before the first $20 Trillion is gone, look for an invoice for the second $20 Trillion. ***"Shovel-ready was not as shovel-ready as we expected."*** – **Barack Obama.**

So there is the ETC gang that is looking to pull off the biggest smash-and-grab propaganda-driven heist in human history, rivaling the American Social Security Ponzi scheme and the 1960s "War on Poverty" in size. Bernie Madoff looks on at Al Gore from behind bars with envy.

Aside from the greedy opportunists like Al Gore, *"global warming"* is the greatest Bolshevik hoax since communism. The goal of its advocates is the same goal of the people who brought you communism. Without exception, they are leftists who are obsessed with *control*, which in this case is a euphemism for global economic slavery. $20 Trillion here, $20 Trillion there and pretty soon you are talking about *real* money. Without question, the goal of Mr. Gore and his merry band of pirates is to bleed the great American "cash cow" dry, utilizing fear mongering.

They will do this via the *control* of carbon dioxide (CO_2) emissions. This is the same evil environmentally-destructive greenhouse gas that you and I exhale many times per minute. Worldwide CO_2 emission quotas will be issued through negotiation by a leftist America hater like Obama. The economy of the United States will be disproportionately penalized for its liberal imagined colonialist past, which is only *fair*. A global CO_2 market will emerge to swap CO_2 credits for CO_2 debits plus *cash*. The black market opportunities are unfathomable. When there is this much money involved, can drug cartel "investors" be far behind? Al Gore will operate the market and collect a transaction fee, which is his motivation.

In his 2006 book, *An Inconvenient Truth*, the Profit (sic) of Global Climate Disaster made a number of predictions which were to occur within 10 years:

1. Rising Sea Levels – inaccurate and misleading. Gore actually purchased a $9M oceanfront mansion in Montecito, CA, in 2010, defying his own propaganda.

2. Increased Tornadoes – declining for decades.

3. New Ice Age in Europe – never happened.

4. South Sahara Drying Up – completely untrue.

5. Massive Flooding in China and India – didn't happen.

6. Melting Arctic – false – 2015 represents the largest refreezing in years.

7. Polar Bear Extinction – the polar bear population is increasing significantly; they appear to be having a good time at it in the process.

8. Temperature Increases Due to CO2 – no significant temperature rise since 1998.

9. "Katrina" was a harbinger of the future – false. During the period 2006-2016, precisely <u>*zero*</u> major (Category 3 or greater) hurricanes made landfall in the United States, the longest major storm drought ever.

10. A *"true planetary emergency"* within a decade unless drastic action was taken to reduce greenhouse gasses. On January 26[th,] 2006, the Washington Post reported that America's resident bloviating blowtorch Al Gore *"believes humans may have only 10 years left to save the planet from turning into a total frying pan."* – Needless to say, January 26th, 2016, came and went; nothing happened.

None of these disproven errant predictions of gloom and doom are going to stop Mr. Gore, a former tobacco farmer, cattle rancher, and divinity school dropout, from attempting to scare America into forking over more cash…that's what he does. ***Liberals are too stupid to be embarrassed.***

Gore simply needs to revise his predictions from 2016 to 2026 and fire up his Elmer Gantry medicine show for another tour. His predictions need to have a horizon within *his* anticipated lifetime to preempt procrastination; otherwise, *he* cannot cash in…and that's what it is all about. There are plenty of the old Obama *Coalition of the Gullible* who are yet in search of a cause to give a modicum of meaning to their otherwise meaningless lives. As it turned out, Obama the Messiah didn't work for them. There is still a market for Gore's evergreen doomsday happy horsecrap. And remember, like the radical Islamic terrorist, Gore only has to be right *once* sticking quarters into his prediction slot machine.

It hasn't happened yet, but Gore now has a net worth in the 9 figure range. Like most Democrat politicians, being wrong seems to have worked out quite nicely for him.

Although the end-desired "Global warming" result is the same, Obama's motive is quite different from the Gore-Clinton style personal greed. In an uber-sized case of OCDL ego, Obama wants to *control* the lives of every human being on the planet. This may largely be accomplished through *control* of the energy sector. He already gave America a preview of his expertise in macro operational control with Obamacare, which was a beyond clumsy attempt to annex one-sixth of the American economy into the same government that runs the IRS.

When Obama disrupted the world's greatest healthcare system with his failed Obamacare, the impact of his socialist antics was contained within America. With "global warming," Obama can extend his reach to disrupt the *global* energy supply/demand market. The result would be an Obamacare economic catastrophe of a world-scale magnitude, brought to you by the same people who thought Solyndra was a good idea.

The concept of "global warming" has been rebranded to "climate change" to cover the anomaly that the earth stopped its apparent warming cycle near the turn of the last century. Now in classic form-over-substance maneuver, the re-labeled "climate change" justifies carbon emission *control* for either observed warming *or* cooling trends...clever indeed!

The "global warming" carnival barkers claim their warnings of pending Armageddon are based on science. Should we trust our energy and economic future to ShamWow® salesmen who think that a Bernoulli balance is an Italian family high-wire act over Viagra (sic) Falls?

Or someone whose sole claim to scientific knowledge is to start a sentence with *"97% of all scientists say blah, blah, blah,"* as though he had actually canvassed *all* scientists. Prior to 1492, 100% of all scientists agreed that the world was flat.

It is particularly troubling when you understand that their motives are greed, power, and *control*. It is troubling when you realize this is the same individual who *Grubered* you with *"If you like your healthcare plan, you can keep your healthcare plan...period!"* and *"ISIS is the JV team."* And *"The shovel-ready jobs were not as shovel-ready as we thought <giggle snort>,"* a trillion dollars later. Oh, by the way, Jeffrey Dahmer was the world's greatest chef and Al Sharpton is a reverend when he is not winning a spelling bee ("R-E-S-P-I-C-T").

The same guy who weaponized the IRS to corrupt the 2012 presidential election and then the FBI, DoJ, and FISA courts to corrupt the 2016 presidential election continues to peddle "global warming," er, "climate change" to you and the rest of America. The same guy who takes a separate jetliner to the same vacation location as his wife.

The "climate change" hoax is *not* based on science. That is part of the hoax. It is based on a combination of Marxist socio-economic goals and a faith that could best be described as the "Church of Global Warming," the Reverend A. A. Gore Jr. presiding.

The Marxist socio-economic goal assertion is easily demonstrable: name one prominent "climate change" activist who is *not* a socialist. Their motive is socialism, not climatology, which is merely a means to their selfish end (Chapter 3).

A refresher on a couple of Obama quotes: *"Growing income inequality is the defining issue of our time."* (12.04.13); and *"Today, there is no greater threat to our planet than climate change."* (05.16.15). We combine these two quotes to fully understand the left's motivation for the "global warming" hoax.

While the hoax leaders are universally socialists, the followers are more varied in motivation. Of course they are *all* liberals. Some are looking for something, anything, to give meaning to their meaningless lives. We think back to the followers of Jim Jones who drank the cyanide-laced Kool Aid back in the late 70s. Apparently the idea of volunteer work is not appealing to them, either. Some want to showboat their moral superiority with a magnanimous public display for the future of our planet and mankind (or "humankind" as Canadian Prime Minister Justin Trudeau would correct us). They are motivated by *ego*. Some actually think the sky *is* falling. They are driven by paranoia.

No need to dwell on their motivation. The *Coalition of the Gullible* would gladly vote for an Obama third term if given the chance...or another Hillary run in 2020 if she is able to evade federal lockup. And of course there are always the parasites who think they will be on the receiving end of wealth re-distribution, the underlying motive for "climate change." Their motive is greed. They obviously do not understand that *global* redistribution means *from* the United States *to* the Third World, and *everyone* in America, including parasites, will lose. They will find this out too late.

One thing should be quite clear to the reader: the leftist zealots who promulgate the "global warming" hoax are attempting to sell you something; I am *not*. They are re-vending the same Marxist socio-economic slavery through energy *control* that was born in the early 20th century (circa 1918 in Russia) and died 71 years later in the late 20th century (circa 1989 in Berlin, Germany).

Yet again, their target is *you*. The scam resurfaces because although communism *per se* was defeated, OCD and its insatiable opiate—*control*—was not defeated and cannot be defeated.

The "global warming" scam is a "buyer beware" situation of the *nth* order. It rates right up there with the e-mail from the Nigerian prince that used to land in my inbox about every full moon.

The hoaxters are not looking to score another mom-and-pop heist like Solyndra. They are looking to convert Western capitalism into socialism under *their control* in the name of saving the planet from an imaginary menace. The economic stakes could not be higher. The "global warming" hoax is their ticket to this economic disaster, which would be a replay of the 20th century communist disaster. This is why I have deemed *"global warming"* the greatest Bolshevik hoax since communism.

The burden of proof is upon those who want to destroy the greatest economy in the history of the planet, not upon those of us who do not want to "fix" what ain't broke in the first place.

Although the primary driver of the "global warming" issue is *political* or *economic*, for many liberals it is *religious*. They take it on *faith* that they are participating in a cause that is larger than themselves in lieu of conventional religion.

It is also psychological. As previously discussed, OCDLs have an obsessive compulsion to be in *control*. Seizure of the world's energy sector to save the world from fantasized lethal overheating puts them in *control* of the looming climate disaster through CO2 emissions. Your basic issue OCDL is now at ease; all is well.

Whether the motivation is economically, politically, religiously, or psychologically based, they all *want* to believe. Liberals are an easy mark for Al Gore and his merry band of doomsday deceivers.

Therefore, it takes very little "science" to make them believe...and that is precisely what they get. The "global warming" technical issue can be reduced to two questions: (1) is the earth's temperature rising? And (2) if so, is it *anthropogenic* ("man caused")? Liberals intent upon separating you from your money and freedom will answer both questions with an emphatic "YES!" I answer the questions with a "Probably not." And "No."

Liberals bet the farm on the 1998 alarmist and now discredited "hockey stick" graph.

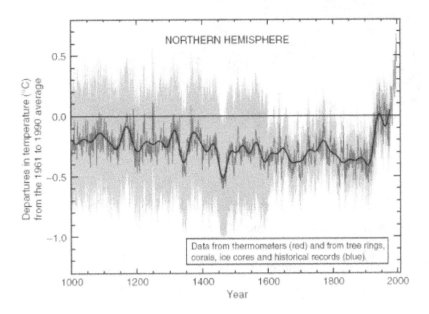

This graph, along with a couple of hyper active Atlantic Hurricane seasons in 2004 and 2005, led to the opportunist Al Gore book *An Inconvenient Truth* in 2006. At this point, the "global warming" movement had momentum. The road ahead for Gore was gold and marked with dollar signs.

But tragically, reality dumped on Gore's parade. First meteorologists and climatologists alike noticed that around the turn of the millennium, the earth's temperature was no longer warming. That has continued through today. Various "scientific" ("political" is closer to the truth) theories were postulated to explain this aberration away, e.g., the heat was hiding at the bottom of the earth's oceans...like next to Jimmy Hoffa's body?

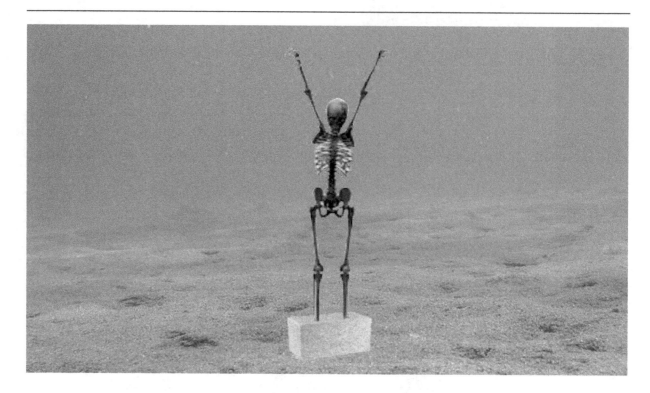

Yeah, right! For the first time ever cold water rises to the surface of the ocean displacing the denser sinking warm water. Or maybe it's just hiding at the bottom of my swimming pool.

Then in late 2009, a series of emails among the scholars at the prestigious East Anglia Climate Research Unit (CRU) was leaked revealing trouble in paradise. Apparently these keepers of the climate had:

- Conspired to hoard the raw data from which they formed the basis for the "hockey stick" graph to preclude any independent analysis. At one point the claim by CRU Director Professor Phillip Jones was that the data was *"lost."* And coincidentally, the dog ate my homework.

Where have we heard this lame escape ploy before?

- They manipulated the data to lower past temperatures and to "adjust" recent temperatures upwards, producing the alarmist result they wanted. In accounting vernacular, they "cooked the books."

The self-described *"hockey team"* conspired to viciously discredit and ostracize the work of any dissenting scientists, or journals that published their critics' work. It would appear our trusted "hockey puckers" read Saul Alinksky's *Rules for Radicals* somewhere along the way.

- To further confound the liberal "Global warming" believers, the continental United States did not experience a *major* hurricane (defined as Category 3 or higher storm on the Saffir-Simpson scale) for almost 12 years after the hyperactive 2005 Atlantic Hurricane Season that Gore so gleefully celebrated on film and in print. Hurricane Wilma made landfall in South Florida on October 24, 2005, as a Cat 3 storm. It was not until Hurricane Harvey made landfall as a Cat 3 storm on the Texas Gulf Coast on August 25, 2017, that the 48 contiguous United States experienced another major hurricane.

The sole scientific premise of the "global warming" movement is that the observed warming is directly related to an atmospheric concentration of the "greenhouse gas" carbon dioxide ($CO2$). This is demonstrably false. ***Never accept any liberal premise because it is based on liberal logic, which does not exist.***

During the course of a calendar year, the earth will tilt about its polar axis toward the sun (spring and summer in the Northern hemisphere) and then away from the sun (fall and winter). On June 21, the sun reaches its point of maximum northward travel at the Tropic of Cancer. This the longest day of the year and also the first day of summer. Then the trip southward begins until the sun reaches its point of maximum southern location at the Tropic of Capricorn on December 21.

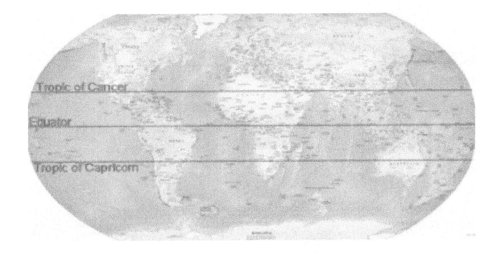

Other than at equatorial locations, the temperature swings between summer and winter can be dramatic, due to the quantity (amount of daylight) and quality (angle of incidence) of solar radiation that falls upon each hemisphere seasonally. The climate "changed" dramatically, but the atmospheric CO_2 concentration did *not*. Even liberals would concede seasonal climate change, although they do it via verbal shape shifting: in the summer when it is warm in the northern hemisphere, the seasonal temperature increase is referred to as "global warming"; in the winter when it is cool, the observed temperature phenomenon is called "climate change". Pretty clever, huh?

The relationship between solar irradiance and the surface temperature of the earth gives us the temperature difference between summer and winter. The same thing happens on a daily basis, *vis a vis* night vs. day...or intradaily between sunlight and shade.

The purpose of this discussion is to demonstrate that the incidence of solar irradiation is a *far* more important factor in determining global temperatures than tropospheric CO_2 concentration. The sun is an approximately 4×10^{26} watt nuclear-fusion-powered light bulb 93M miles from earth. Who among us thinks this *ultimate* source of the earth's surface warmth burns at a constant rate?

It is proven *science* that the sun experiences increased solar flare, sunspot, and aurora activity in 11-year intervals called the *"solar cycle."*

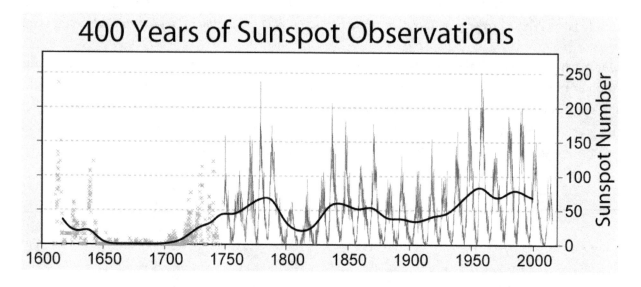

These variations in solar activity can have marked effects on the earth's surface through changes in solar irradiance. Solar irradiance, measured in W/m² can then be correlated directly to the earth's surface temperature.

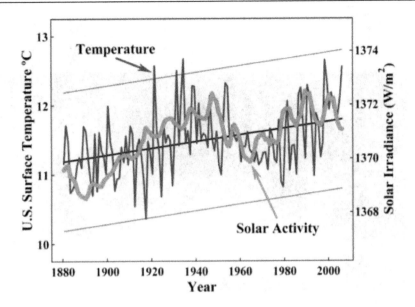

* Graph source is the Global Warming Petition Project.

I find better correlations among the tropospheric CO2 concentrations and the S&P 500 history or the price of gasoline history than the earth's surface temperature:

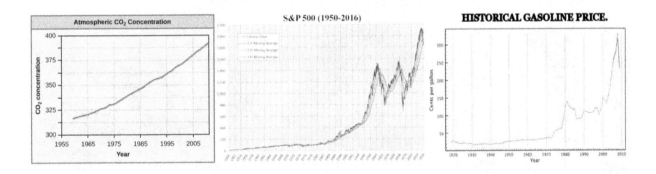

I suspect CO2 concentration could also be correlated "successfully" with Major League Baseball salaries and the price of coffee. You get the idea.

In passing, the maximum solar irradiation occurs annually on June 21 in the Northern Hemisphere. Maximum enthalpy (intensive measure of thermal energy content based on temperature and heat capacity of fluids on the earth's surface) occurs annually on September 10 as indicated by the midpoint of the Atlantic Hurricane Season.

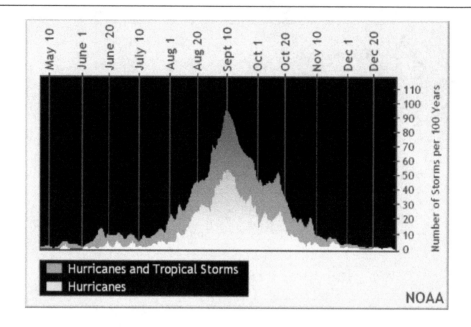

The lag between the two dates is because, while the sun begins its annual journey southward after June 21, it continues to heat water in the North Atlantic Basin from directly overhead until the Autumnal Equinox on September 22. This warmed water flows northward toward the United States due to the clockwise rotation (caused by the earth's rotation about its polar axis) current in the North Atlantic Basin (the "Gulf Stream") causing the September hurricane season peak.

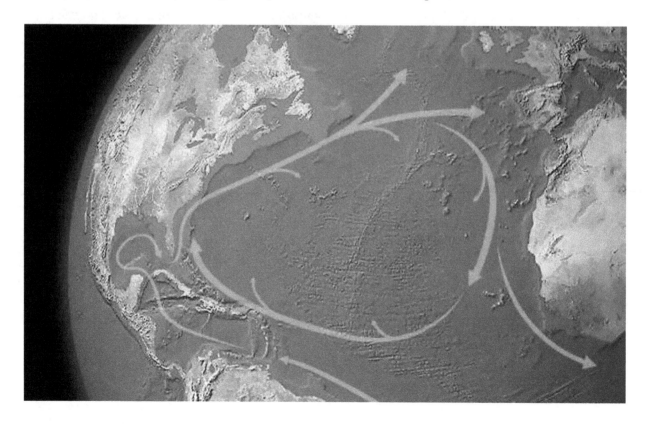

This "enthalpy time lag" is why the official meteorological "Hurricane Season" occurs from June 1 – to November 30, significantly lagging the months of maximum daylight.

The liberal hoaxters choose to "focus" on atmospheric CO_2 concentration while ignoring solar activity as a source of global temperature variation, which they now term "climate change." Why is that?

Remember the "climate change" advocates' *motivation* is varied, but in all cases, it returns to the OCDL primal motivation of *control*. Those who advocate for political or economic reasons want to *control your* CO_2 emissions for fun and *profit*. They cannot control solar radiation flux…only God can. Those who advocate for religious or psychological reasons also need something they can *control* for their mental health. "Climate change" via CO_2 emissions gives them a cause within their reach. Obviously, the sun is out of their reach.

Despite the setbacks, "climate change" will be with us until the next Bolshevik scam aimed at enslaving *you* surfaces. Although the late 90s "hockey stick" conspiracy has been exposed, we will continue to be confronted with computer models predicting the end of the planet by year 20xx. "What else does Al Gore have to do?" the author asks rhetorically.

Yes, the same models that cannot predict whether it is going to rain Saturday or where Hurricane Maxine is going to hit until after it has happened are going to predict the unbearable temperature in Del Rio, TX, five decades from now. Of course, all of these models include the next 10-mile wide meteorite striking the earth like the Chicxulub meteor which ended the Dinosaur Age with a global ice age 66 million years ago. They all include the next Krakatoa (which is actually *west* of Java) explosion like the one in August 1883 that dropped global temperatures by 2+ degrees Fahrenheit. They all include the next Mt. St. Helens eruption like the one in May 1980 that blew a cubic mile of earth into the stratosphere cooling the troposphere beneath its stratospheric dust plume. And of course, they all include the eruption of the Yellowstone Supervolcano, which has the eruption potential of Krakatoa (or significantly *greater*) and could have the climatic impact of a global volcanic winter.

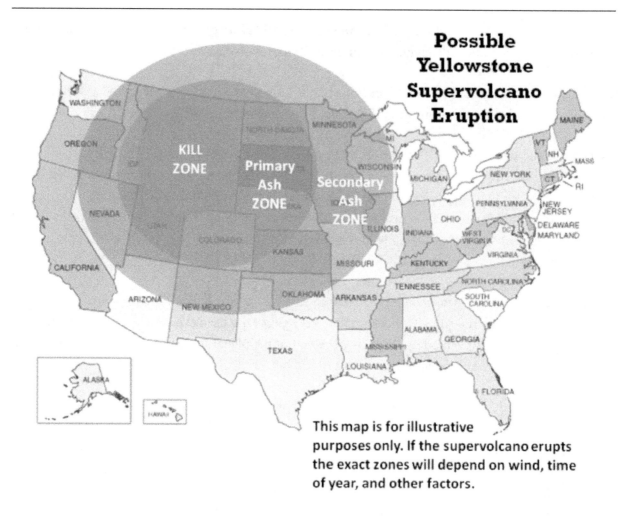

Possible Yellowstone Supervolcano Eruption

This map is for illustrative purposes only. If the supervolcano erupts the exact zones will depend on wind, time of year, and other factors.

They include *nothing* of the like. They are merely extrapolations of the spurious "hockey stick."

But to advance our discussion, let us momentarily accept the liberal premises that (1) there is global warming; and (2) greenhouse gases are the cause; and (3) mankind ("peoplekind" if you live in the domain of Pierre Trudeau) is the malefactor. Examination of atmospheric greenhouse gasses in a recent Department of Energy study reveals the following breakdown:

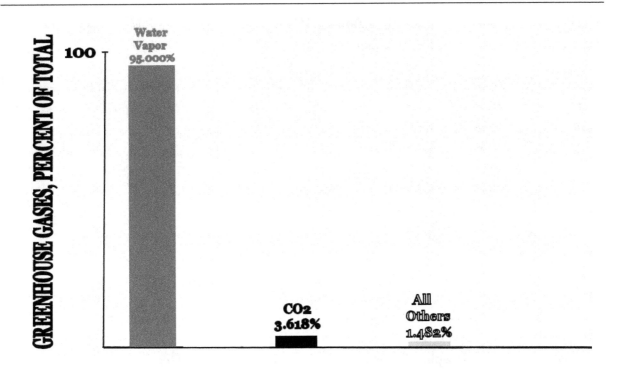

From this, we conclude that by far the most abundant greenhouse gas is water vapor. Almost none of the water vapor (0.001%) is man-caused. The primary source of water vapor in the earth's atmosphere is solar radiation striking open water. CO_2 comprises only 3.618% of the total greenhouse gas portfolio. Of this 3.618%, the *man-made* contribution is only 3.225%:

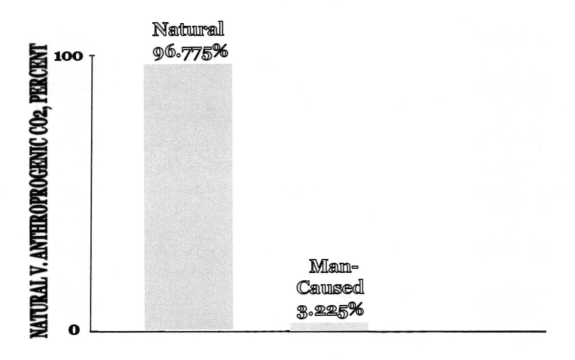

The product of these two very small fractions (.03618 x .03225) gives the miniscule man-caused CO2 contribution to the atmospheric greenhouse gas total, 0.117%.

Of course, when the people who are peddling the "climate change" charade talk about greenhouse gases, it is strictly on a water vapor-free basis. This deceitful mathematical manipulation increases the *apparent* CO2 contribution by a factor of 20 (literally). And when they address CO2 sources, they ignore the 96+% of natural sourced CO2. Same deceitful tactic, same alarmist mathematical result.

This is a lot of data to digest. Unfortunately, that's the way science works...or so it is rumored. It does not work based on rhetoric read off a teleprompter that starts off with *"97% of all scientists...."* by someone who has already *Grubered* your healthcare into ruination with Obamacare. Now ask yourself *"Is this 0.117% of anthropogenic greenhouse gas contribution worth paying Al Gore and his cluster of "hockey puckers" the $20 trillion signing bonus they demand?"*

This chapter was not intended to be a primer on climatology. My college curriculum was littered with Calculus, Physics, Statics, Dynamics, Stoichiometry, Organic Chemistry, Quantum Mechanics, Differential Equations and Laplace Transforms (i.e., "beyond calculus"), Heat Transfer, Mass Transfer, Fluid Mechanics, Thermodynamics, Chemical Reaction Kinetics, and other assorted coursework rooted in science *denial.* ***Rocket scientists are chemical engineers who flunked chemistry.*** My most important takeaway from my college career was not my pedantic transcript. It is the capacity for critical thought.

Weather patterns have been a lifetime personal interest. Although I have no *formal* education in the field does not mean that I cannot opine on climatology perspicaciously.

My parents grew up in mid-America during the Great Depression. That was *the* formative event of their lifetime. They had nothing but the clothes on their back, a roof over their head, three hots and a cot. Their prospects for a future were extremely poor to non-existent.

When it became time for them to defeat Nazi Germany and Imperial Japan in World War II as young adults, they were ready for that reality. They were well battle-tested for the Cold War next. They *were* "America's Greatest Generation." I absorbed my values as a conservative and a conservationist from my parents, who led by their example.

In 2005, I lost my home and everything in it to Hurricane Katrina. No, I am not advocating "victimhood" status for myself. It was a loss but it was also an opportunity to build a hyper energy efficient *total* electric replacement home, which I did (data below).

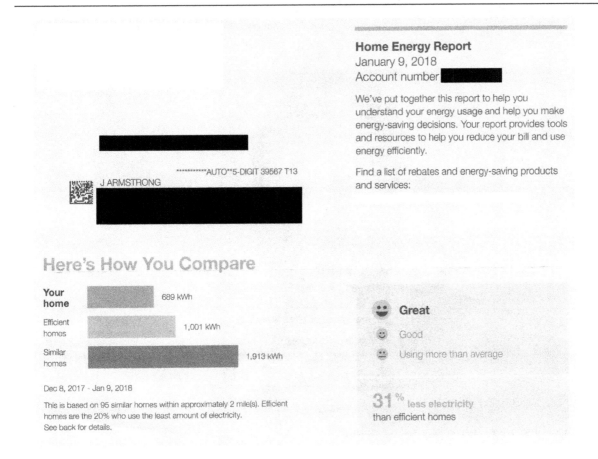

Home Energy Report
January 9, 2018
Account number ▮▮▮▮▮▮

We've put together this report to help you understand your energy usage and help you make energy-saving decisions. Your report provides tools and resources to help you reduce your bill and use energy efficiently.

Find a list of rebates and energy-saving products and services:

***********AUTO**5-DIGIT 39567 T13

J ARMSTRONG

Here's How You Compare

Your home	689 kWh
Efficient homes	1,001 kWh
Similar homes	1,913 kWh

😃 **Great**
🙂 Good
😐 Using more than average

Dec 8, 2017 - Jan 9, 2018

This is based on 95 similar homes within approximately 2 mile(s). Efficient homes are the 20% who use the least amount of electricity.
See back for details.

31% less electricity than efficient homes

The bottom line is that my new home uses only 36% (689/1913) of the electrical power of similar homes within a 2-mile radius; and 31% *less* electrical power than *"efficient homes,"* which are the *best* 20% power consumers of the similar homes within the same 2 mile radius.

I contrast *my* home energy consumption with that of environmentalist *emeritus* Al Gore's Nashville, TN., home. The National Center for Public Policy Research obtained Gore's electricity usage through Freedom of Information Act (FOIA) requests and by talking with the Nashville Electric Service (NES), which services Gore's home. It reports the former vice-president averaged a whopping 19,241 kilowatt hours (kWh) every month, compared to 901 kWh for the average American home. Gore's power usage is 21+ times the national average. His Nashville home is one of three that he owns. The other two may be worse.

My new home is my humble contribution toward saving our planet from energy pigs like Al Gore.

If the ideas in this discussion have merit, feel free to use them. Remember, I am *not* trying to sell you anything. If instead you find the CO2 that you just exhaled the same global menace that liberals do, it may well be the costliest decision of your life: first your money, then your freedom. Don't bother waiting around for a "Thank you!" from Al Gore…he will be too busy congratulating himself at his next awards ceremony.

A final disclaimer: I am not a proctologist, but….

EPILOGUE: LAST CALL FOR COMMON SENSE

Originally I had planned a couple more chapters, but the book is running long because liberalism is a target-rich environment. One chapter was to be titled "Newly Elected President John L. Armstrong." No, it was not to be an egotistical self-tribute. Rather, it was to be an exposé on the policies I would pursue if elected president.

For example, in the area of foreign policy, I describe my first meeting with Russian President Vladimir Putin. In "Godfather" speak, this is known as "making him an offer he can't refuse." It could also accurately be deemed "Reading him the Riot Act."

The location is irrelevant. No handshake.

John L.: "Don't bother sitting down, this isn't gonna take that long. I talk, you listen."

Putin:

John L.: "I am the president of a nation with an $18 Trillion per year economy. You are the pipsqueak dictator of a failed compost heap with a $1 Trillion economy. Your puny economy is dependent on one thing and one thing alone: the price of crude oil."

Putin:

John L.: "In the 80s Ronald Reagan bankrupted your country by forcing you into an arms race which your country could not afford. The same thing would work again today."

Putin:

John L.: "But I don't want to be labeled a copycat, I'm a little more creative than that. What I will do is unleash the full oil production capability of the United States which will drop the price of crude oil worldwide. When the price of crude drops, your $1 Trillion a year economy turns into a $0.5 Trillion economy. Your economy will tank and take you with it."

Putin:

John L.: "But just to prove to you I can walk and chew gum at the same time, I could do both the arms race AND the increased oil production…should compound the results. The point is I can take you out like a cockroach racing across my kitchen floor anytime I want."

Putin:

John L.: "For the cherry on the doggie do sundae (in America we call this "Pelosi-speak") I will force feed you, I will flood Western Europe with cheap American LNG. You can take *your* over-priced gas and pipe it up your posterior…or drop the price and try to compete…your choice, I really don't care."

Putin:

John L.: As your economy sinks into the quicksand, I will make certain every single Russian knows why…YOU!

Putin:

John L.: "I will be keeping an eye on every move you make starting NOW. DON'T PISS ME OFF! Nod if you understand."

Putin silently nods.

John L.: "You are free to go. Don't call me, I'll call you."

No handshake.

In the area of domestic policy, newly elected President John L. Armstrong proposes one sentence legislation to balance the budget: "Congress shall be paid a salary during the current year *only* from a budget surplus from the preceding year." Voila! The budget is balanced instantly!!! I then take my case directly to the American people, who will let Congress know if they agree. Same approach on introducing term limits, including federal judges.

I also planned a chapter titled "The Liberal Hall of Shame," describing some of the leftists who have turned America into the mess it is today. A few examples:

- Saul Alinsky. Patron saint of the contemporary American left, author of the community organizer's handbook *Rules for Radicals*. His approach to everything was that he could get anything he wanted if he just became annoyingly disruptive enough. OWS, BLM, Antifa, the School Kids March for Gun Control all reek of the Alinksy stench almost a half century after his death.

- George Soros. Hungarian born financial manipulator of currency on the global scale. Alleged Nazi collaborator who stripped fellow Jews of their valuables on the way to execution. He later described the experience as *"actually probably the happiest year of my life."* Now resides in the United States financing ultra-leftist causes aimed at the destruction of America as founded with the profit from his currency manipulation antics.

- Margaret Sanger. The godmother of "Planned Parenthood," which performs 300+K abortions annually (a thousand per day!). Author of *"Colored people are like human weeds and need to be exterminated"* quote. Eugenics advocate. Liberals love her, Hillary Clinton in particular.

- Dr. Kermit Gosnell. The poster star for modern liberal abortion. Convicted of 1st degree murder in May 2013 for severing the spinal cords of the infant survivors of his botched abortions with a pair of scissors. Also convicted of involuntary manslaughter, performing illegal late term abortions and federal drug charges. Currently serving a life plus 30 years in a Pennsylvania correctional facility. He plea bargained to avoid the death penalty ostensibly because he values his *own* life. There was a virtual liberal MSM news coverage *blackout* not because it was a "local" story as described but because it elucidated how hideous liberalism is.

- Valerie Jarrett. Iranian born senior advisor to President Barack Obama. Source of much of the heinous advice that blossomed into the eight years of Obama regime total failure, including the Iranian nuke deal.

- Earl Warren. Chief Justice of the SCOTUS (1953-1969). Ruling by his court in 1962 effectively eliminated prayer and Christian morality from the American public school system. Our public school system has never recovered.

- Lyndon B. Johnson. U.S. President from 1963-1968. Author of the modern American welfare system which destroyed the black family in America.

- Timothy Leary. Psychologist and writer known for advocating the exploration of the "therapeutic potential" of psychedelic drugs in the early 1960s. He helped usher in the Baby Boomer drug epidemic by romanticizing drug use, particularly LSD, with his high profile endorsement. His contribution to America's youth meshed nicely with the Warren court's eviction of God from the public school system and LBJ's wanton destruction of the black family unit.

- Richard Cloward and Frances Fox Pivin. These two liberal masterminds authored the Cloward and Piven Strategy to collapse the American socio-economic system through ever expanding welfare entitlement, dependency and abuse. The goal of the strategy was anarchy, from which

Cloward and Piven would be heralded as the kingpins of the utopia that would emerge from the turmoil. Without question, these two Columbia sociology professors influenced Barack Obama, who was once an alleged student there. Obama attempted super-size the Cloward-Piven strategy to a global basis in his second term.

- Joseph Stalin, Mao Tse-dong, Pol Pot. These were standard run-of-the-mill Asian communist dictators who managed to disarm their respective populations, then collectively murder well over 100 million citizens who might have inferred some sort of dissent at totalitarian slavery. The modern American liberal has no particular problem with the astronomical body count because it all occurred in "gun free zones."

Of course there are *many* others, these are just a few liberal "stars" from yesteryear who come to mind first after the latter- day titans of liberalism, Hillary Clinton and Barack Obama.

Running out of space to do them justice here…perhaps a sequel?

ACKNOWLEDGEMENT

A well-deserved acknowledgment to editor Gayle Nolan whose content and organization input was crucial to this final work product.

CPSIA information can be obtained
at www.ICGtesting.com
Printed in the USA
LVHW101132300720
661958LV00019B/152